Also by Ann Ormsby

The Recovery Room

"Ormsby has a wonderful eye for character and detail, as she fleshes out a keenly observed portrayal of small-town life."
Kirkus Reviews

Reader Reviews

"This is both a page-turner and an important dramatization about the complications of personal choice."

"The author is skilled at showing the complexities of people's lives…"

"The Recovery Room moved me to think deeply about my own beliefs and reminded me that everything is not always black and white."

"All of the characters just come to life and pull you into their stories."

"Ann Ormsby delivered a thought-provoking and entertaining novel about the ongoing societal trauma over the rights of women to control their own bodies."

LIVING IN THE RAIN

A Novel

ANN ORMSBY

This is a work of fiction. Names, characters, places, and incidents are products of the author's imagination or are used fictitiously and are not to be construed as real.

ISBN: 978-0-578-80212-1

Cover design by: Robert Dweck

Formatted by: Lois Hoffman

Great South Bay Press
Westfield, NJ

For Mary
Mother—Sister—Daughter
At some point we were these things to each other.

Why Black?

Cassie Pennebaker had met Joe Darby at Kent Community College two years ago when they both took a class on the elements of style in creative writing. They were sitting next to each other, and when Professor Miller gave them a writing prompt and twenty minutes to create a character, Cassie couldn't help but notice, as she looked around the room for inspiration, that Joe's middle finger on his right hand had been cut off somewhere between the first and second knuckle. Intrigued, she stared at the beheaded digit. Was he born that way? How had the tip of the finger been severed? Distantly, she heard Professor Miller clear his throat. She tried to turn her attention back to the prompt. A grocery list, a bicycle, a dog. She couldn't think of anything but Joe's finger. She slouched down in her seat and held up her blank piece of paper to hide her face.

After the class was over, Cassie emerged from the classroom with her determined stride. Although she was looking down, her hair falling in front of her face, she was aware that Joe was standing down the hall by the water fountain. She thought he was waiting for her. As if on cue, he fell in step with her as she walked by him. She reached up to pull her hair back from her face, and she felt his eyes taking in her collection of earrings—hoops, studs, and jewels—that climbed up the curve of her ear. Peering at him out of the corner of her eye, she saw his gaze travel down her neck to her Flogging Molly T-shirt, white belt, and black skinny jeans, and then back to her face with its pointy little nose. She could sense that he liked what he saw.

"What happened to your finger?" she asked as they walked through the hallway and out into the parking lot.

"I noticed you staring at it," he said. She looked up at his smooth mocha-colored face, his startling blue-green eyes, and his big white teeth.

"I was. I was trying to imagine what happened to it," she said.

He threw back his head and laughed, and his corkscrew curls fluttered around his face. His laugh started out loud and ended in a high-pitched chortle. "Let's get coffee," he said. "How about Dunkin' Donuts?" She agreed and followed him out to his car. On the short ride into town she looked at him and noticed that his lips were the color of nutmeg, a rich brown with shades of purple. He pulled into the Dunkin' Donuts parking lot. They jumped out of the car, walked into the store, and ordered. She went to find a table.

As he carried their coffee and donuts over to her on a tray, she studied him and wondered about his parents. "So, who's black and who's white...I mean, if that's okay to ask," she said as he placed a pumpkin-flavored latte and a cinnamon apple donut in front of her.

"My mom's white. My dad's black. I guess that makes me black."

"Why? I don't understand why having one black parent makes you black. You're fifty-fifty. You're mocha. You're coffee with cream. You're wh-ack. You're bl-ite. Like Obama. Why is he black? I've seen pictures of his mother. She looks like my mother. And she left him just like my mother left me." Cassie twirled a piece of her metallic pink and blue hair between her slender fingers.

"It's the one-drop rule," he said.

"The what?" she asked, her lips covered in cinnamon and sugar.

He chewed his donut before he said, "If you have one drop of black blood you can never be white."

While Cassie pondered this "rule," she studied Joe's beautiful face. "Wouldn't it be great if we were all tan? Then it wouldn't matter," she said. "We could all have tan babies." Joe laughed his hearty laugh. She liked the sound of it. It made her remember the feeling she had when her mother would come and sit on her bed as she fell asleep. A blend of happiness and security. When he didn't answer, she asked, "Are they still together?"

"My parents, you mean? Are anyone's parents still together? Are your parents still together?" Joe finished his chocolate-covered donut and started on a glazed cruller.

She noted his cynicism. "No. My dad died when I was two. Then my mom up and married an Aussie when I was fourteen and she left me here with my grandmother when she went to live in Sydney. To be close to his family, she said. Haven't seen her since." She picked up her coffee and took a sip. "It's weird, you know, I hate her, but I miss her." She paused and he nodded. "So, I thought I was going to hear the story of your finger." She locked her eyes on his and took a bite of her donut, licking the sweet cinnamon sugar from her lips in a quick little movement. She saw how his eyes followed her tongue.

He chuckled. "I accidently stuck it in a lawnmower when I was ten. It was the year my dad left us and my mom said it was now my job to mow the lawn. So I went to the garage and got the lawnmower out and was cutting the grass in the backyard when a branch got stuck in the machine, and without thinking, I stuck my hand in to pull it out. Hurt so much I passed out, and when my mom came home she found me lying there with my finger chopped in two. Too much time had passed and they couldn't reattach it."

Cassie listened to Joe's story and tried to visualize the little boy with the lawnmower. The sound of the engine, the pungent smell of the cut grass, the spray of blood on the metal. She smiled in amazement. "Wow. That is really crazy. Just like that. Gone. A body part. No more. You know, sometimes I think about death and how one minute the person is here and the next minute they're not. Like your finger. Poof. Like my mother. Bam. Gone." Her cheeks were flushed and little beads of sweat had formed on her upper lip. She reached out and pulled his hand toward her. She examined the tip of the finger as if it were a priceless piece of art. She ran her finger gently and slowly over the tip of his damaged finger.

"Okay. Cut it out," he said, trying to take back his hand. She could tell he was excited. In an attempt to change the conversation, he said, "Do you hear from her? Your mother, I mean?"

"I used to get a monthly check, but when I turned eighteen she sent a note saying that I should take care of myself now. Ha, what a joke. Like I wasn't already taking care of myself. She'd been gone for four years. She liked to think that she had been taking care of me by sending a check. What bullshit." Cassie's small blue eyes were bright.

"Yeah, that is bullshit," Joe agreed.

"Enough about her."

"Yeah, enough," said Joe and laughed into the silence that sprang up.

Cassie suddenly felt like she knew enough about Joe to make a move. "Who do you live with?" she asked.

"Just me and Weezer, my cat," answered Joe.

"Weezer?"

"Yeah. Like the group."

"I love Weezer." She smiled.

"They're my favorite. Do you want to come over…and listen to them?" He didn't laugh as he said it, and she knew he was afraid she'd say no.

"Yeah. Now?"

"Yeah. Now."

They eyed each other over the Styrofoam cups and crumpled tissue papers, collected their garbage, grabbed their backpacks, and headed out the door.

Clippings

I t was a warm September night as Cassie walked home and tried to remember where she had put the nail clippers. Noting the eerie blue light of the television in the window of her apartment up ahead in the distance, Cassie hastened her pace. Her grandmother, Sally Bishop, never bothered to get off the couch and turn on the lights as the afternoon faded into dusk and then into night.

Cassie mentally ticked off all of her chores that needed to be done in a matter of minutes before Joe picked her up. She knew she had to hurry and the pressure to do it all made her feel squeezed. Still searching her brain for a visual of where she left the nail clippers, she trudged down the street, with the garden apartments on one side and the modest split-level homes on the other. Glancing at her phone for the time, she picked up her pace. As she skipped up the few stairs to her door, she could see Sally through the window staring at the TV.

Cassie Pennebaker had lived in Kensington Garden Apartments for eighteen years. Since she was only twenty, she felt that she had lived there her entire life, although her mother used to tell her stories of the house they had lived in when she was born. A house that Cassie did not remember. She also used to tell her stories of her father. A man she did not remember. No, Cassie felt that 765A Kensington Terrace had been the only home she had ever known, and the one constant person in her life had been her grandmother, Sally Bishop, or Gram, as Cassie called her.

Sally had always been different from the other grandmothers that Cassie saw in the courtyard in the back of her apartment. She rarely went out and never socialized with the other older ladies who gathered out back gossiping and sharing stories of their grandchildren. Sally spent her time watching TV and was prone to sudden outbursts, paranoia, and angry tantrums. Without warning or provocation, she would scream and throw the nearest dish or hairbrush, whatever was in arm's reach. Cassie's mother, Jillian, had told her that Sally suffered from mental illness. Actually, Jillian had said that her mother was "bat-shit crazy," and that was all she said. No further explanation. No treatment plan.

Cassie reached the door to the apartment and shifted the weight of her heavy backpack on her back and hung the grocery bags off her wrist. As she struggled to get her key out of her tight jeans, one of the flimsy plastic bags broke and the Perdue chicken nuggets and two rolls of toilet paper fell to the ground. "Shit!" she said under her breath. She put her key in the lock and realized that the door was open, and a wave of frustration reverberated through her brain.

As she kicked open the door she said angrily, "Gram, you have got to lock the door when you're here by yourself." She twisted out of her backpack and dropped it and the remaining bags on the floor before going back out to get the chicken nuggets and toilet paper that had rolled down the steps. As she reentered the apartment, she flicked on the foyer light switch and looked at her grandmother sitting on the old worn couch with her feet up on the wooden coffee table that was littered with catalogues, newspapers, and last night's Chinese food containers. She closed her eyes and counted to ten. Their two cats, Stripe and Bossy, eyed her warily as they sat, one on each of the two mismatched chairs in front of the window.

"I did lock it," said Sally with conviction.

"No, you did not. It was open. I told you someone broke into the Garcia's apartment a few nights ago and the Nowak's the week before. Do you want to be sitting here in the dark when a robber breaks in?" asked Cassie, her voice filled with exasperation.

"Is it raining out?" asked Sally, her eyes never moving from the TV.

Cassie grunted under her breath and carried the grocery bags into the small galley kitchen. She turned on the oven to cook some French fries and started to wash just enough dishes for the meal they were about to eat. Two plates, two forks, two glasses. Mechanically she arranged nuggets on a plate, French fries on a cookie sheet. She briefly looked in the cabinets over the microwave for some canned vegetables, but finding none, made a mental note to buy some tomorrow and then rifled through the fridge for the ketchup.

"Can I have some Coke, Cassie?"

Cassie poured two glasses of Coke, grabbed the ketchup and salt between her arm and her stomach, took the two glasses, and walked into the living room, handing a glass to her grandmother. "Thank you." Sally gave Cassie a grin. She had lost her two front teeth and the next two were brown and broken. Cassie looked away. After watching her sixty-three-year-old grandmother lose her teeth from lack of care, Cassie was fastidious about dental hygiene. Brush, floss, gargle with fluoride rinse twice a day.

"I've got to eat fast tonight and I want to clip your nails. It's been on my mind all day." Sally made a face and put her hands in the pockets of her housecoat. "Joe will be here to pick me up in half an hour. I have a test tonight," said Cassie, walking through the living room to the hallway that led to their bedrooms.

At the end of the hall there was a tiny bathroom. Cassie noted that the faded blue wallpaper was peeling away from the wall over the toilet. She sighed. Another thing she should attend to. She washed her hands and combed her straight, shoulder-length, multicolored hair. Leaning toward the mirror, she pulled her hair taut on either side of her jagged part and looked at the two inches of light brown growth that became bleached blonde with stripes of magenta, purple, and blue. She still liked the bright colors. Joe said they looked cool, but she needed a touch-up. Another mental note, another thing to do on Saturday. After the wash and changing the beds and doing all the dishes. She looked down at the toilet and added scrubbing the toilet to her list. Weren't these supposed to be her carefree years?

She looked at her frowning face in the mirror. Her small, blue almond-shaped eyes looked back at her. They were dull, lifeless, tired. She tried to

7

stand up straighter. *Oh, who cares?* Disgusted with her hair, her face, and her life in general, she opened the drawer under the sink and was happy to see the nail clipper. She shoved it in her pocket and marched back through the living room to the kitchen.

She finished heating up the food and then plated the nuggets and French fries. "C'mon, Gram. Dinner," she said as she put the plates on the table. It took Sally a few minutes to get her legs off the coffee table, hoist herself up out of the couch, and arthritically move over to the table and sit down. They ate and watched the weather forecast. Clear and mild. Cassie was hungry, and the greasy fries tasted good and salty.

"Ouch! Ow!" Cassie watched Sally spit a tooth into her hand.

Cassie gagged on a nugget. "Jeez, Gram." Cassie went to the bathroom and wet a soiled washcloth lying by the side of the sink, then went to the kitchen to get ice. She came back into the living room with the cloth wrapped around a plastic bag of ice, a bottle of Tylenol, and a glass of water. As she handed them to her grandmother, Sally looked up at her with tears in her eyes.

Cassie frowned, wishing she had time to tend to Sally. "Here. Take two Tylenol and put this on to keep down the swelling. You have got to go to a dentist." Something she had been saying for years but never came to pass. As she sighed she heard Joe honk his car horn outside as he had done for the last two years. It was hard to get parking on the street at night, so Cassie hurried to get out the door. "Damn, now we don't have time to clip your nails. Gram, I have to go. I'll be back by ten."

"I prayed for you today. I prayed that you got to work safely and that you had a good day and that you got home safe, but God told me that he didn't hear me. He said I was just talking to myself." Sally held the cold cloth to her cheek and a little drizzle of blood flowed into the wrinkles that started at the corner of her lips. The broken tooth sat next to her dinner plate. It looked like a pebble—brown, gray, and yellow, with a silver filling and a blood-stained root.

Cassie looked at it and retched. "Try to clear the table while I'm gone," she said. As Sally stared up at her, the cold cloth against her cheek, Cassie heard Joe honk his horn again. "I gotta go, Gram. Keep ice on it. You'll have to put yourself to bed." Cassie grabbed her backpack and jacket and headed to the door. She looked over her shoulder at her grandmother and sighed. "I love you, Gram," she said and left the apartment, locking the door behind her.

Home to Australia

C assie often thought about the night when she was just fourteen and her mother, Jillian, had sat down on her bed and told Cassie that she was leaving and she wasn't coming back. When Cassie closed her eyes at night, she could still smell Jillian's spicy perfume and hear the creak in her old bed as her mother sat down—not near Cassie's head in order to stroke her hair and kiss her goodbye—but near her feet in order to leave quickly afterward.

"Jake is taking me home to Australia to be closer to his family," Jillian had explained. Even though her mother hadn't said it, and Cassie hadn't asked, Cassie knew that she was not being asked to go with her mother. Cassie often wondered why her mother had bothered waking her up at all. Why not just go, abandon her in the middle of the night, and let Cassie figure it out on her own? At least she hadn't told her she would be back, which would have been easier for Jillian. She hadn't apologized or given Cassie any advice about taking care of her grandmother, but just matter-of-factly told her she was leaving. Au revoir. Arrivederci. Ciao. Jillian had just squeezed Cassie's foot, tossed her long hair over her shoulders, grabbed their shared cell phone and charger, and left forever.

After the door closed, Cassie turned on her side, face to the wall, curled up, and cried deep sobs that she muffled in her pillow. She finally fell asleep by telling herself that her mother would be there in the morning, sitting at the old wooden dining table, smoking a cigarette in her baggy gray sweats. But when she went into the living room the next morning it was empty. Only the cats and an overflowing ashtray greeted her. She sat down at the table and pulled a half-smoked butt out of the pile. Dusting off the ashes she lit the cigarette and took a deep drag. Jillian had forbidden her to smoke, but now she was gone and Cassie would do as she pleased. Exhausted from the act of defiance and light-headed from the smoke, Cassie put out the butt and got back in bed.

Cassie and Sally stayed in the apartment for a whole week after Jillian left. They ate whatever food was in the refrigerator, then the cabinets, and then they ate nothing for a day. Sally never mentioned Jillian, Cassie never explained where she had gone. That week it felt like they were in mourning. Then, on the day that marked one week after Jillian left, Cassie woke up starving. She decided that today was the day she needed to get food. First, she went and took a long, hot shower, the first she had taken in a week. While she was towel drying her hair and thinking of what she would buy at the store, she realized there was a flaw in her plan. She had no money. Fear gripped her and made her feel light-headed. She took a deep breath and tried to think clearly. Surely, Sally had some money.

"Gram!" she said loudly entering her grandmother's bedroom, still dark from the drawn blinds. Sally opened her eyes and stared at the girl. "Gram, do you have any money? Money. We need money so I can go to the store."

"Is it raining?" asked Sally, pulling the blanket up to her chin.

"Gram, wake up. No, it is not raining. Where is the money? Do you have any?" asked Cassie, going to the window to open the blinds and let the bright light in.

"Ask your mother," said Sally, turning over to shield her eyes from the light.

Sweat drenched Cassie's armpits as her fear started to turn to panic. "Where's your purse?" Cassie asked, scanning the room until she saw the ancient black bag that Sally had always used on the chair. She grabbed it and dumped it out on the bureau. The wallet was empty and so was the change purse. She found one dollar and eighty cents in coins in the lining.

Throwing the purse on the bed, Cassie demanded, "Think, Gram. Where do we keep the bankbook? Do you have a bank card? Where do we keep the checks?" Cassie started going through the old wooden desk beside Sally's bed. The drawers were stuffed with old papers, emery boards, playing cards, pens, crayons, tissues, tubes of Blistex, but nothing that looked like a bank statement. "Gram, where are the bank statements? I need the account number. I have to go to the bank."

"Are you sure it's not raining? You better not go out in the rain," said Sally, who had placed the pillow over her face.

"It is *not* raining!" yelled Cassie. "Gram, I need you to think. Where are the bank statements? Where is the checkbook?" Getting no reply, Cassie went into the living room and started to look through the piles of old mail on the coffee table. She started to sort. Catalogues, bills, menus. She noticed an envelope from the apartment complex and tore it open. In big bold red letters, the statement had been stamped "Past Due."

Panic gripped Cassie's intestines and she ran into the bathroom. She sat on the bowl, her bowels emptying, sweating and crying, and hating her mother. How could she have left them without money? Without telling Cassie how to live without her? She realized in that moment that their survival depended on her, and the weight of it was crushing. She would have to take charge. When she couldn't cry anymore, she got up and washed her face in the sink with cool water.

She went into her bedroom, the room she had shared with Jillian, and the first thing she saw was a framed photograph of her and Jillian at the beach. She picked it up and looked at the happy smiles on both of their sunburned faces. Jillian had her arm casually placed around Cassie's shoulders. "Fuckin' bitch," Cassie muttered and threw it in the garbage can. "You had to be closer to *his* family. What about *your* family? What about us?"

Pulling the drawers in the dresser open one by one, Cassie saw that Jillian had taken all of her own clothes. She must have packed them when Cassie was at school the day she left. Cassie realized then that Jillian had been planning to abandon them, never dropping a hint. Never explaining anything to Cassie that she might need to know. Like where the money came from.

How to pay the bills. How to take care of Sally. The top two drawers were empty, but when Cassie opened the third drawer she found Jillian's suede jacket with the long fringe and knew that Jillian had left it for her because Cassie had always wanted it. Cassie slammed the drawer shut. "More trash," she mumbled.

The bottom two drawers were hers, so Cassie knew that the bank statements weren't in there. She sat down on the bed and looked around. The only furniture were the two beds and the dresser. Cassie realized she hadn't looked in the closet. She got up and opened the door. Everything belonging to Jillian was gone, but on the top shelf was a box covered in green foil. A pang of hope struck Cassie's heart. She went and got a chair from the dining room and climbed up on it to get the box.

She sat down on the bed with the box in her lap, biting her bottom lip. She stared at the shiny green foil. She remembered that she had wrapped the box one Christmas to give Jillian her gift. She took a deep breath and slowly picked up the lid and found what she was looking for. Bank statements for the last few years were neatly stacked in date order. Last month's on top. Thank goodness.

Cassie picked up the unopened envelopes and hugged them to her chest, relief overwhelming her. She tore open the one on top. Her eyes searched for the place on the page that would tell her if they had any money. The amount of $1,358 from the Social Security Administration had been deposited on the third of the month. She scanned down until she saw the word "Balance." Yes, that sounded right. She used her index finger to cross the page and see how much was in the balance column: $2,379. Closing her eyes, Cassie exhaled long and hard. But her chest tensed up again when she realized only Jillian's and Sally's names were on the account.

Taking the statement with her, Cassie went to find her grandmother, who was now sitting in the living room. "Gram, how do you take money out of the bank?" Cassie asked, sitting down on the old couch next to her grandmother.

Sally stared hard at the opposite wall, and Cassie knew she was thinking. Trying to remember. Jillian had always handled their finances. "Fill out the slip," she finally said.

"The slip?" asked Cassie.

"The withdrawal slip. At the bank." Tired now, Sally leaned back against the ancient, sagging couch.

Cassie tried to remember going to the bank with Jillian, but she never had paid much mind to what her mother was doing. The amazing neon fish in the tank by the service desk had always drawn her to them, or she had filled her pocket from the bowl of lollipops and chocolates that sat unguarded on a table in the waiting area. She did remember vaguely that her mother would go over to a counter with little cubbies, fill out some papers, and then go up to one of the tellers.

She scanned the statement again and found the account number. With the number and the bank statement she felt that the bank would have to give her some money. She would find the checks later and pay the rent. "Gram, I'm going to the bank and then the store. I'll be back later," she said, as she slipped on her flip-flops and perched her sunglasses on top of her nose.

"Bring your umbrella," was all Sally said as she turned up the volume on the TV.

Cassie sighed. She started to think about the bank. Should she pretend she was her mother? Should she confide in the teller? As she walked into the center of town she debated the pros and cons of each approach. She didn't really look like her mother. Her mother was taller and dyed her hair blonde, while Cassie was smaller, shorter, and had light brown hair. And then there was the age difference. Nineteen years.

By the time she reached the bank she had decided just to present the withdrawal slip and see what happened. The bank was crowded, and Cassie felt herself sweating as she filled out the withdrawal slip. How much money should she get? What was she buying? What could she cook? *Stop. Stop. One step at a time. Get the money first.* A hundred dollars. That should do it.

The withdrawal form called for a signature. Cassie thought about her mother's distinctive signature. The one Jillian was so proud of. The capital "J" just perfect. Each letter round and beautiful. Then she thought of Sally's signature. A mess of squiggles and loops. Yes, she would forge Sally's signature, and if caught, she would say that her grandmother was sick and couldn't make it to the bank.

Taking the withdrawal slip in her trembling hand, Cassie got in line behind a mother and her three fighting brats. Cassie watched as the older boy repeatedly poked his younger sister in the ribs and then turned away as the girl squealed and the mother reprimanded her. Cassie wanted to reach out and smack the boy in the head. When he turned around again their eyes met and Cassie scowled at him. He moved closer to his mother. *Baby!* Cassie thought to herself.

Happy for the distraction, Cassie watched as the mother was called to the next available teller. She was next. Her heart started to race. She felt it beating so hard against her ribs that she thought she might pass out. She reached out to the stanchion to steady herself as the young teller with the polished smile called to her, "Next!"

Cassie smiled as she approached the teller's station and heard herself say, "I'd like to make a withdrawal." Sliding the withdrawal slip and the bank statement under the plexiglass, she tried not to make eye contact with the teller.

"Are you Sally Bishop?" asked the teller.

"No, she's my grandmother. She's too sick to come in." Cassie stared at the teller with desperate eyes.

The teller sighed. "Doesn't your mother usually come in?"

"She's in Australia," said Cassie.

Again, the teller hesitated. "Okay. I'll do this one time but next time your grandmother needs to come in. Does she have an ATM card?"

Cassie shrugged. "I don't know. I'll ask her."

Why didn't she get two hundred dollars or five hundred dollars? That way she wouldn't need to come back to the bank again so soon. Cassie berated herself, but then thought, *One day at a time. At least we'll eat today.* The teller counted and recounted five twenty-dollar bills and then pushed them under the glass toward Cassie.

The teller watched Cassie scoop up the money. She reached under the counter, pulled out a form, and shoved it under the glass. "In case your grandmother's too sick to come in, have her fill out this form for an ATM card." She smiled at Cassie, and Cassie gratefully smiled back.

Nothing Scares Me Now

"**S**o, you've never even asked me if I use birth control," said Cassie as she looked down on Joe's naked back. She was sitting on his butt, straddling his body as she gave him a back massage.

"Mmmm. What?" mumbled Joe, who had lapsed into a semi-comatose state from the massage. "A little lower, baby."

"You don't care if I use birth control?" Cassie dug her nails into the soft skin under Joe's arms. He jumped and groaned, turning over beneath her.

Cassie slid off Joe, lay down beside him, and waited.

"So, what kind of birth control do you use?" he finally asked.

"So now you're assuming that I do use birth control," Cassie said with a tone of outrage. "Typical man. Just assume that the woman is taking care of it."

Joe looked confused and a little hurt. "Well, you are the one who gets pregnant. I just guess… You haven't gotten pregnant, so I thought you were already on something. You know, like the pill. Are you on the pill?"

"I have an IUD."

Joe picked up his head to look at Cassie, his hair a wild mane around his face. "A what?"

"An IUD. An intra-uterine device. I got it after my abortion when I was fifteen and it lasts for ten years. It's a hundred percent effective."

"You had an abortion when you were fifteen?" Cassie nodded. "Jeez, I'm sorry, babe." Joe slid his arm under Cassie's neck and pulled her toward him in a bear hug. "I hope the guy helped you out."

"He did. He brought me to the clinic and got me home before his wife got home from work," said Cassie. "He was our neighbor, and after my mother left he pretended to help me. Glenn—that was his name—told me that he and his wife were on the verge of divorce. He was unhappy, he said. He used to drive me to the store, and he was the one who taught me how to balance a checkbook. He even helped me get a part-time job at the laundromat. And then it came time to pay the bill." Cassie's voice caught in her throat, but she had a hard look in her eyes. "We started going to his friend's apartment in the afternoon when I got home from school and one thing led to another. Then I was pregnant. Puking all over the place. It sucked."

Joe hugged Cassie to him. "Did you think of keeping the…it?"

Cassie pulled back and hoisted herself up on one elbow to look at Joe. Her cheeks had turned red. "Joe, I was fifteen! So, no. I never for one minute considered keeping it. I already had enough responsibility. I was taking care of myself, or trying to. I had Gram to take care of. There was no room for a baby and Glenn was freaking out. He was so afraid I would tell someone. He could have been arrested. I was only fifteen. A minor." Cassie was trembling. She stopped talking abruptly and stared straight ahead as if she was in a different place. "But honestly, who was I going to tell?"

"I am so sorry you had to go through that, babe. I wish I had been there to help you." Joe looked at Cassie with the saddest eyes.

Cassie kissed Joe and gave him a resigned smile. "In some weird, twisted way, having to deal with such an adult problem so young helped me to understand that I could take care of myself. That no matter what life threw at me, I would get through it. I know that having an abortion at fifteen should be traumatic—and it was—but it was also empowering. Between Jillian leaving and getting knocked up, I had bottomed out, you know? Nothing scared me after that."

"No one but you would see it that way. I love that about you. How you look the worst times right in the eye and find something good to take away.

Not everyone can do that." Joe looked at Cassie with respect. "So what happened to Glenn? I hope he's not still around."

"No. He packed up his family and moved away and I never saw him again. Thank God." Cassie rolled over, grabbed her pack of cigarettes from the nightstand, and lit one up.

Joe rolled away from Cassie. "Damn, girl! Why do you do that? I'm sorry, but that is a disgusting habit. I'm taking a shower." Joe got up and went into the bathroom, and Cassie could hear the water in the shower running. She sat up and looked around the room for the ashtray she had bought for Joe's apartment. A pile of mail was next to the bed on the nightstand and on top was an envelope from Boston University. *Admissions Information* was written in bold red letters. The envelope was open, so she pulled out the slick catalogue and letter. Her heart started to race. Unable to stop herself, she started to read the letter as Joe came back into the bedroom with a red and white striped beach towel tied around his waist. He looked at Cassie, sitting naked on the edge of the bed and saw what she was reading. She took a last drag on her cigarette, spotted the ashtray under the other mail on the nightstand, and stubbed out the cigarette.

"Applying to BU?" asked Cassie, looking up at him with a glint in her dark blue eyes.

Joe closed his eyes for a moment before going over to the laundry basket piled high with clean clothes. He picked up a pair of blue boxers and put them on. "We'll go together, Cass," he said as he walked to her. "Come on. It'll be great. At least go up there with me for a visit." He reached out and stroked her hair, choosing a bright magenta piece to twirl in his fingers.

"I don't need to visit, I was already accepted two years ago," she said, throwing the papers on the bed and reaching down for her clothes, pulling on her panties and a short, ruffled skirt. Joe tugged on his jeans.

"Are you ever going to do anything you want to do? In your whole life?" Joe asked irritably. "Are we never going to be..." His voice trailed off.

"Joe, don't. You know I have...obligations." Cassie suddenly felt claustrophobic in the small bedroom. Since the bed took up most of the floor space, they had to keep their movements close to keep from hitting each other when pulling on their shirts, but that had nothing to do with the pressure that tore her in half every time she felt trapped between Sally and Joe. Joe reached out and tried to pull Cassie toward him, but she shook her head and sat down on the bed to pull on her socks and boots.

Joe leaned back on the dark wooden bureau that ran parallel to the bed and folded his muscular arms across his chest. "Is she always going to come first, Cass?"

Cassie finished pulling on her boots and looked up at Joe. "I don't have time to talk about this now." She got up brusquely and walked into the hallway.

He followed her into the living room doing a dance to put on his socks, hopping on one foot, then the other. "I'm applying and I want you to go with me."

"Can we talk about this tonight?" Cassie asked, putting on her coat. "Are you driving or am I?"

Joe pulled on his shoes, leaving them untied. "You drive so I can finish getting dressed."

Cassie grabbed the keys from the small table by the door and headed out of the apartment. Joe trailed behind her with a sour expression.

Married Men

Sierra Kole liked older married men. "I like my meat aged with a lot of green," she told Cassie. She liked the thought of them going home to their wives smelling like her. She had purposely wiped lipstick on many a collar. Once she even sprayed her perfume on a guy's jacket when he had fallen asleep in her bed.

She didn't take the time to figure out why she liked married men, she just knew she did. No boyfriend for her. She didn't want to hold hands in public or go grocery shopping together, she wanted the urgency of the secret encounter. She liked to think about the lies they had to tell to meet her at her apartment. And most of all, she liked knowing how guilty they felt when they snuck in the door at home. When they tucked in their children. When they told their wives they were just too tired tonight.

When an attractive man entered the pharmacy, she always looked to see if he was wearing a wedding ring. Of course, many men didn't wear rings, but she could always sniff out a married man. Usually they were at the pharmacy to buy something specific. Shampoo. Razors. Deodorant. They came in on a mission. As soon as she approached them, she could usually bring them down with one look. One unexpected look that told them she was available.

She knew how sexy she was. Not really beautiful, but very sexy. One victim had told her that she "exuded sexuality." She had had to look up the word "exuded" but when she did, she had to agree with his assessment. She had perfected a move—practicing it in the mirror—where she let her long, thick dark hair fall strategically forward, obscuring her face, and then she would toss it back to reveal her big, round dark brown eyes, tiny upturned nose, and thick, luscious dark red lips.

"Can I help you?" never sounded so dirty as it did when Sierra whispered it between the feminine products and the condom display. Letting her eyes drift ever so subtly to the Trojan packages. She loved the way they would get. All nervous. Without waiting for an answer, she would then turn and walk away from the man, swinging her ample buttocks and maybe sliding one manicured hand into the back pocket of her tight jeans.

Sierra also liked an audience and knew that Cassie, who worked behind the counter at Jenkins Pharmacy, got a kick out of watching her work over the men. She heard Cassie chuckle as she put on a show for Mr. Trench Coat. She and Cassie always gave her targets a name. As Mr. Trench Coat watched, his mouth slightly open, Sierra bent over without bending her knees, her curves on full display, to ever so slowly take one bottle of Pantene shampoo out of the box on the floor and place it perfectly on the shelf in front of her. Swishing her heavy curtain of shiny hair to the side to show off her perfect profile. The man literally shook his head to clear it so that he could pick up the Old Spice deodorant from the shelf and place it in the red plastic basket he was holding in his other hand. Sierra turned her head just enough to catch his eye and smiled. The man walked over to Sierra as if she was pulling him on a string and stood in front of her as Sierra heard Cassie sing the refrain from "Another One Bites the Dust."

Just then the bell jingled, signaling the door opening, and Mr. Trench Coat looked over to see who was coming in, his face covered with guilt. Sierra bent down again to get another bottle of shampoo, now looking bored. It was Mr. Ladinsky, the pharmacist and owner of Jenkins Pharmacy, returning from lunch. He was a sturdy-looking middle-aged man with pitted skin who himself was not immune to Sierra's charms. He was, however, one man who Sierra would never go for. She told Cassie that she "wouldn't shit in her own bed." And besides, Mrs. Ladinsky also worked at the pharmacy, and actually *seeing* her anger was not what Sierra was after. She wanted to imagine the pain. The tension. The fight that would ensue.

"Good afternoon, Cassie," said Mr. Ladinsky as he walked past the counter and turned down the cosmetics aisle toward the back of the shop where the pharmacy counter was located.

"Hi, Mr. Ladinsky," said Cassie as she watched Mr. Trench Coat nod to Sierra, make a wide semi-circle around her, and continue to the food aisle two lanes down. Sierra, now that her target was gone, bent down to pick up the box of shampoo and quickly stocked the shelf. Mr. Trench Coat filled his basket with milk, Cheerios, and a loaf of bread, then made his way to the counter to pay and escape the vixen in the shampoo aisle. A thin line of perspiration stood on his upper lip as Cassie rang him up.

"Warm today," she said as she placed the milk in a bag.

"Yes, warm," said the man, looking desperate to leave the store. He paid with his debit card, grabbed the bags, and headed out the door.

Sierra approached the counter holding a number of empty boxes.

"Literally saved by the bell, that one was," laughed Cassie.

Sierra struck a pose in front of her, fixing her enormous eyes on Cassie with an innocent expression. "Whatever do you mean?" she asked, adopting a Southern drawl. Sierra shared her exploits generously with Cassie, never holding back on any of the details. "He obviously wasn't worth my time if he was scared off by the tinkle of a little bell and the appearance of old Mr. Ladinsky. He wasn't really my type anyway. A little too clean… Now Joe. Your Joe. Mmmm, I'd break my marriage rule for a roll with him." She stopped there to consider Cassie, and then her face brightened as she said, "Cass, let's do him together. What do you say?"

Cassie wrinkled her nose. "Gross. I wouldn't go near you with a forty-foot pole. After watching the parade of men you've had and knowing all their ailments from their prescriptions? You better be careful. Why don't you get a nice young guy? One without kids and baggage?"

"That's just it. *I* don't want any baggage. I want them to take their bags and go home to their problems and just leave me with the sweet afterglow of knowing how lucky I've made them feel. I'm only twenty-two. I don't want a real boyfriend. Now, if you'll excuse me, I have to take out the trash." Looking back over her shoulder, she said, "But if you change your mind, let me know."

"Yeah. I'll think it over, but don't hold your breath," Cassie said with a smile.

As the afternoon wore on, the girls took turns standing at the counter checking out customers and restocking shelves. When it was Sierra's turn to stay at the counter, she was tired from carrying boxes and lining shelves with product. As she slowly approached the front she noticed that Cassie, as usual, had her eyes glued to a book. She read the title, *The Handbook of Journalism Studies*, and frowned.

"Why are you even bothering to go to school?" she asked as she walked up to Cassie.

"I know it seems weird, but I like it. I've always dreamed of being a journalist. Going around the world, covering important stories. Joe and me…we're thinking of applying to school in Boston," replied Cassie, nervously putting her hair behind her ear and exposing an interesting collection of studs.

"All studs today?" asked Sierra, tipping her chin toward Cassie, approving of her earring selection. "I don't know. College just seems like a waste of time to me. I hated school. All that sitting and listening to boring people blab on about other boring people who lived a long time ago and then testing us on it. Of course, there were a few teachers who I found inspirational," Sierra said with a wink. "Besides, who's gonna take care of your crazy old grandmother if you go off to Boston?"

"That's what I like about you, Sierra. You never hold back. But that is a good question. That's my problem," Cassie said with a frown. "There's no one else but me. Since my mom left it's been me and Gram. I love her, but she is zapping the life out of me, and now Joe really wants to go to Boston."

"Not you?"

"I don't know."

"Tell you what, I'll take Joe to Boston and you stay here with Grandma," said Sierra with a wicked smile.

Cassie looked down at her watch. "And it's five o'clock. I am so out of here," she said as she grabbed her backpack. "And you, Sierra, you are never leaving Tinden and you are never going to have Joe."

Sierra took Cassie's place behind the counter. "You never know," she called after Cassie.

Chores

"Cassie, I'm hungry. Let's go to Wendy's," moaned Sally.

"Gram, life is made up of chores," said Cassie, frowning. It should be her trying to get away on a Saturday afternoon without doing the chores, not her grandmother who she brought with her to the store and now was sorry that she had. Joe had let her borrow his car for a few hours, and she had decided it would be good for Sally to get out of the apartment. But ShopRite was crowded, and Sally was embarrassing her by commenting on other people.

"Cassie, look at that fat woman. So many of these women have such fat asses," Sally exclaimed loudly pointing to an extremely obese woman who had made the unfortunate decision of stuffing herself into black leggings and a tight bright red T-shirt. As the woman started to turn around, Cassie quickly steered Sally behind a large display of Ragu spaghetti sauce that was on special.

"Gram!" Cassie hissed. "I am not going to take you with me anymore. Stop embarrassing me. Don't point and don't insult anyone. I don't know why I try. I could have just left you home and shopped in peace." Cassie threw four boxes of assorted pasta into her cart.

"Cassie, do you think it's raining outside?" asked Sally.

"Gram, the sun was shining when we got here. I don't think it's going to rain today. We need cat food," said Cassie, turning down the aisle with pet supplies.

"I want chocolate pudding. It's probably raining. The sky looked a little dark," said Sally.

As Cassie loaded up the cart with cat food and litter, she said, "Gram, please, let's just get through this. Go to the checkout and read the magazines while I do the rest. Okay?"

Sally shrugged and shuffled off toward the checkout. Cassie sighed and headed toward the frozen food aisle for a few minutes of peaceful shopping. She just wanted to try to buy enough food for the week ahead so that she wouldn't have to come back to ShopRite. She could get milk and bread at the pharmacy.

As she was hurling frozen pizzas, mozzarella sticks, peas, and French fries into her cart, she could hear Sally offending other shoppers. Cassie decided right there and then that this was the last time she would bring Sally to the store. *Two more aisles,* she thought to herself. She now regretted that she had promised Sally Wendy's for lunch. *Maybe the drive-through and then I'll bring her home,* she thought.

As she rounded the aisle to the homestretch of the checkout counter she could see a situation unfolding. Father Cruz, the priest at the Catholic church around the corner, was in line, and Sally had his ear. Cassie, a devout nonbeliever, had to endure daily questions from Sally about God's lack of intervention in her life. Cassie could see Sally's fingers counting the buttons on her coat while she asked the priest questions. It was hard to explain to people about Sally's habit of counting the buttons on her sweater or coat to receive God's answers to her questions. If she counted three buttons then the answer was no. She always counted three buttons and therefore the answer was always no. Then, after being rebuffed in this way, she would accuse God of not listening to her, although according to her, he always did answer.

Of all the people in the world, Cassie felt that the clergy were expected to have patience for her grandmother, to take time for her, to listen and answer her questions. One look at Sally and it was obvious that she struggled with mental illness. She wore a kerchief on her head over her short gray hair, her coat was too big, her pants were too short, her teeth were unsightly, and she smelled like she needed a shower. But Father Cruz was not up to the task. He squirmed and cleared his throat and could not answer Sally's questions on the nature of God's work.

"I don't think he really hears me. I think I'm just talking to myself," Cassie could hear Sally saying as she looked for the shortest line to get on to check out. "Does he hear me, Father? Do you think he hears me? I've counted my buttons and they're telling me he doesn't. Do you talk to him? Does he answer you?"

At this point, all the shoppers reading the magazines at the checkout turned their attention to Father Cruz, who shifted his weight from one foot to the other. "Sally, we all hear God in our own way. God loves you. You're not talking to yourself," said Father Cruz in his official sermon voice.

Sally was not to be dismissed. "But the buttons tell me otherwise. I count three buttons and that means no. I don't like the rain, Father. The rain makes it gray and I always feel gray to begin with. Please tell him not to let it rain and tell him to have Joe drive safely when Cassie's in the car. And—"

"Gram, let Father Cruz do his shopping and we'll do ours. Okay?" said Cassie, taking Sally by the arm.

"Yes Sally, get your shopping done. Maybe we'll see you at church on Sunday," said Father Cruz, looking relieved now that Cassie had Sally in hand.

"We don't go to church. Cassie doesn't believe in God," said Sally as Cassie started to load her groceries onto the conveyor belt in the next lane down.

"Let's just get out of the store, Gram. Look at the magazines while I do this," said Cassie, tossing their groceries onto the conveyor belt and then moving to the end of the counter to quickly bag her own things. When she paid the cashier, he scowled as Sally absent-mindedly picked her nose.

"C'mon, Gram," she said as she headed out the door.

Cassie heaved a sigh of relief as she helped Sally into Joe's car and slammed the door. She loaded the grocery bags into the trunk and returned the cart to the cart station. As she got into the car she mentally went over the list of chores she still had to do before she picked up Joe at five o'clock. Next, she had to get Gram lunch and bring her home, then she had to go to the bank, then she had all the cleaning to do, and she wanted desperately to deal with her hair. She sighed. *Maybe I should just bleach the whole thing blonde.* Although she loved the magenta, blue and purple accents, dying all those different colors was time-consuming.

Time she didn't have. No, she never had any time for herself. All the things she *wanted* to do were overridden by what she *had* to do. When could she focus on herself? How would she get all the chores done in a few short hours? And if she didn't get them done, then what would happen? Cassie felt herself becoming light-headed. She was hyperventilating and she hadn't even realized it.

"The light's green," said Sally.

"I'll drive the car, Gram," she snapped irritably.

She remembered she had also promised to fill Joe's tank for him, so she pulled into the Exxon station. She looked at her watch. It was already two thirty. Sometimes she felt trapped between Joe and Sally. Taking care of Sally was a full-time job and being Joe's girlfriend was a full-time job. Joe had asked her many times to move in with him, but she couldn't figure out how to take care of Sally while living full-time at Joe's. She looked over at her grandmother as they waited for the man to pump the gas. She was picking her teeth with her dirty nails. Cassie looked away. Why did she have Sally to take care of? What would life be like without her? How would it feel to be free of her? To think of nothing but herself?

"I'm thirsty, Cassie," complained Sally, sounding like a child.

Cassie looked out the car window. She felt small. Alone. Lost. Singled out. Unfairly burdened. She thought about Sierra and how free she was to do whatever she wanted. Resentment, anger, and jealousy boiled up. They were unwelcome emotions but frequent companions. She was so deep in thought that she didn't realize the gas attendant was banging on her window.

"What's a matter, sweetheart?" he asked when she finally rolled down the window.

"You don't wanna know," she replied as she handed him her debit card.

Makeup Sex

Joe hit the disconnect button on his phone. It drove him crazy when Cassie didn't pick up. Why pay for a phone when you never answered it? It was five ten and Cassie was supposed to pick him up at five. He took a seat on one of the benches outside The Home Depot and watched the shoppers choose their fall annuals, mostly mums, from the huge selection that had been categorized by color. Yellow, maroon, white, burnt orange, purple. His knee bobbed up and down impatiently, and he wished he had brought a book with him to work today so he could be reading it now.

With nothing to do but think, his mind focused in on his predicament. How could he get Cassie to go to BU with him? He was going, with or without her. This was the year to do it. He had saved some money for the move and to get settled in Boston, and he was turning twenty-four. He couldn't wait much longer. He had retaken the SATs and scored 2360. *Pretty good,* he thought, although it did bother him when Cassie reminded him that she had scored a perfect 2400 without any prep. She was smart. He had to give her that, but her refusal to leave the old lady was getting in the way. He hoped that she was able to work out some plan with the home health aide she was meeting with this afternoon. *Put her in an institution, for Christ's sake, and live your life,* he wanted to yell at her. He absent-mindedly kicked at a large potted tree by the bench.

But what if she didn't? Would he go without her? He wasn't sure. He really did love that skinny little girl with a perfect moral compass and a great sense of honor. Damn, life would be perfect without Sally. *Maybe she'll die in her sleep,* he thought. That would be great. He closed his eyes and envisioned consoling Cassie, then packing the car and going off to Boston, where they would go to school, get their degrees, and become foreign correspondents, traveling to Africa and Bosnia, Paris and Frankfurt, Italy… They would roam the world with nothing to hold them back. He would win a Pulitzer…

"What's going on in your head that's so wonderful?" a voice asked, bringing him back to reality. Joe opened his eyes and took a minute to figure out what was going on. He realized he had been so deep in his daydream that he had forgotten where he was and hadn't noticed that a very pretty young woman had sat down beside him. Blonde, blue-eyed, and buxom with long legs and a great smile.

"Oh, wow. I was dozing off, I guess. Daydreaming. I wasn't snoring or anything, was I?" he asked, chuckling and giving her a big grin.

"No, just smiling," said the girl. Joe looked at the girl, who smiled a shy smile and adjusted her short skirt. "What were you daydreaming about?"

Joe laughed. "Do you really want to know?"

"Yeah, sure."

"Winning a Pulitzer."

"A what?" the girl asked, looking confused. Her big blue eyes searched his face for a clue. She looked totally baffled. Blank. How different from Cassie's sharp look. *What a boring girl,* thought Joe.

"It's a prize for writing," he said, stretching. He could feel the girl watching him with interest. Her eyes moving down his chest to his flat stomach and powerful thighs. Joe knew that in a minute or two she would mention some party or event and invite him to meet her. He started feeling uncomfortable knowing that Cassie was going to drive up at any minute. "My girlfriend is supposed to pick me up here. I'm going to…" But he was too late. As he started to get up, Cassie was pulling up in front of them. "Uh, bye," he said.

"See ya," said the girl, looking disappointed and kind of superior when she saw Cassie's crazy-colored hair, earrings, and tats.

As Joe got in the car he could sense that Cassie was pissed. "So that's what I get for rushing here? Throwing the nurse guy out of the house. Thinking you were waiting for me. I'm glad you didn't have to wait alone. Really!" Cassie took off out of the parking lot, just missing a minivan.

"Whoa! Slow down. I mean literally—slow down. Let's not kill ourselves because a girl said hello to me. Shit, Cassie," said Joe, throwing his orange Home Depot apron in the backseat and buckling his seat belt.

"Shit, Cassie," she mimicked.

"Don't be a bitch." Joe knew how this would end and he was looking forward to it. They would get back to his apartment, Cassie would slam the car door, and the second they were inside they would be at each other. If they made it to the couch they would be lucky. Even the erratic driving was turning him on. He egged her on. "She was just this beautiful girl who sat down next to me. Wanted to know what I was thinking about."

Cassie answered by making a sharp turn onto Joe's street, coming just a hair's breadth from a white SUV parked on the street. She pulled up in front of his apartment, threw the keys at him, got out, slammed the door, and started walking down the street away from Joe's apartment.

Joe got out, ran after her, picked her up over his shoulder, and carried her kicking and complaining back to his door. The minute he put her down she threw her arms around his neck, jumped up, and wrapped her legs around his waist. He fumbled with the key. She fumbled with his belt. They literally fell into the apartment and never made it past the small entryway.

When she regained control over her breathing, Cassie fell off Joe and rolled into the living room. Joe crawled along after her. She punched him in the chest one last time before she curled up with his arm under her neck. "Beautiful, my ass," she said. Joe reached down and squeezed her ass. One whole cheek fit in his hand.

"You do have a beautiful ass. Kinda scrawny, but beautiful," said Joe. "I love you, Cass."

"I love you, too." At some point, they made their way into the bedroom, ordered Chinese, watched old movies, and fell asleep in each other's arms. When the alarm went off at five thirty in the morning, as it did every morning so that Cassie could be there when Sally woke up, it was all Joe could do not to smash the clock on the floor.

Club Car Relay

F rank Jaworski knew every inch of Kensington Garden Apartments. All two hundred acres. All four hundred units. He made it his business to know every tenant and their habits. He went out early every day, around six o'clock, to check the grounds for any mischief that may have occurred during the night. Frank's enemies came in the furry variety—raccoons and feral cats—and the much more onerous kind, the human teenage variety. The raccoons made a mess of the garbage, and the cats left pieces of their kill all over the sidewalks, which was a nuisance but could be cleaned up quite easily. However, the teenagers did their mischief with spray paint which was hard to clean up, or discarded used condoms which was just disgusting.

Frank rode his club car around the grounds noting what had to be cleaned up, repaired, or tended to once his team arrived at eight o'clock. Frank loved his club car and was quite a sight with his beady eyes and leathered skin showing underneath his painter's cap, a woolen scarf flying out behind him as he pushed the club car to its maximum speed. It was the best part of his job. He loved to take it out and ride the grounds before the dog walkers got up. There were a lot of dogs in Kensington Garden Apartments, but the owners were pretty good about cleaning up after them. The dog walkers were followed by the high school kids, then the guys who worked construction, then the moms and the younger kids, then the nine-to-fivers. Frank knew everybody's schedule. He also knew everybody's business. He knew who was sick, who was cheating, who was pregnant, unemployed, re-employed, getting married, getting divorced, shacking up, moving in, moving out. He made it his business to know what was going on.

As he rounded the corner on his first surveillance ride of the morning, he saw Cassie Pennebaker coming home again at the crack of dawn. Why was that girl giving it away to that black boy? If she would just get rid of that crazy-colored hair and all of the hardware she wore in her ears, she could be a good-looking girl. And smart. He remembered when she was a little girl she could recite the alphabet and count way before she went to school. He remembered her mother, before she ran off with that Australian guy, bragging about her report cards and all the A's she would get. Some of the other kids used to call her "99" because that was the lowest grade she ever got. But Frank had to credit the girl for taking care of Sally.

Frank had known Sally for forty years. Ever since he came to work at Kensington Apartments when he was twenty years old and just stepped off the boat from Poland. Sally was a sad case. She was always crazy, crying and throwing things. Got herself knocked up and had her daughter, Jillian. The girl was a piece of work. Only cared about herself. Although, he imagined growing up with Sally as your mother would have been hard. And now here was Cassie with that black boy. What a shame. Frank shook his head as he watched her kiss Joe and then slowly climb the few steps up to her apartment. He decided to go and talk to her.

He pulled up on the sidewalk in front of her just as she was about to go in. "Good morning, Frank," Cassie said without smiling.

"Mornin', Cassie. When are you going to straighten yourself out and get a nice Polish boy?"

"I'm not Polish, Frank. I'm American," said Cassie with an exasperated tone. "I have to go in. Gram's waiting for me."

"What does Sally think of the boy?"

"Frank, please. I'm going in," said Cassie, turning the knob and opening the door.

"It's a damn shame, that's all," said Frank as he stepped on the pedal and the club car moved away.

The apartment complex was cut in two by Mountain View Drive, oddly named because there were no mountains to view, however, the road provided more parking for residents. Frank crossed Mountain View and was nearly at the last apartment on the property when he smelled it. Pot. Marijuana. Mary Jane. Reefer. Weed. Whatever the kids were calling it these days, the substance had been a problem at Kensington Apartments since Frank got there. Frank stopped and sniffed the air like a terrier. Where was it coming from? He closed his eyes and breathed deeply, trying to decide if the smell was coming from a car parked in the road, an open window in an apartment, or from behind the hedge that ran across the far boundary of the property.

He opened his birdlike eyes with a determined stare and rode his club car quickly over the grass toward the hedge. As he did, a cloud of smoke emanated from between two firs. *Caught ya,* thought Frank. He ran the club car right up to the hedge, shaking it with the fender. Two boys wearing black hoodies over their heads ran down the length of the hedge and out onto the sidewalk and down the street, away from Kensington Apartments. Frank gave chase, flooring the club car, driving in mad pursuit along the hedge and making a sharp right down the street after the hooded kids. The boys, looking back, dodged between two parked cars and headed across the main avenue. Frank stopped the club car at the spot where the boys had run between the cars. He knew he couldn't follow them across Randall Road, the main drag.

Damn, he swore, feeling exhilarated and making a mental note to check the hedge for the next few mornings. He loved the chase. He hadn't had a good one in a while. He smiled to himself as he turned the club car around and continued on his rounds.

Broken Plates

As Cassie pushed open the door and stepped inside, a plate hit the wall next to her head with such force that it shattered, the white porcelain falling in shards on the floor.

"Whoa, Gram! What the fuck?" swore Cassie, turning her face away from the spray of cheap china that fell like shrapnel around her feet. Strands of spaghetti from the night before flew off the plate and stuck to Cassie's thigh.

"You slut! Leaving me here alone. I didn't know if you were ever coming back," screamed Sally, her thick, wiry gray hair sticking straight up, her sleeveless nightgown slipping off one boney, wrinkled shoulder.

Cassie turned and shut the door. "I don't know why I *do* come back. You should be nothing but grateful when I come home. You should thank me every time I walk in the door, but instead, I get this," she screamed back. Anger and frustration welled up inside her chest. "I don't need this shit! I could leave right now and go live with Joe and go to Boston and go to college like I want to, but I don't because of *you,* and this is how you treat me? Fuck you! Do you hear me, Gram? Fuck you!" Cassie faced Sally, her muscles quivering, pulse speeding. Her cheeks were flushed and she was breathing heavily.

"You're just like your mother! She's a slut too." Sally looked around and picked up the first thing she saw. She hurled the television remote at Cassie's head. Cassie ducked, but the remote caught her shoulder.

"Stop it! Do you hear me? Don't throw things at me. Go back to bed." Cassie took a few steps toward Sally with a menacing look on her face and pointed toward the hallway. "Go! Go back to bed while I clean this up. You have no shoes on. You'll cut yourself."

Sally's mouth hung open in a toothless grimace. She reached out to the back of the couch to steady herself. The fight had gone out of her. "Don't leave me, Cassie. I'm scared when I'm all alone."

"I *should* leave you. You're ruining my life," Cassie screamed, then, under her breath, "but for some reason I stay." In a voice Sally could hear, she repeated. "Now, go back to bed." Cassie went into the kitchen to get the broom as Sally turned and shuffled, head hung, into the hallway on her way back to bed.

Cassie took a minute to collect herself. She steadied herself by putting a hand on the back of one of the old chairs by the windows and rubbed her eyes. This had been her life since her mother left six years earlier. Cassie had always known that there was something wrong with her grandmother when she was growing up, but she never knew exactly what it was. Sometimes Sally would cry for hours, never getting out of bed or coming out of her room, or sometimes she would fly into a rage, screaming, throwing things. Other times, she would act like anybody else and could carry on a relatively cogent conversation. Cassie never knew who she was going to find at home.

Jillian had taken her mother to many doctors. Cassie remembered as a little girl sitting in various waiting rooms and hearing her mother repeat strange-sounding diagnoses. Schizophrenia. Post-traumatic stress disorder or PTSD from abuse as a child. Manic depressive. There had been many different diagnoses, but putting a label on whatever tormented Sally had not helped to cure her.

Cassie remembered Jillian trying to sedate Sally, putting mashed-up pills in her food. Sally wouldn't take them herself, and when Jillian begged her to, they would fight, cursing and shoving each other, until Jillian would storm out of the apartment. Sometimes Cassie wished that she and Jillian could run away to Florida, where a neighbor had told her it was warm and sunny all the time, but Jillian never talked of leaving—until she did.

Sally had scared off a lot of Jillian's boyfriends, but Jillian would just go out and get another. Cassie had stopped counting the number of men who dropped by the apartment to pick up Jillian, leaving Cassie and Sally alone for days sometimes. Cassie noticed that Sally was calmer when Jillian was gone. She remembered Sally had been the one to teach her the letters of the alphabet and how to count to ten, how to tie her shoes and brush her hair. Sally had taken care of Cassie while Jillian was at work. They would eat cereal and watch Kelly Ripa in the morning. They would laugh at Cookie Monster and follow the adventures of Dora the Explorer. Sally put Band-Aids on her knees and kissed her good night. But over the years, Sally had deteriorated to the point where now she was not even able to tie her own shoes or button her own shirt.

The details of Sally's early life were sketchy. Cassie knew that Sally had been expelled from high school when she was sixteen, but she didn't know why. She knew her parents had died in a car crash when she was twenty and that she had married Ernie Bishop when she got pregnant. In an old cardboard box in the hall closet, there were black-and-white photographs of Sally as a child and as a teenager. Cassie had looked through them one day and saw her grandmother as a child, smiling, waving, with her arms around another girl. At the beach. Eating ice cream. She looked so normal. She was pretty. Prettier than she was herself, Cassie had thought, with long wavy golden hair, twinkly eyes, a strong nose, and a wide, happy smile with big white teeth.

But by the time she was in middle school, it was clear that something had happened. Her bright smile was gone, the sparkle of youth had left her eyes. Cassie was struck by one photo of Sally and a friend. "Susan" it said on the back of the photo. Two young girls, maybe twelve or thirteen, similar in height with bodies just budding. But the difference between the two girls was obvious. Sally radiated sadness whereas the other girl was bright, happy, carefree.

Cassie sighed and finished sweeping up the broken plate and the spaghetti, then went back into the kitchen to get a wet paper towel to wipe the wall and floor. As she scrubbed the wall she looked down at the floorboard and saw old splatter from other plates Sally had thrown at the wall. Spots of brown gravy. Something yellow. A touch of green. Cassie closed her eyes and took a deep breath.

Sally never fought with Cassie when she was little, but when Jillian left, Sally began to lash out at her. It was like their relationship had replaced the relationship Sally had with Jillian. Cassie sank to the floor, leaning against the stained wall, and let her exhaustion seep in. She felt defeated to her core. Why was this her life? The ramifications of the damage done to Sally decades ago were still here, living on in Sally's mind and impacting Cassie's life. Sally had never been able to heal. What would it be like to live a life without Sally's pain in it? Cassie closed her eyes and tried to focus on something positive, anything, so that she could summon the strength to keep going. She thought about Joe's smile, his beautiful nutmeg-colored lips, and she felt a little better.

She got up and walked back into the kitchen and stuffed the dirty paper towels into the garbage can, which was already overflowing. She pushed the garbage down and then pulled the plastic bag out of the can and tied it. She looked at the clock on the microwave. Eight o'clock. She had to be at work at ten. She picked up the bag of garbage, walked over to the back door, and peered through the blinds to see if the dumpsters in the back of the apartments were full. She saw that they had already been emptied, so she opened the door and went out onto the small back porch they shared with their neighbor, Rick Smollett, a thirty-five-year-old ex-Marine.

As soon as Cassie opened the back door, Rick opened his. This happened a lot and Cassie suspected that Rick somehow watched her every move. She imagined a small hole that he had drilled in the wall they shared between their kitchens. As she turned to close the door behind her, she immediately regretted not throwing a jacket on over her thin white T-shirt. In her haste to get home this morning, she had shoved her bra in her backpack.

"Good morning, sexy lady," Rick said with a grin, slowly looking her over from neck to toe. Cassie heaved the garbage bag into her arms to cover her chest and started to walk toward the stairs. "No hello?" he called after her with a bit of an edge.

"Hello," muttered Cassie without looking back over her shoulder, and kept walking to the dumpster. She would have to walk back to her apartment without the cover of the garbage bag, so she decided not to throw the garbage away. She turned around, still holding the bag, and started back to her apartment. Rick was sitting in the old wooden rocking chair that Cassie had bought at a garage sale for Sally. She felt him watching her and kept her eyes on the ground.

"Keepin' that garbage?" he asked as Cassie climbed the stairs.

"I think I threw out a knife," she said.

"Ha!" Rick said, spreading his legs far apart to make it impossible for Cassie to get to her door without touching him.

"I'm late for work, Rick," Cassie said as she brushed past him.

"But you just got home," he said, leering up at her. He was wearing a dirty wife-beater and she noticed the words "Semper Fi" tattooed on his bicep. She remembered him telling her that it was the motto of the Marines. "I heard the fireworks when you walked in. Thin walls," he said with a sneer.

Cassie looked down at Rick, all of her favorite curse words streaming through her head. She couldn't seem to put enough of them into one sentence, so she said nothing as she felt the blood flowing into her cheeks and knew that they were getting red. Rick smiled at her, his eyes mocking her. "Is that what you look like when you're hot?" he smirked. She noticed his heart-shaped face, the way his cheekbones eased up into his eyes when he smiled. He reminded her of the Grinch. She wanted to kick him but decided to walk away and slam the door as hard as she could behind her instead.

More Like Your Mother

oe's desk, which was really a slab of wood held up by two sawhorses, was covered with Boston University brochures, postcards, maps, copies of the Common Application, marked-up copies of essays, and transcripts. He had been working on his essay for the Common App for a few hours now. Five hundred words that would sum him up, make him special, and get a college admissions officer to admit him to the university six years after high school graduation.

This was his fifth draft of his third attempt at saying something insightful. If he wanted to be a writer, the essay was all the more important. If he couldn't write a persuasive essay about a subject he knew a lot about—himself—then maybe his goals were out of whack with his talent. He didn't have any extracurricular activities or community service, but he was poor and black. *That's good,* he thought, chuckling to himself. *What else do you do in life that makes being poor and black a good thing?*

As his mind wandered, he thought back to the time he was in a department store with his mother and he had decided to play a prank on her. He was maybe six or seven years old. While his mother stood in front of the mirror and held up clothes to see how they might look, he had quickly taken a dive into the middle of a circular clothes rack. Then, when she realized he was gone, he had watched as she went from annoyance to panic.

At first, she just called his name, but when he didn't come back to her, his mother's voice took on this desperate quality, and then he was afraid to come out. Afraid of her anger, so he just curled up in a ball and stayed where he was. The store manager, a clerk and a few customers all started to call his name and look for him. Finally, a woman who later said her own small son had played the same prank on her parted the dresses on the circular rack and found Joe. His mother put her arms around him in relief, but what he remembered most was the tone of the store manager when she asked, "*This* is your son?" Her voice was filled with disapproval. She had pointed to Joe, and then one by one the other adults who had helped his mother just walked away. No one said, "Thank God you're safe," or, "Don't play pranks on your mother again." They did not seem relieved that he was found. They just walked away.

Joe shook his head at the memory. He looked around the room for inspiration for the essay; his eyes stopped on the corkboard that Cassie had hung over his desk and decorated with an assortment of photos. In some, they were together. Others he had taken just of her. His favorite showed them together at the beach: he was coming out of the waves with Cassie riding him piggyback, her head thrown back, laughing. He remembered his mother had taken that one. Another showed Cassie in her dark purple thong with a bright round rhinestone in her belly button, all tanned at the end of the summer.

He looked at his watch. Damn, it was four o'clock. She had promised to be there by three to read his essay. Rubbing his tired eyes, he thought again about how to get Cassie to leave her grandmother. How he had grown to hate that old hag. If she was a good and kind person, it would be different, but the way she treated Cassie, he just couldn't understand it. Cassie said she was sick, but he didn't care anymore. He *had* to persuade Cassie to go to Boston with him and live her life. Cassie needed to realize that she shouldn't give up her whole life just because her grandmother was crazy and her mother had run off. He had to get her to come up to Boston with him to visit the campus. He had cousins in Boston and they would go out and have a blast.

Cassie was the reason he had zeroed in on Boston University. She had told him about her junior year of high school, and how her guidance counselor had insisted that she apply to college. The counselor, Ms. Levine, had good connections with the admissions officer at BU and she knew Cassie well enough to know that the Ivy League schools would intimidate her. With a 4.0,

2400 on her SATs, and her story of caring for her mentally ill grandmother after they were abandoned by her mother, Cassie had a shot to go to any school she wanted, but Ms. Levine thought she could help Cassie get a full scholarship at BU.

Cassie hadn't even wanted to apply. Ms. Levine had practically tied her to a desk and made her write her essays, and then she had filled out the application for Cassie. And she was right. BU had offered Cassie a full scholarship. Then, Cassie had deferred a year. Then another. Now they were saying they understood the situation with her grandmother, but this was their last offer. Joe hoped that he, too, could get a full ride, and he thought he could.

The time to act was now. He was twenty-four and working at Home Depot. Joe looked around his tiny apartment with the dirty walls, the faded rug, the scratched coffee table, and the recliner he had picked up at a garage sale, and thought, *I can do better than this.* He had written a few articles for the *Tinden Record,* but writing freelance articles didn't earn him enough to pay his rent. At least they were the beginning of a portfolio.

Joe yawned and went over to the leather couch—the one nice piece of furniture in his entire apartment—and picked up Weezer, his old white and marmalade-colored cat, laid down on the couch, and settled the cat on his chest.

He must have fallen asleep, because the next thing he knew, Cassie was coming in the door. She had dyed her hair again, adding a green stripe.

"Hey, babe," she said.

"What time is it?" he asked.

She took off her jacket, threw it on the recliner, and squeezed onto the couch next to Joe. She pulled on one of Weezer's ears as he purred. After a while, Cassie said, "So I finally cut her fingernails."

Joe winced. "Sometimes I wish you wouldn't share these things with me."

"I'm getting really good at it. Maybe I'll become a manicurist," Cassie said, picking up one of Joe's big hands and looking at his nails. "Do you want me to clip yours? All but your sorry little beheaded finger?"

Joe took his hand back and petted the cat. "I'm good. So…I've been working on my essay. Actually, I've written three different ones and I think I've settled on one. Will you read it for me? For grammar and, I guess, organization?"

"Did you notice the green stripe in my hair?"

"I did. It looks cool, babe. I like it. Will you read it?"

Cassie sat up, giving Weezer's ear one more tug. The cat looked at her and yawned. "Joe, I'll read it, but does that mean you're actually leaving if you get in?"

Joe sat up next to Cassie, dismissing the cat, who slunk off to the bedroom. They sat there staring straight ahead in the fading light. His muscles tensed as he tried to hold back his anger at the situation, at Sally, but when he looked at Cassie his heart broke. He loved her so much and he just wanted her to be free, to be happy. He took her hand. "Cassie, I want us to go to Boston together. This is your last chance to get a full ride. They said so. We can go to school. Become journalists. Let's live our dream, babe." He reached over and took Cassie's pointed little chin in his hand and gently pulled her face to look at him. "Babe?"

Cassie closed her eyes. "And what am I supposed to do? Just leave her in that apartment to die? She can't live without me." She pulled her face away from him. "What about Rutgers? Maybe we can go to Rutgers together. I think they'll take our credits from the community college."

"You don't have a full scholarship to Rutgers—"

"Maybe I can get one—"

"We need to get out of here. Start over—" Their voices grew louder and louder with each interrupted sentence.

Cassie stood up and screamed, "Joe, you need to understand, I have a responsibility. I can't just leave. Do you want me to bring her with us?"

Joe jumped off the couch, his frustration bubbling over inside; his cheeks felt hot. He towered over her. "Cass…I gotta tell you…it's our turn. It's our turn to live. Your mother left. She didn't feel this responsibility that you feel. Why? Why is Sally your responsibility? Why can't you be more like your mother?"

Cassie's face was bright red and tears started streaming down her cheeks. "Really? You want me to be more like my mother? Wow, are you kidding? You don't know what you're saying. Jillian thinks of herself 24/7. What's best for Jillian is what's best for everyone. Should I leave you when things get hard? If you get sick. Should I just move on and leave you? Huh? Well, I'm sorry. I'm not like her. She is a selfish bitch. Is that you want? To be with a selfish bitch who only cares about herself?" She whirled around, picked up her jacket, and started walking to the door. She turned and faced him. "Joe, I know you can't understand this, but Gram's the only one who has stayed with me." Cassie looked down. She took a deep breath that made her slight chest heave. "And now you're leaving." She took a step toward the door and put her hand on the doorknob. "You know, sometimes, after we have dinner, just Gram and me, I cut up a banana for her and she sits and eats it, and I can remember her doing that for me when I was little. And it's just the two of us. And she's quiet. I feel some kind of peace—"

Joe pulled on his curls. "Are you sure she was there for you, or were you there for her? Cass, you've been the adult since you were fourteen with adult responsibilities. Don't you just want to be young? Now, when you *are* young?"

"Of course I do. I want to go to Boston with you. I want to go to college. I want to see the world, but you just don't understand. What am I supposed to do with her?" Cassie closed her eyes and ran her hand over her brow as if to soothe the pain in her head. Then she turned and opened the door.

"Cassie, wait…" Joe started toward her, but she held up her hand.

"Joe, you need to do what you need to do." She looked at him with her clear blue eyes, and he turned and sat down heavily on the couch. She opened the door, took a deep breath, and walked out into the night.

Young and Free

Growing up Cassie never had any girlfriends. She never felt comfortable enough to invite a girl home with her. She didn't want to answer questions about her grandmother, plus she didn't want to risk a friend having to deal with Sally's unpredictable behavior. Boys were happy to be with her even if she had a crazy grandmother because she was willing to experiment with sex, but girls did things like staying up all night gossiping or painting each other's toenails or going shopping for fun. Things Cassie never did. She didn't know any gossip, she rarely painted her nails, and the only shopping she ever did was for groceries.

Once, in the tenth grade, she had joined a study group that met at the library. She thought maybe she could find other smart girls who didn't like these girly things, but she soon realized even the smart girls liked to talk about clothes, pop stars, and kissing. None of these girls had had sex, which she already had. None balanced the family checkbook, which she did. None cooked dinner, did the dishes, and washed the clothes. No, as soon as her mother left Cassie had to take on all the responsibilities of a full-grown adult, and there was no time for trivial girl friendships.

But tonight, she was going out. She had called Sierra, the only young woman she ever spoke to, and they were going to the Dragger Inn. A working-class bar that she used to go to before she and Joe started going out. The bartenders at the Dragger Inn rarely carded young women: they were happy to see them. Cassie was dead set on going out and getting drunk and forgetting about Joe. Forgetting about BU. Forgetting about Sally. Forgetting about her fucked-up life. Tonight, she was going to be young and wild and free. Just like Joe said she should be. She was going to try to be more like her mother, even though the thought of that turned her stomach.

Joe had called her a bunch of times and left messages, and she was worried that he would show up at her apartment before she could leave, so she had made Sally eat dinner early, afterward throwing the soiled plates and silverware in the sink for tomorrow. Sally had watched her, over her meatballs, chewing slowly, knowing something was up. Any deviation from the routine was suspect.

Cassie retreated from Sally's disapproving stare to her room. She opened the small closet and turned on the light. A lone bulb in the ceiling. She hadn't gone out in a long time. She and Joe usually stayed in watching movies, having sex, and doing homework. She searched out her tightest low-rise jeans, a black long-sleeved T-shirt, and her Free People tunic. She rarely had money to buy such extravagant clothes. It had cost her eighty dollars and was made of sheer white muslin with red embroidery on the shoulders and down the front. She and Joe had gone to the mall just to walk around one day, and she had seen it in the window of the shop. Joe had encouraged her to buy it, and she had, but she rarely wore it. She didn't know what she was saving it for, so she pulled it off the hanger and put it on. She pulled on short black boots and closed the closet.

Looking at herself in the old mirror on top of the ancient dresser that Sally always insisted was an antique, she liked the look, but now she needed jewelry. On the dresser was her jewelry box, another prized possession. Joe had given it to her for her birthday. It was made of cherry wood and opened like a small closet. Inside was a revolving rack for necklaces and two drawers where she kept her earring collection. First, she popped out all of the everyday studs. In the bottom hole on each ear she inserted thin silver hoops with long white feathers hanging from them, followed by an assortment of small turquoise shapes that moved up her ear. She slipped silver rings on both of her thumbs. Next, she made up her eyes with black kohl and lots of black mascara, finishing with clear gloss on her lips.

48

She tried to smile at herself in the mirror, but the thought of Joe knocking on the door and spoiling her plan made her hurry. Tonight was her night. She was going to be a girl with no responsibilities tonight.

As she came back into the living room, Sally was settling herself on the couch between Stripe and Bossy.

"Cassie, I think it's raining out. Bring your umbrella. Where are you going?" asked Sally suspiciously.

"I'm just going out, Gram. It's Friday night," Cassie said, still trying to pretend that she was a normal girl.

"I'll pray for you then. Can you hand me the remote? God doesn't hear me anyway." Sally held out her hand for the remote. "The buttons tell me so."

Cassie felt her imaginary normal world slipping away. She grabbed the remote and handed it to Sally. "I gotta go. I'll be late," she said and kissed Sally on the top of her head. She grabbed her knock-off North Face fleece out of the hall closet and slipped out into the cool night air, locking the door behind her.

She had told Sierra that she would meet her at the 7-Eleven on Route 11, the major highway that ran just north of Kensington Apartments. Cassie didn't think Sally and Sierra would get along. Sierra would think Sally was disgusting and Sally would probably insult Sierra. Sierra would insult her back and things would go south from there. Neither of them had any filters. Better to keep them apart.

The night was quiet as Cassie walked down Kensington Terrace and turned left to walk up Boxwood Row toward Route 11. On the corner was the 7-Eleven, which was always a hub of activity. Teenagers milled around smoking and looking at their phones, moms ran in for milk, dads ran in for beer. Cassie went inside and bought a pack of cigarettes. Six dollars and seventy-five cents. What a rip-off. But tonight, cost was no obstacle. Tonight, she was going to smoke and drink and be irresponsible. She went out, passing a group of young punks who looked her up and down.

"Hey, sweet hair," said the leader of the group, a tall, lanky boy of sixteen or so. "What's up?"

"Go home to your mommy," Cassie said and walked over to where two broken pay phones hung on the brick wall. Their cords hanging without receivers. She opened up her pack of cigarettes, pulled out the foil, and lit one up. As she waited, she felt relaxed. She had left her cell phone at home on purpose, turned off. No one in the world except Sierra knew where she was. No one could bother her. No one would ask her to do something for them or make a major life-decision. There was only tonight. As she was stamping her cigarette out with her boot, she saw Sierra's bright yellow Beetle pull into the parking lot. She waved and Sierra pulled up and Cassie got in the car. The boys watched, and when they saw Sierra they started to hoot and whistle.

"Who are your friends?" Sierra asked as Cassie got in and shut the door.

"Just the local riffraff," Cassie said as they headed out of the parking lot.

"Nice. So I thought we'd go back to my place first. I have a six-pack of Corona so we can drink it before we go. One beer at the bar costs as much as the whole six-pack."

"Sounds great," Cassie smiled and nodded at Sierra.

Sierra lived in Freemont, the middle-class community next to Tinden. They blasted Rhianna as they drove along, singing "Umbrella" as loud as they could. Sierra pulled off the parkway and drove to her apartment complex, pulling into the parking lot. As they got out of the car, Cassie said, "So, this is where all those guys in the pharmacy end up. This is the place where their marriages come to die?"

"I don't think of it that way. I think this is where they come to keep their marriages alive. They have me. They feel sexy again. And guilty. I'm doing a public service, really." Sierra inserted her key in her first-floor apartment.

"A public service! I love that! You are so twisted. I can't believe their wives would see it that way." Cassie stepped inside and looked around. "Wow! This place is nice! How do you afford all this? I know you work a few more hours than I do, but not enough to have all this stuff." Sierra's apartment was spotless and decorated in a contemporary style with two sleek white leather couches, a glass coffee table, and a soft gray carpet. A large flat-screen television hung on the wall.

"Many of my friends help me out," said Sierra with a wink. "And there's the money that my father left me." Cassie sat in one of the two tall chairs at the counter that divided the kitchen from the living room. She had never seen anything as beautiful as the white marble countertop with the muted gray and black swirls. She kept running her hand over the smooth, cool surface. This was the nicest apartment she had ever been in. She tried to imagine living here. Closing her eyes, she imagined Joe coming home from work and hanging his coat on one of the hooks Sierra had by the front door and coming into the kitchen where Cassie would be cooking dinner at the stove. He would put his arms around her from behind and lean in close to kiss her neck.

Sierra got two Coronas out of the fridge, cut a lime into thin wedges, stuck one in the neck of each bottle, and placed one in front of Cassie.

"You falling asleep?" Sierra asked.

Cassie opened her eyes and smiled. "No, just trying to imagine living in a place this nice." She picked up the beer and tipping the bottle at Sierra. "Thanks. Cheers! I'm sorry your father died."

"Don't be. It's the best thing he ever did for me. He was rich but such a shit. Had a heart attack in between marriages, and I'm the only kid. The only legitimate one anyway." Sierra sat down next to Cassie.

"So, why do you work at the pharmacy? I mean, you could work at the mall in a clothing store and get a discount."

"Yeah. But then I'd have to deal with all those snotty little bitches looking for clothes. *Do I look fat in this?* Barf. I couldn't do it. And there are no men in women's clothing stores." Sierra looked closely at Cassie. "So, what are you doing out without Joe? We've been working together for a year now and this is the first time you've ever called me to go out. Did you guys break up?" Sierra wore a hopeful look. "You know I want to have that man even though he has no money."

Cassie smiled. "No, we did not break up. We did have a fight though." Cassie took another swig of her beer and felt a slight buzz go to her head while she tried to decide whether or not to confide in Sierra. "He wants me to move to Boston with him and go to school, which means leaving Gram. That's the problem in a nutshell."

Sierra drank from her beer. "Why can't you just leave her? She might surprise you and be able to do more for herself than you think."

Cassie considered what Sierra just said. Something she never thought about before. "Anyway, I'm not thinking about it tonight. Put on some music. Let's get this party started."

Sierra got up and disappeared down the hallway to the bedroom to find her iPod. Cassie looked around the apartment at the nice things Sierra had. From the soft pink blanket that hung off the back of one of the couches to the fancy coffee maker on the kitchen counter. How much had it all cost? When Sierra came back, she said, "Why don't you just smother the old bitch when she's sleeping and put her out of her misery and go live your life?"

Cassie laughed. "Now you sound like Joe. He wants to leave her to die. But I'm not going to do that and I am not going to worry about it tonight."

Sierra answered by cranking up the music and got them each another beer. As she handed the cold bottle to Cassie she started to dance and Cassie laughed. Sierra pulled her to her feet, and as she swayed to the music she felt all the tension that she carried around every day start to magically leave her body. She felt light. She felt free. She closed her eyes and let the music move her body. When she opened them, Sierra was smiling at her, and when the song ended they fell on the couch hooting and laughing. Cassie felt her skin tingling: every inch of her was alive. When the beer was gone, the girls brushed their hair, reapplied lip gloss, and headed out into the night.

The Dragger Inn was down the street from Sierra's apartment, which was a good thing because both of the girls were tipsy by the time they left. They swayed and weaved a little as they walked, bumping into each other and laughing about it. As they walked into the dark, crowded bar, Cassie saw Rick Smollett sitting at the first table by the far wall. *Damn,* she thought, *he could be a problem. I don't want to deal with any problems tonight.* She wanted to disappear into the safety of the crowd without him spotting her.

Sierra had headed into the swarm of drinking, laughing, flirting young people, and Cassie followed her. They made their way to the back of the bar and lined up behind a group of young men to order a beer from the bartender. Cassie saw Sierra scanning the room for a victim, a man to buy her drinks and take her home. They made their way up to the bar to place their order, and when the bartender came back he said, "Compliments of the guy at the end of the bar," and slapped two Coronas and two shots of lemon vodka on the bar. Sierra and Cassie looked down the bar to see who it was. Cassie was afraid she already knew.

Sitting at the end of the bar wearing his most sinister Grinchy grin was, of course, Rick Smollett. Sierra raised her shot and toasted Rick and downed the vodka. Cassie downed the shot without acknowledging Rick.

"That's my lecherous neighbor," she shouted into Sierra's ear above the music.

"He's coming this way," Sierra shouted back.

"He's all yours," Cassie replied.

"Is he married?"

"Divorced." Sierra wrinkled her perfect nose at Cassie's reply. As she did, Rick worked his way sideways into the space between Sierra and the back of the man beside her and leaned on the bar.

"Well, well, well," he said slowly, looking at Cassie. "What have we here? My little neighbor without her bodyguard." He inspected Sierra and broke out into a huge grin. "And wow. What a replacement! Hello! Cassie, who's your friend?"

"We're taken, pal. Thanks for the drink, though," said Sierra, and she turned her body toward Cassie as a shield.

"You're not even twenty-one. You shouldn't even be in here," she heard Rick yell in her direction from behind Sierra, as he left and melted into the swarm.

Cassie and Sierra continued to drink and played pool with a couple of guys until last call. Men of every description had been hitting on them all night, and Cassie knew that Sierra was trying to pick which guy to take home. There was the handsome guy in construction boots, the fireman with the bright blue eyes, the pseudo-preppy guy with his pink collar flipped up and his perfect teeth, and then there was Rick, who kept circling back to the girls throughout the night, biding his time like a fox. Cassie thought she could detect some attraction between Sierra and Rick. Rick had been coming on to

Cassie for a long time, but she had never taken his advances seriously. She thought of him as a lecherous old man. Way too old for her. Part of her wished that Sierra would choose him so that he would leave her alone, however, she was just beginning to realize that she had to get home somehow, and it would be convenient to get a ride from Rick.

As Cassie sat on a barstool in the very back of the bar pondering, in her drunken stupor, what to do, Rick appeared in front of her. In a minute he had pushed her back against the wall and was trying to kiss her. His hot, thick breath covered her nose and mouth. It disgusted her and she tried to turn her face away from him, but he grabbed her hair in his fists on both sides of her face and held her head still while he tried to push his tongue in her mouth. Cassie was too small and drunk to fight him off. She grabbed his wrists and tried to push him back, but his arms were like steel and she was defenseless against him.

She was kicking and squirming when Rick got pulled off her by the back of his shirt. Cassie's heart skipped a beat when she saw it was Joe. He punched Rick square in the nose. Blood sprayed and splattered all over Cassie's face and white tunic with Joe's first blow. Rick ran at Joe and pushed him back hard onto the pool table, but Joe quickly rolled over and off the table as Rick's fist came down and hit the felt. Joe was younger, stronger, and sober. Rick was no match for him as Joe hit him squarely in the face again and he went down in a heap on the floor.

Joe grabbed Cassie by the arm and dragged her out of the Dragger Inn, practically carrying her by the scruff of her neck as they went out the door. Neither looked back to see if Rick got up.

When they got out to the parking lot, Cassie struggled to get away from Joe. "Joe, stop pulling me. What are you doing here anyway?" she asked slurring her words together.

Joe stopped and faced Cassie and stared at her. "Who are you right now? And the question is, what are *you* doing here?"

Only Herself to Depend On

assie woke the next morning, but the pain in her head was too great to open her eyes. After two or three attempts she opened one eye long enough to figure out that she was in Joe's bed. She uttered a sigh of relief, which was quickly followed by disjointed memories of the night before. Drinking with Sierra. Shots of lemon vodka. Rick. His tongue in her mouth. Rick hitting the floor. Joe yelling. It was a montage of images that ran through her mind. She gently slid her hand toward Joe's side of the bed, but it was empty. Another sigh of relief. Maybe he had gone to work. What time was it? What day was it? Gram.

She raised her arm to her eyes to look at her watch, and when she did, she realized that Joe was leaning on his dresser watching her. He wore only his underwear. Neither of them spoke. Her frayed nerves, sour stomach, and throbbing head were making it hard for Cassie to focus. She gave Joe a wobbly smile.

Sounding more like her father than her boyfriend, Joe asked, "So, you want to tell me what you were doing last night?"

Cassie mumbled something indecipherable.

"Excuse me?" Joe said with attitude.

"Being young."

"Being young."

"And irresponsible."

"Irresponsible. That's sounds about right," said Joe with a shake of his head.

"You told me to be young and live my life." Cassie tried to lift her head, but the room started to spin and she sank back into the pillow.

"So it's my fault?" Joe scoffed. "I didn't tell you to let that drunken asshole slobber all over you."

"I didn't invite that…How did you know where I was?" Cassie squinted at Joe. His normally sparkling eyes were the darkest forest green, and he wore a serious look that Cassie had never seen before.

"He could have hurt you. He was all over you. It was disgusting," he said, turning to sit on the bed.

"It *was* disgusting. What I remember of it, that is," said Cassie. "I don't really remember much. I do remember you punching him. I hope that was a good idea. He was a Marine, you know."

"So? He didn't fight like a Marine. He went down on the second punch, he was so drunk. Asshole. And you have to see him every day. You said he lurks around and waits for you to go to the garbage. Cass, you gotta get out of there." Joe reached out to push a lock of hair off Cassie's cheek.

Suddenly, Cassie sat up straight. "Oh my God! What day is it? Saturday? I have to go home and meet with the home health aide. She's coming today…" Her head was spinning. She slumped back onto the pillow.

"Here we go. Run. Run home. You don't even care about patching things up with me…"

"Of course I care, but Joe, I have to get some help with Gram. Then maybe we can spend more time together. The woman is coming at eleven. Isn't that what you want, Joe? What time is it?"

"I guess…"

"If it works out I'll go to Boston with you to see the university," said Cassie, knowing this would make Joe happy. Maybe help him forget about Rick and the bar.

Joe was too smart to be manipulated so easily. "Really? You think a trip to Boston should make me forgive you?"

Cassie maneuvered herself around so that her head was lying on Joe's thigh. "Would it?" she asked, but when she tried to look up at Joe's face the room started to spin. "I think I'm gonna be sick," she said as she tried to sit up. Joe got up fast to let her pass through the tiny room to the bathroom.

Cassie just made it to the toilet, slumped down on her knees, and emptied her stomach. After each hurl, she took deep breaths to try to steady herself. When there was nothing left to come up, she stood up on shaky legs and pulled herself over to the sink to wash her face. *I am never drinking again.* She looked at her reflection in the mirror and noted that only one of her feather earrings had made it through the night. As she looked at the mascara smudged under her eyes and her pale cheeks, she wondered, *Is being young overrated?* She had never felt so old and sick from trying to be young. She ran Joe's brush through her hair and went back into the bedroom.

"You look like shit," Joe said.

"Don't be mean. Will you take me home?" Cassie got dressed. When she picked up her Free People tunic from the floor to turn it right-side-out, she saw that her treasure had a tear at the shoulder seam and a spray of blood across the front. When Joe looked at her with her ripped shirt and one earring the anger melted off his face, and he went and took Cassie in his arms for a hug. "I'm coming to your apartment with you and I'm gonna listen to the aide and help you work this out. You're in no condition to understand everything she says, and Sally is usually scared of me. She won't put up such a fight. And I'll be there if Rick shows up. C'mon, I'll help you. Okay?" Joe looked down at Cassie and she merely nodded her head. She felt too sick to fight him.

As they got in Joe's car Cassie looked over the roof and asked him again, "How did you know where I was?"

"Sierra texted me. She said she was leaving the bar with some guy, and you were so drunk that she didn't want to leave you there alone. She's a good friend, Cass."

As Cassie bent her head to get into the car she muttered, "Yeah, I'm glad she texted you."

It was just eleven o'clock as they pulled up in front of Kensington Apartments. Saturday was the worst day to park, but Joe insisted on finding a spot and going to the apartment together. Cassie knew Joe wanted to be with her if Rick confronted her.

Cassie felt nervous. She had never come home so late before. What would she find? Would Sally have broken all the dishes? Would she be frantic? Still in bed? Crying? Yelling? Cassie had no idea. As they drove by the apartment, she noticed that all the shades were still drawn. She was glad that Joe wanted to come with her. It felt good to rest some of the burden on him.

"There's a spot," she said, pointing up the street. Joe pulled in and they got out of the car and walked to the apartment.

An eerie silence permeated the air as they walked in. Sally was nowhere in sight. Cassie took a deep breath, wondering where she was. There were no broken dishes or spilled food in the living room or the kitchen. The apartment had an empty feeling.

"I'll go look for her in the bedroom." Cassie went through the apartment and down the hall. When she opened Sally's door she was relieved to see that her grandmother was still in bed. But as she walked into the room she noticed blood on Sally's forehead. Dried blood dripped down the side of her head, into her left eye, and down her cheek.

"Gram!" Cassie rushed over to the bed. She reached out to shake her grandmother and watched her grimace. "Gram! What happened?"

Joe came running into Sally's room. "What happened?" he asked, looking from Sally to Cassie.

"Gram, are you okay?" Cassie asked again.

"I fell and hit my head…last night… You never came home. Cassie, you never came home. I was all alone," cried Sally, her breath coming in wheezing bursts. Tears mixing with the dried blood as they ran down her cheeks.

"I'm sorry, Gram. I'm sorry. I overslept." She turned to Joe. "Can you get a wet cloth?"

"Should we take her to the emergency room?" Joe asked. Cassie saw genuine concern on his face. As he spoke the doorbell rang.

"Oh God, it's the aide. Maybe she can help us. Go let her in, please." Cassie motioned to Joe.

"Who's here?" demanded Sally, but without her usual bite.

"Stay right here. I'm going to get a wet cloth," said Cassie. She hurried to the bathroom to get the cloth. She wanted to see how big the cut was. She knew that face wounds tended to bleed a lot. As she came out of the bathroom, the aide was standing by the door.

"I'm so glad you're here. I just got home and found my grandmother with blood all over her face. She says that she fell. Maybe you can help us." Cassie looked up at the stern-faced woman wearing a pink sweater, her hair in a tight bun.

"I haven't been hired yet," she said curtly.

"Please help us," said Cassie. She could feel the tears coming on. It was all too much. The drinking, the fight, Rick's forcing himself on her, now the blood on Sally's face.

"Let me look," said the woman.

Cassie led her down the short hallway and into the small bedroom. The smell of Sally's unbathed body filled the room. The aide put a hand to her nose. Without looking at Sally she went and opened a window. Then she turned to look at Sally. "When did she last bathe?" she asked Cassie, bringing her hand up to her nose again.

"Is that really the most important question right now? Please look at her face. Look at the cut," pleaded Cassie.

"No, I can't work in these conditions. I'm sorry. Take her to the hospital." The aide backed out of the room.

Joe placed himself in front of the woman. "Wait a minute. You do this for a living and this is how you act? Can't you show some compassion?"

"Please. Get out of my way. I'm sure the agency will send someone else."

"I can't believe this," said Joe, raising his voice.

The aide looked surprised, and when Joe didn't move out of her way, she started to look scared. "Excuse me," she said, but Joe didn't move.

"Let her go," said Cassie. "She doesn't want to help us."

The aide quickly skirted around Joe and made for the door. Joe shook his head but let her go.

Cassie sat next to Sally and started to wash her face and tend to the cut. All she really wanted to do was to curl up in her own bed and go to sleep. She couldn't remember ever feeling this tired, this hopeless. In her mind she had created a world where the aide would show up and solve all her problems, but that woman had given her a reality check. Once again, she only had herself to depend on. The aide had made that clear.

When she cleaned the blood off Sally's face the cut itself was small. Right above Sally's left eyebrow. She brought Sally some tea and toast. When Sally drifted off, Cassie took Joe's hand and led him into her room. She hoped that he had seen that she had tried to get help for Sally and what she was up against. It wasn't that easy to give your burdens away. As soon as they lay down Cassie was sound asleep.

Semper Fi

Rick Smollett was an early riser. After eight years in Afghanistan he was a jittery, paranoid insomniac who slept with one foot on the floor so he could spring out of bed at the slightest sound. A twig breaking. A throat clearing. Cassie's key in her door. Ever since his wife left him the year before, taking their two daughters with her back to Iowa, he had lived in Kensington Apartments. Since the first time he had seen her, he had been drawn to Cassie's firm little body and her complete lack of interest in him. Actually, he could tell that he made her nervous, and he liked it.

Now, after that son of a bitch had given him a swollen eye and a fat lip, he couldn't leave his apartment. He didn't want Cassie to see him this way. He'd called into the job sick; told the boss he had the flu. Twice in the last week, in the pre-dawn hours, he had snuck out to the all-night bodega and loaded up on beef jerky, mac and cheese, Coke and cereal. It was lucky that he had made a beer and tequila run the day of the fight and stocked up. He had been holed up for a week, so his supply was getting thin; garbage filled his small kitchen.

He liked the gray light of the night when the moon was his guide. It reminded him of being on the base in the Afghan desert where he had been stationed for three deployments, until the incident that had earned him a dishonorable discharge. He'd been sent back to civilian life ill-equipped to be a husband, father, and nine-to-fiver. He tried not to think about what had happened, how he had been caught doing what all the soldiers did, but he had been caught literally with his pants down, and so he had been court-martialed and discharged. The big double D—Dishonorable Discharge—no pension, no benefits.

The missus had not taken kindly to the news, and he had not taken kindly to her reaction. He had taken a good look at his supposed daughters before they left, and he wasn't really sure they were his. They were both blonde, and true, their mother was blonde, but he certainly wasn't. Didn't it take two parents with blonde hair to make a blonde baby? He was sure he had read that somewhere. He didn't care for their high, screechy voices and their crying and their mess of dolls and crayons and had uttered a sigh of relief when he saw them pile into his wife's car and leave. Good riddance!

Best not think too long of her abandoning him after he had risked his life for her and this country. It only made him angry. His mind flipped to Cassie, and from her to the fight. If he hadn't been so drunk, and if Joe hadn't attacked him from behind when he had his mind on kissing Cassie, he would have killed that bastard. He still had his Beretta M9 pistol hidden in his dresser. He could feel her there. Feel her power. See her shiny black body and feel her kick back. Smell her gunpowder, a mix of chalk and burnt paper. Rick loved his Beretta, more faithful than any woman he'd ever had. Always ready to go. Always happy to see him.

Stuck in his apartment he started to fantasize about taking Cassie away with him. They'd go to Mexico where he had ex-Marine friends. She had to want to get away from that old woman. God, she was a sight, and the stink and the screaming and the throwing. Yes, Rick should take Cassie away from all that. They'd buy a motorcycle and ride it down to Mexicali, where Stan and Jake had ended up after it all went down. He just needed to talk to her and maybe play the victim now that she had seen Joe knock him out. Joe was violent. He would beat her too, Rick would tell her. Rick would convince Cassie to leave the old woman and Joe. He had a bullet for each, if need be. He didn't have many bullets left and couldn't chance trying to buy any online. She didn't have to know; it would be a surprise. A gift. Maybe he didn't even need a bullet for the old lady. Just a pillow placed gently over her face until she stopped struggling. He laughed to himself. Yeah, he could fix all of Cassie's problems, and she didn't even know how easy it would be.

Deciding to have another beer, Rick got out of the lawn chair in his living room—the only piece of furniture in the room—and walked to the front windows to see what was going on. Using two fingers, he pried the blinds apart just as Joe was emerging from Cassie's apartment. *Bastard's living there now,* he thought to himself, and spit on the floor. *Disgusting how she degrades herself.* He watched Joe bounce down the steps, his girly curls flying in the wind, and get into his Honda.

How could he get Cassie alone so he could talk to her? He needed a plan. Wiping his mouth with the back of his hand, he went into the kitchen to get the beer.

Three's a Crowd

During Sally's recovery, Joe moved in with Cassie. Actually, he used Sally's recovery as an excuse to protect Cassie from Rick. He knew Rick would want to retaliate for getting knocked down in the bar, and Joe didn't want the retaliation to involve hurting Cassie. He was also finding it nice to come home to Cassie at the end of the day. Cassie got off around the same time, and they would go home and make dinner. The nights they had class they ate fast and then drove to the school and came home together. He fantasized about them being married. There was only one problem, and that was Sally.

The first week everything was fine. The second week he could tell Sally was feeling better but getting cranky that he was still there. Then, on the Monday of the third week, Joe got home before Cassie and was met with a bowl of cereal flung like a Frisbee at his head. Caught off guard, he reacted without thinking and lunged out and pushed Sally back. She fell into one of the old chairs by the front windows just as Cassie walked in the door. Sally tried to blame everything on Joe, but Cassie had come home to too many flying plates to believe her. However, Joe couldn't push Sally, even when she threw something at him.

The accusations and counter-accusations went on and on, and Joe suddenly realized he could use a night off. Sure, he felt guilty leaving, but enough was enough. Thoughts of his bed at home, peace and quiet, and tranquility overwhelmed him. He went into the bedroom to pack his stuff.

Cassie did not come after him. Joe realized that they could all use a night off. Rick had lain low the entire time Joe was living with Cassie, and Joe thought maybe he had been wrong, maybe Rick would stay away now.

❀ ❀ ❀

"I'm going home for the night," Joe told Cassie when he came out of the bedroom. She was on her knees mopping up cereal and milk. Sally sat eyeing Joe from the chair. She looked at him as if she had won. He scowled at her.

Cassie's shoulders slumped forward and her eyes fell to the floor. She had liked Joe living at the apartment, helping her with chores. Having Joe and Sally in the same place had consolidated her life. Less running back and forth from apartment to apartment. Sleeping warm and safe in his arms every night. Why had Sally ruined her little bit of happiness? But Sally was always the victor. She did whatever she wanted to do and Cassie was defenseless. Counselors had told Cassie to dispense "tough love." Tell Sally that *if you do this, I'm going to do that.* To Cassie it seemed like advice from people who had never actually dealt firsthand with a mentally ill person. Sally's mind couldn't process the relationship between her actions and Cassie's actions. She didn't really understand rational reactions. Cassie had learned that lesson a long time ago.

"Okay," was all she said to Joe.

Once Joe left, the apartment felt empty. Cassie looked over at Sally and Sally gave her a defiant stare. "Well, thank God he's gone," Sally proclaimed.

Cassie looked at Sally. "Gram, you do know that I love Joe, don't you? He's my boyfriend, and maybe someday he'll be my husband."

"Oh Cassie, marriage never works out. People are never who they seem to be."

"I know it's hard for you when I'm with Joe, but you need to know he's a part of my life and will be forever."

"Are you making dinner?" Sally asked, closing her eyes. "I need some aspirin. He hurt me."

"Then don't throw things at people," Cassie said, raising her voice.

"I didn't."

Tired of arguing, Cassie picked up the dustpan full of cereal, the wet paper towels, and the brush and slowly walked into the kitchen. Feeling like she couldn't take a full breath, like there wasn't enough air in the apartment, she opened the back door and found Rick sitting in the old rocking chair with a Budweiser in his hand. *Jesus Christ! When am I going to catch a break?*

Startled and then frightened, she shrieked. "Rick, what are you doing sitting here?"

Rick smiled his sickly grin, and Cassie noticed that his face had healed. "Unlike some folks, I actually live here," he said. Taking a long pull from the Budweiser he looked up at Cassie. "What do you see in that boy anyway when you could have a man?"

"Rick, don't. Joe and I are together and that's that. I am not interested in you. Leave me alone. Please." Cassie started to shut the door, but Rick jumped up quickly and put his boot on the door frame and his free hand on the doorknob.

"I could help you," he said in a hushed tone.

"I don't need any help. Please, just let me go. I have to make my grandmother dinner," she pleaded, her voice sounding shrill.

"Yeah, that's the problem I can help you with."

Cassie's and Rick's eyes met, and she tried to figure out what he was talking about. "Well, thanks. I don't need any help. Now, please...please let me close the door..."

"Cassie! Cassie! Are you making dinner? I'm hungry. I want an aspirin. Cassie!" Sally's loud wailing interrupted Cassie's pleading with Rick.

Looking desperate now, Cassie whispered, "I have to go," and pushed Rick's hand off the doorknob.

"You think about what I said. I can lighten your load," he said, moving his boot from the door and swigging back the rest of his beer. Cassie closed the door, locked it, and put the chain in place.

One Day at a Time

Before the cereal incident, Cassie and Joe rode home together from Kent Community College every night. This semester Joe was taking Journalism III, Cassie was taking Journalism II, and they both were enjoying Philosophy 101. Because of their part-time schedules it would take them four years to earn an Associate's Degree. Then they would have to transfer to a four-year school to earn a Bachelor's Degree.

Joe was hoping that BU would accept at least some of their credits. He had taken one writing course per semester and thought that he was getting pretty good. His vision of being a foreign correspondent included riding in a helicopter across enemy territory to expose insurgents, covering peace summits, and writing travel pieces from Monaco and Marseilles. He saw himself as the new and improved Hemingway—biracial, sensitive toward women, adorable instead of ruggedly handsome, but also a great writer and hard drinker. He yearned to go to Paris and Barcelona, Prague and Brazil, and he knew that Cassie would love it too. She was tougher than he was in many ways and she had a natural writing style. He could see her staring down dictators and rebels alike, but she also had a tremendous heart and pools of empathy that he wished could be redirected to self-indulgence and ambition to make a name for herself.

Was that what he really wanted? Wasn't her empathy, her sense of loyalty, and abundant heart why he was so in love with her?

They hadn't seen each other since he had narrowly escaped being hit in the head with Sally's cereal and he had left the apartment. That had been a few nights ago. It was unusual for them to spend any length of time without seeing each other, but Joe felt that he needed some space to try to understand his feelings for Sally and how she interfered with his relationship with Cassie. It didn't look like Cassie was leaving Sally any time soon, and Joe had to figure out if he could try to build a life with Cassie at the same time as Cassie took care of Sally. So far, he couldn't reconcile his dreams of being a globe-trotting reporter with taking care of Sally. When he dug really deep he had to admit that he felt sorry for Sally, and, of course, he felt sorry for Cassie having to deal with a sick relative, but he also wanted to live his life and he knew he wanted to live it with Cassie.

He decided to take it one day at a time. She was old. Anything could happen.

Zen Not Prozac

Three days later, Cassie looked down at her phone and saw that Joe was calling. She picked it up immediately.

"Hey," she said.

"Hi."

Pregnant pause.

Joe finally said, "I'm sorry I didn't call."

"I wanted you to."

"I miss you—"

"Should I come over tonight?"

"Yes. I can't wait to see you."

Cassie was glad Joe had made the first move after he had left her the other night. For the rest of the day, after his call, she had felt lighter, and now it was easy to admit how worried she had been about their relationship. She couldn't wait for her class to end. When it finally did, she could feel her pulse racing as she hurried down the main hallway of the glass and steel English building at the college to meet Joe in the parking lot.

As she opened the door to leave the building, she saw Joe standing in the flood of light flowing down from the streetlamp. He was talking to two classmates, and she could hear his wonderful laugh as one of them reached out to touch his shoulder and finish their story. Cassie stopped and watched. She felt like she was floating as he threw back his head, his wild curls momentarily framing his beautiful face, and she felt the same feeling that she felt every time she saw him—that they belonged together. That they were actually born to be together. Some people called this phenomenon "meeting their soulmate" but Cassie just called it lucky.

She jogged toward him, no longer able to wait to feel his arms around her. At that moment he looked away from his friends toward her and a smile appeared on his face. Cassie inhaled deeply, her breath catching in her throat as she ran toward him and he extended his arm to wrap her in his embrace. Without missing a word of the story, he made her a part of the group. She buried her face in his jacket and breathed in the smell of him, detergent and spice.

Warmth crept through Cassie's veins as she laughed at the young man's story. She was really only laughing at the delight of being alive in Joe's presence. But it felt so good to laugh. The story was merely an excuse to hear Joe's laughter. All of the tension of Gram and Rick and BU fell away and only she and Joe were left. The story ended and his friends said their goodbyes and walked away. Joe pulled Cassie in for a long, tender kiss. When they parted, he looked down into her eyes, and for that moment everything in Cassie's world made sense.

"So, ya missed me?" he asked after a minute.

"Yeah, I missed you." Cassie's eyes sparkled as she grinned at him.

Joe turned Cassie in the direction of his car and they started to walk through the parking lot. Most of the students had left and the lot was mostly empty. As they walked, Joe's protective arm around her shoulders, a light snow began to fall, and it was beautiful. Cassie stopped and stuck out her tongue to catch a few flakes and Joe did the same. When they put their heads down to look each other in the eye, Cassie said, "I love you, Joe."

"I love you, Cassie."

"Joe, let's not do anything to ruin this one night. Okay? Let's make this our perfect night."

"Will you still read my essay?"

"Yes, but I won't talk about BU."

"It's a deal." They arrived at his car, and he opened the door for her with a gallant gesture. As she bent her head to get in, he pulled her out again. "Cassie, I always want you to be safe. I only want you to be happy."

"I know." She reached up and put her hands on either side of his face. She looked deep into his eyes and then pulled his face to hers and kissed him before getting into the car.

They drove through the quiet streets listening to Led Zeppelin. Cassie had been thinking about what Joe had screamed at her when they fought: that she should be more like her mother. She knew he was just angry and didn't really mean this—he didn't even know her mother—but it had started her thinking about why she hadn't gone to Boston two years ago after high school. Why she stayed and felt that Sally was her responsibility, when Jillian clearly did not. She didn't know the answers, but while she figured it out she had decided that the only way to live her life was by trying to compartmentalize it. She would enjoy her time with Joe, but then go home and do what she had to do for Sally. It was the only way to balance out the good with the bad. She needed to train her mind to stop going over and over her problems and mentally adding to her ever-present to-do list. Joe would have his time and Sally would have her time.

She knew this approach fell apart when they had to make the decision to go to Boston—or not—but tonight, until she went back to Sally, it was just her and Joe. She looked over at him and smiled, and he gave her a quizzical look.

"Who stole my girl and left this mellow babe in her place? Wait, are you breaking up with me? Are you pregnant? Did you take Prozac or something?" Joe asked, looking genuinely concerned.

"Now that's an idea. Maybe that would solve all my problems. No, I'm trying to find inner peace, be more *zen*."

"Inner peace?" Joe laughed.

"I'm always so intense…"

"Yes. Yes, you are," chuckled Joe. "But that's kinda sexy. I have to get used to your new tranquility, but right now you're making me a little nervous."

"I've just decided to try and find a little happiness when I can. When I'm with you. Is that okay? No talk of Gram or laundry or cleaning the toilet or clipping her nails. When I'm with you we'll talk about you—and me—apart from her. Let's try it." Cassie reached out and put her small hand on Joe's arm.

"Yeah, I can try that. I can pretend she doesn't exist," he said with a huge grin, pulling the car to a stop in front of his apartment.

"I'll bet you can," Cassie said, returning his smile. "C'mon, let's get in before it really starts to snow."

Free as a Bird

Cassie opened her eyes and stared at the face of her old clock. It was so dusty she could hardly read its face. *Add dusting to the to-do list,* she thought. It was Saturday, chore day, and her list was long. Go to the library and get books to research her Philosophy paper; go to the supermarket; call the home health aide agency and ask for another aide and complain about the first one while on the phone; try to get Gram to take a bath; clean the bathroom; pay the bills. Raising herself up on one elbow, Cassie took a deep breath, letting the oxygen filter through her sleepy brain and wake her up.

"Cassie!"

She was immediately awake now. "What? Yes. I'm coming." Cassie moaned as she threw off the blankets and sat up. She was wearing a cotton cami and matching bikini underwear, and the room was cold as she looked around for her old flannel bathrobe. She spotted it at the end of the bed and hurriedly put it on. Shivering, she got up and walked over to the radiator and felt the cool metal, only a hint of heat coming up. Her slippers were on the other side of the bed, and she quickly hopped-jogged over to them.

"Cassie! Are you here?" screamed Sally, her voice piercing the early morning calm.

"Yes! Yes, of course I'm here. I'm coming," Cassie yelled back. "I'm not up two minutes and you have already pissed me off. Quit your yelling!" She walked into the living room to find Sally wearing only a thin nightgown.

"Where is your robe? You'll catch a cold, and I do not need you to be sick." Cassie walked back to Sally's bedroom, got the robe, and returned to the living room. "Here, put this on," she ordered, holding the robe out so Sally could slip it on.

"I'm hungry, Cassie," said Sally, settling into the couch.

"Yes, I know." Cassie walked into the kitchen and turned the switch on the wall lamp. "I have got to get another light for this kitchen. It's too damn dark in here," she said to herself.

"What?"

"Just sit down and watch TV. I have to see what we have." Cassie peered into the refrigerator. "I'll make scrambled eggs." She took the eggs and butter out of the refrigerator.

"I don't like eggs. Yuck," said Sally, sticking out her tongue.

"Well, they're soft and easy to eat and you'll eat them. You *do* like them," said Cassie, breaking four eggs into a bowl.

"I don't like them."

"Okay," Cassie said, melting the butter in the pan. She watched the yellow square of butter melt into a pool of liquid and then start to bubble; she beat the eggs until they were foamy and then poured them into the pan. While she waited for the eggs to start cooking she emptied yesterday's coffee grounds from the coffee maker, put a new filter in the basket, and poured in new coffee. Then she stirred and flipped the eggs. She poured water into the coffee machine. Stir and flip. Rinse the coffee pot. Stir and flip. *Eggs are done.* Cassie mentally checked breakfast off her to-do list.

By the time she walked into the living room—with the eggs in the pan in one hand and the plates and silverware in the other—the heat had started coming up and Sally had settled into watching a cooking show. For a moment, Cassie felt okay. Able to breathe.

"Breakfast, Gram," she said, setting the table.

"I don't want to eat over there," said Sally, her eyes glued to the TV.

Cassie looked at her grandmother. One bony shoulder sticking out from the bathrobe, vein-covered legs showing below. "Fine." Cassie pulled a small end table over and placed a plate of eggs in front of her grandmother, who stared at the eggs and then picked up the fork and dug in. She went back to intently watching TV and Cassie went and sat at the table. As she took her last bite, she heard a sound at the back door. A scratching. No, a knock. A rapping. Fingers tapping. Now what?

Hesitantly, Cassie walked into the kitchen and toward the back door to the sound. She knew in her gut it was Rick. What was he doing? She knew he could hear the TV, but still she could pretend it was just Sally home alone. He watched her. She was certain of it, but she didn't know how. What did he want? Fear enveloped her as she walked slowly past the stove, the sink. His shadow was silhouetted outside the door, and still she kept walking, knowing it was him. She wanted to tell him one last time to leave her alone. She opened the door and he leaned in with his hands on both sides of the frame.

His quick movement toward her made her breath catch in her throat and she instinctively took a step backward. "Rick! What do you want? I want you to leave me alone. Do you hear me? I am not interested in you in any way. Now get out of here or I will call the main office and report you and get you evicted. Evicted!" Her voice grew louder and louder as she spoke.

Rick squinted at her, his tremendous shoulder muscles bulging through the material of his long-sleeved T-shirt, one boot firmly planted on the threshold of the door. Cassie looked down at his massive thigh muscles and started to regret her outburst. How could she save herself and Sally from him? Instantly, she decided an offense was better than a good defense. Looking him straight in the eye she said, "Get out!"

"Cassie! Who is that?" Sally croaked, sounding irritated. "Shut the door. The cold's coming in."

Rick smiled and put a finger to his temple and pulled an imaginary trigger. "Bang. Gone. You would be free as a bird," he whispered.

Cassie quickly put her foot on his knee and kicked with all her might, but Rick wrapped his huge hand around her tiny ankle and pulled her toward him. She struggled not to fall backward and he reached out and pulled her to him.

"Rick!" It came out as *Reek*. Frank Jaworski had pulled up in his club car at the foot of the steps to Cassie's porch. "Get your hands off her! Now!"

Cassie took this unexpected interruption as her opportunity to pull free and dive back into her apartment, slamming the door and putting on the chain lock as fast as she could. Pulling her bathrobe around her frail frame she realized now how cold she had been. Her teeth chattered from the cold or from fear—she wasn't certain which, or was it both—as she tried to gain control of her breathing. She could hear Rick cursing at Frank and Frank threatening to call the police. Finally, a door slammed shut and Cassie heard nothing but the sound of the television.

"Cassie! Cassie! What's going on? What's all the racket?"

"Everything's fine, Gram," Cassie answered, walking into the living room and curling up on the couch under the afghan, trying to gain control of her shivering. She decided that she had to avoid Rick at all costs. She would come and go quickly and never confront him again. Sally was watching a rerun of *Modern Family* and Cassie tried to lose herself in Sofia Vergara's ridiculous problems. Wasn't that what sitcoms were for?

Let's Celebrate

"I pressed Submit. It was terrifying! I reviewed the application four times. Then I sent the most important piece of correspondence in my life so far," said Joe, grinning, as he deposited the grocery bags on the counter in his kitchen.

Cassie, who had pleaded exhaustion and not gone to the supermarket with Joe, sat curled up on his leather couch painting her toenails. "You know you're in, Joe. They'd be crazy not to want you and give you a full ride. Your essay was awesome. You have the grades and they like oldsters like you," she said with a smile.

Joe stuck his head out of the kitchen and gave Cassie a menacing look. "I think I might have to spank you for saying that." He walked toward her aggressively.

"Not while my toes are wet!" squealed Cassie as Joe picked her up, spun her around, and then sat down with her in his lap.

"Yes, even when your toes are wet. Before I get any older." Joe had a broad smile on his face and happiness beamed out of his eyes. "Cassie, I have applied to college. After six years of farting around, I have applied to college. I feel great. Over the moon. Let's celebrate."

"Yes, let's celebrate. I'm so proud of you." Cassie put her arms around Joe's neck and kissed him. "Congratulations! It's really great!"

"I feel like I've taken a tremendous step. And I have to say thank you. Before I met you, I thought about college, but there was no one to believe in me. You know?" Joe's full lips turned down in the saddest frown.

Cassie kissed both sides of Joe's mouth hoping the frown would go away. "Your mom believes in you. She knows you're smart."

"Yeah, she knows I'm smart but she also thinks the job at Home Depot is great. Great benefits. Her goal was to get me to be self-sufficient as soon as possible. She never thought going to college was worth it. Just get a job, she told me. So I did." Joe sighed and nodded his head. "And…you called and left a message at the Admissions Office. Did they get back to you?"

"No, not yet."

"You did call. Right?"

"Yes, I did," Cassie said unconvincingly, avoiding Joe's eyes.

Joe put his head back on the couch and sighed. "Cass, I thought you said you called. You lied to me."

"I just bought a little time, Joe. I'll call. I promise."

Joe looked skeptical. "You know what, Cassie? I'm going to celebrate tonight because I'm twenty-four years old and I just applied to college. I just took an important step toward realizing my dreams, so we're gonna celebrate, and then on Monday we are going to call Admissions together, and that's how it's gonna be." Joe gripped Cassie in a tight bear hug.

Relief and gratitude spread through Cassie's body. He wasn't going to start a fight. He was mad, but he was putting his anger on hold until Monday. "Yes, we'll call together on Monday," she agreed.

"Great! I'm hungry. Just wait until you see what I bought. I really splurged!" Joe's eyes sparkled with joy.

Joe had bought lamb chops—the tiny ones that look like musical notes and that were gone in one bite but tasted so good. They prepared dinner, dancing around each other in the small kitchen as two people get used to doing. She squeezed lemon on the meat as he cut the rough ends off the asparagus. Usually their meals together consisted of pizza, Chinese food, chicken nuggets, or the rare homemade burger, but tonight Joe had told Cassie that he wanted dinner to mark the first day of his new life. She watched him as he rummaged around under the sink and found a candle and stuck it in an empty salt cellar. It made Cassie smile when she saw it lit up on the table and she went and put her arms around his neck. "So romantic," she said before giving him a kiss.

"We'll dine by candlelight every night, my dear," Joe said, smiling back at her.

They ate the lamb chops, her two to his seven, and the rice and the asparagus and drank a bottle of wine. Cassie felt like she was in a movie. The heroine. A sought-after woman, young, beautiful, light dancing in her eyes. Her other reality, her life with Sally, melted away and she was free to be happy, to laugh, to think of the future.

"You look beautiful tonight, Cassie. Everything's going to be okay," Joe reached across the table and took Cassie's hand. "I promise. We're gonna work it all out. By this time next year we'll be living in Boston. Studying. Maybe writing for a local paper."

"Maybe," said Cassie, but Joe's planning was ruining the moment, and she wished he could just be here with her now without thinking about what came next. To change the subject, she asked, "Have you started your philosophy paper?"

"I've made some notes. It's due next Monday. Right?"

"Yeah. I can't decide between Confucius and Hannah Arendt. Who are you writing on?"

Joe was busy getting every morsel of meat from his last lamb bone. "These are so good." He smiled sheepishly. "Sorry I ate most of them."

"That's okay. You're bigger," she said, nodding and leaning in toward Joe.

"I kind of like Noam Chompsky. Maybe Hegel. Where's that book you had with short descriptions?" asked Joe, glancing around the apartment.

"I think it's at my place. I'll bring it over tomorrow," she said, eating the last bite of asparagus.

"Yeah, tomorrow we'll work on our papers, but tonight let's have another glass of wine." Joe got up and went into the kitchen for the second bottle.

As Cassie watched him walk across the room she tried not to think about Joe's dream of going to BU. She tried to just feel happy for him tonight, knowing that his acceptance to the school would drive them apart.

I Need You

The alarm started to beep its annoying and persistent beep at five thirty the next morning, and Cassie quickly turned it off, wishing she could somehow have an alarm that only she could hear, one that wouldn't also wake Joe. Sleepily, Joe put his arm around Cassie's chest and went back to sleep. She felt so warm and wonderful and wished with all her heart that she could just stay where she was, but she knew she couldn't. She had to go home and feed Sally and the cats. She had decided to ask Sally how she felt about Cassie going away to college. Cassie assumed that Sally didn't want her to leave, but what if Sally surprised her and told her to go and live her life? That she would try to take care of herself. Maybe Sally wouldn't want to hold her back. Cassie wasn't getting her hopes up, but she felt she needed to at least hear what Sally said.

She started to wriggle her way out of Joe's grasp but he just hugged her tighter. "I've got to go," Cassie whispered.

"Stay a little."

"I'll be back later," she said, slipping out of bed, searching for her sweater and jeans. Joe rolled over and closed his eyes. When she was dressed she lightly kissed his forehead. "See you this afternoon."

Joe ignored her and Cassie grabbed her boots, put them and her coat on in the living room, and left the apartment. The morning air was bitter cold. It was mid-December, Cassie reminded herself as she took her hat out of her pocket and pulled it down around her ears. Joe had told her to take his car, so she quickly slipped into the Honda, started it up, and then yanked on her gloves, the steering wheel too cold to touch, and drove home.

The car was just heating up as she made the turn onto her street and saw Frank Jaworski rounding the corner of the apartments in his club car. *Damn*, she hadn't decided if she wanted Frank's help with Rick or not. Well, there was no getting away from him now. He had stopped his club car in front of her apartment.

Cassie parked, pulled her collar up around her chin, and got out of the car. "Good morning, Frank," she said tentatively.

"Good morning, Cassie. How are you doing?"

"Besides being cold, I'm okay."

"Cassie, what do you want me to do about Mr. Smollett? I think I should report the incident to management. Yes?"

"No. I mean...yes. Frank, I don't know. I don't want to make it worse." She was afraid that Rick was watching them right now from his window.

"If I don't report him and he hurts you, it is my fault," said Frank.

The raw wind blew and Cassie shivered. "No. He won't hurt me," she said, but she didn't sound like she believed it. She climbed the steps toward her apartment.

"Next time I won't ask," said Frank and pushed the pedal of the club car and went on his way.

Cassie hurried up the remaining steps and stuck her key in the door. As she did, Rick's door started to open. Cassie fumbled with the lock and panic gripped her chest as she finally threw open her door. As she passed inside, she quickly looked over her shoulder and caught a glimpse of long black hair. She quietly closed her door and leaned against it, breathing heavily. A woman. Cassie went to her own front window and peered out between the slit in the closed blinds. She uttered a guttural sound as she watched Sierra Kole walk in her black suede coat toward her yellow Beetle. How had Cassie missed the car? And what was Sierra doing with Rick? Obviously, she knew what they were doing, but she couldn't believe that even Sierra would stoop so low. Rick was nothing like the men that Sierra went after. The other men were married and rich, and Rick was divorced and dirt poor. Cassie shook her head—it was too disgusting to even think about.

Cassie took off her coat, and the cats swarmed around her legs. It was clear that Sierra had a very dark side to her and would enjoy the depravity of sleeping with Rick. But she also wondered if there was an element of competition. Rick had come after Cassie in the bar, not Sierra. Was she with Rick to prove she could steal him from Cassie? Prove she was more attractive? *He's all yours!* Cassie thought with a snort. She couldn't wait to hear Sierra's story on Monday at work.

As Cassie made breakfast she heard Sally shuffle in from the bedroom. She thought about what to say to Sally about going away to college. It made her nervous and sad to talk about leaving Sally all alone. She bit her cuticle and thought about going out back for a cigarette, but she couldn't risk seeing Rick. She wondered if Sally would start cursing and screaming, or worse yet, would she cry and beg Cassie to stay? The cold butter kept sliding off the dish as Cassie tried to butter the waffles. She stopped for a minute and shook out her hands and stared out the small window by the back door into the deserted courtyard. Two huge dumpsters were the only things in the courtyard. No wooden benches. No picnic tables or jungle gym for the kids. Just two green dumpsters. She sighed, closed her eyes, and sliced up a banana to go with the waffles.

"We're having waffles, Gram. Do you want syrup?" she called, wondering if she would be able to swallow a few bites and have a serious conversation.

"Yes, syrup," Sally replied.

They ate in silence, watching MTV. Song after song of young people gyrating, swooning, falling in love, falling out of love. Cassie looked at Sally and tried to decide how to bring up the subject. Finally, knowing there was no easy way, Cassie just spit it out. "Gram, if I got into college would you want me to go?"

Sally's shaky hand had speared a slice of banana and her mouth hung open waiting for her hand to make it up to her mouth. As she looked up the banana slice fell in her lap. "You are in college. Aren't you?" she asked, trying to spear the slippery banana slice off her bathrobe but squishing it into goo as she did.

Cassie got up and took a tissue from the box on the coffee table and scooped up the banana. She took the fork, speared another slice, and put it up to Sally's mouth. Like a little bird, Sally took the slice in her mouth and then reached out for the fork and took it from Cassie's hand.

"I go to community college now, but I mean a real college, like Boston University, for instance. Would you want me to go?" Cassie asked, trying to maintain eye contact with her grandmother, trying to perceive if Sally wanted what was best for Cassie.

Chewing slowly, Sally replied, "I never went to college. I didn't even finish high school. And I was smart, too. Maybe not as smart as you, but smart." Sally thrust her chin out.

Cassie knelt down on one knee so she was eye level with Sally. "I know. But don't you want something better for me? Don't you want me to have a better life than you've had?"

"You've had a better life. I didn't have a chance. I was sick. They made me sick."

Cassie reached out and squeezed Sally's hand. She fumbled for the right words. "Did you want to go back to high school? Maybe get your GED? Did you ever try?" Cassie asked, her eyes soft and encouraging.

"First, when they died I tried to put myself back together, but it was hard. I could hear their voices in my head. I could still smell him. And then I got pregnant and had other problems like trying to raise your mother. She was a handful. I never got a chance to catch my breath. But I survived. I'm a survivor, Cassie," she declared, crossing her arms over her chest and staring straight into Cassie's eyes.

"I know you are, Gram, and I'm so sorry about everything that happened to you. I am so very sorry, but…" Cassie tried to choose her words with care. "What do you want for me?"

Sally closed her eyes. "I never had much of a life. You work, you go to school, you have that boyfriend. You already have so much more than I ever had. I don't want to talk about it anymore. Turn up the sound. I can't hear the song," said Sally, craning her neck to see beyond Cassie to the television.

Getting slowly to her feet, Cassie felt defeated. She tried so hard to take care of Sally, and this was what she got for her devotion. She went in the kitchen to finish cleaning at least one room, too hurt to even cry. When the room was tidy, Cassie stood staring at the garbage, knowing that it was not a good idea to go out the back door and have a fight with Rick.

As she stood there contemplating her options, Sally shuffled over to the doorway. "Cassie, I do want you to have a better life than mine, but the trouble is I need you." Without waiting for an answer, she went back to the couch.

No Prep

As Cassie drove back to Joe's apartment, she thought about Boston University and got furious. Joe was fixated on BU because of events that Ms. Levine, Cassie's high school guidance counselor, had put into play years ago. Everything was harder now because of the day when Cassie had found out about her SAT score. She could remember the day as if it was yesterday.

"Will Cassie Pennebaker please report to Guidance? Cassie Pennebaker." The disembodied voice crackled through the PA system and caught Cassie in the locker room changing for gym, a class she hated. With a small smile, she put her shirt and boots back on and went to find Ms. Coleridge, the gym teacher, to get a hall pass to go and see her guidance counselor. *Perfect timing. No pickleball for me today!* she thought as she walked out of the gym.

It was Cassie's junior year in high school and her classes were filled with students discussing plans for family trips to tour colleges, raising their GPAs, signing up for community service that would look good on their college resumes, and racking up extracurricular activities that would make them look well-rounded. Cassie had never seen the inside of a church, a day care center, or a nursing home where other kids went to do good works. She did enough caretaking every day at home with her grandmother. She didn't need to sign up to do a few hours of service and then get a signature from a minister or organization director to prove it. Her extra-curricular activities consisted of running her household, managing the family checkbook, paying the bills, doing the laundry, planning meals, shopping, and trying to take care of a mentally ill relative. *These other kids don't know the meaning of responsibility,* she thought as she listened to them talk about tutoring kids for a week in Cambodia or banging a nail or two in a hut in Mexico. Vacations— that's what Cassie called that kind of activity.

Cassie had no intention of taking the SAT because she had no intention of going to college, but Ms. Levine, the guidance counselor, had persuaded Cassie to sit for the test. "It will give you options," Ms. Levine had said. "Your circumstances might change and then you'll be ready." Cassie had finally agreed to take the test just to make Ms. Levine feel good. No one else had shown any interest in Cassie's future, so Cassie thought she should show Ms. Levine that she was grateful. They had filled out the paperwork together and Cassie had taken out her checkbook and written a check. Ms. Levine seemed surprised that it was in her own name and Cassie explained that she paid all the family bills.

Most of the college-bound students had been prepping for months with tutors and special classes, but Cassie had just shown up and taken the test. Buying a #2 pencil was her only prep.

Cassie quietly slipped into the Guidance Office and gave her hall pass to the secretary.

"She's waiting for you," said Mrs. Clark with a nod of her ancient head.

The hallway back toward Ms. Levine's office was lined with posters of college campuses, ivy-covered stone buildings, paths through manicured lawns where happy students stopped to chat, cafeterias with delicious-looking food, and classroom shots of engaged young people listening intently to bearded professors in corduroy jackets. Cassie walked by without looking at them. The carefree students in their preppy clothes had nothing to do with her life in the apartment with Sally. Her life experience had made her grow up so fast—she felt decades older than the smiling students. She had every intention of thanking Ms. Levine for her interest in her future and telling her she should focus on other students who were actually planning on attending college.

As Cassie arrived at Ms. Levine's door, she saw her counselor sitting with a stack of official-looking papers. She cleared her throat to get the woman's attention. "Hi. You wanted to see me?" Cassie asked.

Ms. Levine jumped out of her chair, grinning, and crossed the office to shake Cassie's hand. "Cassie! I wanted to be the one to tell you. You got a perfect score on the SAT! The only student in this school—the only student in the county—to receive that score. Congratulations! You did such a great job."

Cassie, not used to praise, stood limp and motionless. The woman's perfume overpowered Cassie's senses until she couldn't think of anything else. She wasn't sure what to say or how to act. No one ever told her she did a good job. Sure, teachers praised her work, but none of them had tried to reach out to her the way Ms. Levine did.

"Wow. Thanks, Ms. Levine," Cassie said, taking her hand back and looking up at the woman's happy smile and swaying silver earrings as Ms. Levine laughed and shook her head in wonderment.

"Cassie, we haven't had a student in many years get a perfect score— and without any prep! You are amazing. I can't wait to tell Principal Bain. He'll be so proud of you. He'll announce it over the loudspeaker—"

Cassie put up her hand in protest. "Please don't do that, Ms. Levine. That would be so embarrassing," said Cassie with a look of alarm on her face.

"Cassie, it's nothing to be embarrassed about. Just the opposite." Ms. Levine's kind blue eyes searched Cassie's face.

"Ms. Levine, we've got to talk," said Cassie as she went over and plopped down in the chair beside Ms. Levine's desk. "Ms. Levine, I can't...go to college. So please...let's not make a big deal out of this..."

"Cassie, why do you say that you can't go to college?"

Cassie looked down at her hands in her lap and studied her nails, bitten down to the quick. Closing her eyes, Cassie said, "You know I..." Cassie opened her eyes and looked at Ms. Levine's kind face, beaming with enthusiasm.

"Money will not be an issue. With your grades and now this perfect score, the money will come rolling in! Are you thinking about big schools? Smaller schools? In a city or a rural setting? What do you want to study?"

Cassie closed her eyes and focused on the question. Pretending that she was just an average kid with an average mom and dad, what would she like to study? She had always liked to write. "I want to be a-a writer. A j-journalist," she finally stammered.

"Yes. Yes! I can see you as a reporter. Traveling the world. I'll tell you what we're going to do. I'm going to research the best schools for journalism and then we'll meet again. How does that sound? I'll help you write your essay, although you probably don't need my help. We'll fill out the applications together. We have time. Just think about it. Okay?" Ms. Levine looked at Cassie with such happiness that Cassie couldn't stand to squash the woman's dreams. To dash her hopes for her prize student.

"Okay, Ms. Levine. I'll think about it." Cassie left the counselor's office trying desperately to cling to the normal girl she had conjured up for Ms. Levine, but as the door to the Guidance Office closed she became herself again.

As she turned onto Joe's street, Cassie snapped back into the present from her memories and silently cursed the guidance counselor. If Ms. Levine hadn't stuck her nose into Cassie's business three years ago, Cassie wouldn't have been accepted to BU and Joe wouldn't be set on going there now. Why couldn't people just mind their own business?

Let's Both Forget Him

On Mondays, the pharmacy received its deliveries for the week. The refrigerator in the back that held milk, butter, ice cream, and cold soda and juices was always empty on Monday mornings. Diapers, candy, and cold pills were running low. Cassie usually hated Mondays at the pharmacy, but today the mindless work of replacing the empty boxes of candy with new boxes had a soothing effect on her raw nerves. She wanted to talk to Sierra about her night with Rick and find out why Sierra would do such a thing. Curiosity was killing her! Rick was neither married nor rich. That left only dangerous as an attraction, or complete drunkenness— so drunk that the alcohol had left her seriously impaired or completely unconscious.

Sierra didn't like refilling the fridge—too cold—so Cassie started in the back when she got to work. The crates of milk—whole, low fat, no fat, half and half—were piled in front of the doors. Cassie pulled on yellow rubber gloves to stock the fridge. She checked her phone for the time and noted that Sierra was twelve minutes late already. If she didn't show up Cassie knew she couldn't possibly get everything restocked.

A few minutes later she heard Mr. Ladinsky whistle, a wolf call whistle, and assumed that Sierra had arrived. Instead of being reprimanded, Sierra was applauded for her tight black leggings, black T-shirt with a metallic peace sign gently riding the cliff of her bosom, and black leather boots with three-inch heels. Cassie considered the scowl on Mr. Ladinsky's face when she was late.

Shaking her head, she wondered why people who didn't need a job, who didn't need the money, who came late, left early, and did a shitty job while they were there, were allowed to act one way and diligent workers who needed their job and their salary, and who worried about being late or absent were held to a higher standard. Obviously, large breasts played a role here, but Cassie felt it had more to do with attitude than cup size.

Cassie finished restocking the milk, piled the empty containers on top of each other, and went to put them in the back room. When she returned to the main room, she saw that Sierra was busy with a line of customers. She headed over to check the candy and wait until Sierra was free. As she entered the candy aisle she saw the empty KitKat box with Hershey's milk chocolate running a close second. Three weeks in a row now KitKat had won. Cassie smiled at her private game.

She started at the top with the gum, peering over the Trident to see when Sierra was free. As soon as the last customer headed for the front door, Cassie walked over to the counter and picked up the latest issue of *People* that had been returned to the wrong spot on the rack in front of the counter. Still rearranging the magazines, she whispered, "So, I know it's none of my business, but Rick? Really? Why?"

Sierra pretended to care about the neatness of the counter. "That's right. It's none of your business." She smiled provocatively when Cassie looked up at her.

"He's crazy," Cassie hissed.

"You have no idea!" Sierra said with a wicked laugh.

"No, crazy. Really crazy. Certifiable. I think he has a gun," said Cassie with wide eyes.

"He does! More than one. He showed me. And crazy tattoos!" said Sierra excitedly.

Cassie stopped organizing the magazines and stared at Sierra, who smiled back at her with abandon.

"What?" hissed Sierra. "You don't want him. Why can't I have him for a while? As a toy? A dangerous one at that. When we did it, he let me hold his gun. Like I was making him do me. It was hot," said Sierra breathlessly.

Cassie stared at the cover of *Vogue,* trying hard to get that last image out of her brain. Finally, she said, "You two deserve each other. You're as crazy as he is. But he scares me. Did he mention my grandmother?"

Sierra's smile faded. "Is he doing your grandmother?"

"Oh my God! Really? Did you just ask that?" Cassie stormed off to stock more shelves.

"Some people are so touchy," said Sierra rolling her eyes.

Cassie avoided Sierra for the rest of the morning, but at lunchtime Sierra went and sat by Cassie at the staff lunch table located in the windowless stockroom. Mrs. Ladinsky watched the counter for forty-five minutes so the girls could eat. Cassie always brought a sandwich from home, and Sierra usually ate a yogurt that she took from the fridge at the pharmacy and rarely paid for. *Another perk of not giving a shit if you're fired,* thought Cassie.

"So, what is it that you're so mad about anyway?" Sierra asked, licking her spoon. "You have Joe. Do you want this guy too?"

"No, not at all. Yuck. It's just that he truly creeps me out. He…says he'll get rid of Gram if I want him to. Who offers to do that?" Cassie took a bite of her bologna and American on Wonder Bread.

Sierra considered it. "Would that be so bad? He would take the fall. You'd be free. You'd get rid of them both. The creepy neighbor and the concrete block around your neck."

"Sierra! We're talking about killing my grandmother."

"I know. I was only trying to help," said Sierra with a shrug.

"And that doesn't scare you? How do you know he won't kill you? Did you fall asleep? I wouldn't sleep in his apartment. Well, let's look on the bright side if you go missing I can tell the police where your body is," Cassie said with a smirk.

"Hey, it was just one night. Not a bad one either. Except the mattress on the floor. That was a little seedy." Sierra looked blank as if remembering something. "He did say he would see me at the pharmacy."

"Oh, great! Now he's coming here. I'm already avoiding him at home. Now I have to avoid him here?" Cassie stuffed the last of her crusts in the plastic bag.

Sierra stared at Cassie. "You know, Cassie, I'm the one he slept with. I think he's coming here to see me. Why do you always think everything's about you?" Sierra's black eyes penetrated Cassie's face.

Cassie stood up and collected her things. Her shoulders stooped and her rainbow hair fell over her face. "Wow. You're right. I'm just so overwhelmed lately that I jump to conclusions. I'm sorry. Of course you're right. If you want to date him or sleep with him or whatever, that's your business. I was just surprised, that's all. He's not your type. Let's forget it," said Cassie. If Rick was interested in Sierra, that was good for Cassie. Maybe he would leave her and Joe alone. Still, Cassie had a nagging feeling that Rick was using Sierra to get to her. Maybe Sierra was right and Cassie was stuck on herself.

Sierra got up slowly and smoothed her shirt. Her eyes softened a little as she said, "Fine. Now that we're clear that everything is about *me,* we're fine." She threw her yogurt cup in the trash with a smile. "Why are we fighting over that man anyway? Neither of us actually wants him."

"Yeah, let's both forget him," said Cassie as she followed Sierra out of the lunchroom. If only she could.

The Dream

Sweat dripped down Cassie's temples and armpits as she woke from the dream. The recurrent dream was only one image: Jillian, her mother, slowly walking away from her toward the bedroom door, the creaking of the door as Jillian opened it, her retreating back as she moved through the doorway, and then the slow shutting of the door as Jillian walked out of Cassie's life forever. The only difference in the dream was the color scheme, many times brown was the dominant color, sometimes shades of deep forest green, versions in blue, purple, red, golden yellow haunted Cassie's nights. The dream was silent. Jillian never said a word or showed her face, just her back. Her thin sweater hugging her slim waist, her long hair glistening in the light coming in from the moon in the window.

Wiping the sweat from her brow, Cassie sat up and stared at the clock—5:05 a.m. Whenever she had the dream she couldn't—or wouldn't—go back to sleep. Fear of experiencing the dream again prevented her from turning over, sighing, and going back into that mysterious dark of sleep. When she had the dream, the color hurt the backs of her eyes and her throat would constrict. When Cassie was awake and thoughts of her mother surfaced, she would curse them to the side and they would disappear into whatever activity she was doing.

Cassie's days were so full of Sally, Joe, work, school, and chores that there was never much time to sit and reflect or ponder why Jillian was able to get up one morning and simply leave her young daughter and her sick mother and go to Australia to start a new life. When she left, Jillian was still young enough to have another family, and Cassie often wondered if she had brothers and sisters. Children that Jillian was now living with and mothering, hugging, encouraging, protecting. Was Jillian right now braiding the hair of another daughter as she used to do when Cassie was little? Or making chocolate chip pancakes for her new family as she had for Sally and Cassie?

As Cassie stood up from the bed, she tried to forcibly expel thoughts of Jillian from her mind. Thinking of what if this or what if that was not healthy, but she wanted to know what it was that made Jillian different. What wall was Jillian able to construct in her heart that Cassie could not? Why were some people able to justify the most irresponsible actions and then go on with their lives? Usually they blamed their actions on other people. *Sally was too much to deal with. That's why I left.* Cassie could actually hear these words coming out of Jillian's mouth even though they had never had a chance to have the conversation.

Cassie liked to think it was possible that Jillian woke up from nightmares, sweating, repenting, waking Jake, swearing to get in touch with Cassie, to tell her she was sorry, to give her back the years of fear and loneliness and struggling to take care of Sally. Did Jillian ever wonder what had happened to her brilliant daughter? Or did she take solace in knowing how smart Cassie was and believing that she would figure it out?

Jillian had always known that Cassie had a gift. In fact, when Cassie was in second grade the school had sent home a letter announcing that Cassie would be placed in the Gifted and Talented program the next year in school. Her IQ was 145, the letter declared. Cassie remembered Jillian bragging about the program to the neighbors as if Cassie's innate intelligence was Jillian's doing.

Her mother's dates would come to the apartment to pick her up, and Jillian would point to Cassie and say, "Isn't she cute? She's also smart. She's going to be in a special program for children with high IQs next year at school!" Then Jillian would toss her long hair and say, "I don't know where she came from. I can't keep two numbers in my head or write a proper sentence!" Her eyes would go all big and gooey as if to tell the man not to worry, that she wasn't smart enough to be a threat.

To her credit, Jillian had read to Cassie every night until Cassie was seven, at which time Cassie had said she could read to herself. There was still a box of picture books in Cassie's closet that Jillian had read to her. Cassie knew that Jillian had been proud of her, the way she got all A's in school and her homework and tests would come home with gold stars and exclamation marks on the top. Jillian would show Sally the papers and Sally's face would light up, and she would go and put the paper on the fridge with a magnet.

At that time Cassie had felt they were a family—that was, until Jake Kelsey appeared on the scene. Tall and broad, blond and jolly. Jake filled a room with his personality and charm and cowboy boots. Jillian was jelly in his hands and regressed overnight into a teenager. Having a fourteen-year-old daughter was a wrinkle in her plan, let alone a crazy and violent mother who smelled bad and who wouldn't go in the bedroom and hide when Jake picked her up. Cassie was scared by his loud laugh and the quick way he would get her mother in a bear hug, sweeping her into his big arms and lifting her off the ground. Kissing her right there in the living room while Cassie did her homework and Sally watched the television.

Cassie remembered snippets of conversation now that she didn't understand then. Jake would say, "We'll go to the beach on the Gold Coast," or "It's a long flight," or "My brother says I can work at his brewery." When Jake would say anything like this, Jillian would change the subject or say it was time for Jake to get going or time to do the shopping, anything to redirect the conversation.

Cassie never really spoke directly to Jake, probably because Jake never spoke to her. Thinking back, it was almost like he didn't want to know her. Didn't want to risk getting attached or knowing her too well and feeling bad about making Jillian abandon her only daughter. Or maybe that was giving her mother too much credit, maybe Jillian was the one who wanted to leave her behind. Cassie would never know the answer to that question. Whose idea was it to leave? Whose idea was it *not* to take Cassie with them? Had they debated it? Fought about it? Argued pros and cons? Cassie assumed that Jake wouldn't even discuss taking Sally, so Cassie had been sacrificed because even Jillian couldn't leave the sick woman all alone. Something Joe wanted Cassie to do now.

Unable to stand her own thoughts, Cassie started to layer clothes on her thin body: flannel pajama pants, a fleece, sweatpants, woolen socks, slippers, and her bathrobe. Then she slowly trudged into the kitchen to make coffee, moving clumsily under all the layers, pushing the sleeves up onto her skinny forearms. Shivering, she cursed the landlord for not raising the heat until six in the morning. Forty-five minutes away by the clock on the microwave. She decided to make a full pot of coffee to get her through the day and mentally noted that she needed to buy coffee. The cats, not used to anyone being up so early, had come into the doorway of the kitchen and looked at her with tired, blank eyes.

Cassie bent down to stroke one, then the other, and then started filling their bowl with dry food. The sound of the dry kibble hitting the empty bowl stirred the silence, and Cassie stopped pouring, not wanting to wake Sally. She watched the cats eat and drink and then switch places as the coffee perked.

Without thinking, Cassie chewed on a nail, a habit that she could not break, and wished that Joe hadn't thrown out her pack of cigarettes. Something he did on a regular basis, and that really pissed her off. At six dollars and seventy-five cents a pack she couldn't afford to throw them away. The last time he had taken her cigarettes she had taken money out of his wallet. He had never mentioned it and neither had she, but last night she hadn't noticed they were gone until after Joe dropped her off.

The coffee pot beeped and Cassie poured herself a cup, smelling the rich aroma before she took the first sip. Her favorite sip. *Mmm.* She went to sit in the living room on the sagging couch in the dim morning light without turning on the lamp. She pulled the dirty afghan that Jillian had crocheted years ago over her lap and placed both of her tiny hands around the hot cup. The cats came and settled down on either side of her, had a short bath, and went back to sleep, their bellies full from the early breakfast.

Cassie wanted to sort out the possible solutions to her problem. How could she leave Sally and go to college with Joe? What strength—or weakness—of character did it take to think of yourself first? To realize your own dreams, even if that meant hurting someone else you cared about. Was it wrong to want to do something for yourself? Her mother had left. Jillian's father had left. Joe's father had left.

Joe wanted her to leave Sally. Did that make Joe a bad person? A callous person? An uncaring person? Selfish? Would he leave Cassie in the future if she got sick? She had tried to explain to him how she felt about Sally. It was more than obligation. More than ordinary love. What was it? Was it Sally's vulnerability? Knowing that she, Cassie, was all Sally had? Did that put a higher moral calling on Cassie? What did that mean anyway, morality? There was no law that said she had to take care of Sally. There were laws about abandoning your children, but people did it all the time. Was the law immoral? The church said honor thy mother and thy father. It didn't say anything about thy grandma. Where could she turn for answers?

Cassie wondered what it would feel like to get up in the morning and have only herself to think about. Light as air. Yes, she thought it would feel light as air to think and plan and dream about only herself. Why did she have this overblown conscience and how could she get rid of it? It seemed to be a part of her that she couldn't banish, couldn't loosen. Like a noose around her neck, her own heavy sense of right and wrong tightened its rope as soon as she started to think of her own freedom.

Was she the defective one or was it the others, like Jillian, even like Joe, who wanted her to abandon Sally? Was it her particular circumstances that made her feel so bound to Sally, or was she the yin to Jillian's yang? Was she compelled to be the opposite of her mother because she knew firsthand the pain of abandonment?

Joe knew abandonment. His father had left when he was ten and had never looked back. It made Joe feel bad to think that his father just got up one morning and split, made a new life for himself. Joe had no idea where he was or if he had a new family, or if maybe he was dead. Cassie remembered Joe saying that if his father had died, he thought someone would let him know. Cassie had asked what for? Joe had shrugged. But somehow Joe didn't seem to think it was so bad for Cassie to leave Sally. Was leaving a child different than leaving another family member? Yes, Cassie thought that leaving a child was probably the worst form of abandonment. But Sally was sick. Was leaving a sick person just as bad?

Cassie went into her bedroom looking for clues about herself, about her relationship with Sally. On the top of the dresser was a stack of children's books. She pulled Richard Scarry's *Funniest Storybook Ever* from the pile and opened to the center spread. It showed the cartoon town with Sergeant Murphy the cop-dog, Huckle the cat, and Lowly Worm. She smiled as she remembered sitting in Sally's lap and looking at the funny characters. Next to the books was a bowl of hair clips and ties and bows. For each one she had a memory of Sally helping her get dressed and putting a matching bow or clip in her hair. When she turned ten, Sally had given her a small wicker basket with ten little presents in it from the Dollar Store. One of the things she gave her was a little picture frame in the shape of a sunflower, and the photo was of Sally and Cassie sitting on the back stoop. They looked happy.

Cassie heard the slow exhale of the radiator and knew that it was six o'clock. The light behind the dusty blinds had turned a soft gray, and Cassie knew that the questions she was struggling with had no single answer, that the answer was different for each person. What she had to figure out was her own answer. She alone had to live with it. She wasn't afraid of being judged by others, just by herself.

Better Watch Out

Sierra came up behind Joe and thrust her long nails into his wild curls in a caress that started out soft and ended with her digging into his scalp in a satisfying scratch. Joe, standing in front of the checkout counter of the pharmacy talking to Cassie, closed his eyes mid-sentence, apparently forgetting what he was saying, and a smile of pure pleasure formed on his face.

"Sierra, you bitch, get your claws out of my boyfriend's hair," said Cassie as she watched Joe's face.

"He likes it," purred Sierra.

"Mmmm. Yes, I do," murmured Joe.

"Joseph," reprimanded Cassie. "Don't encourage her."

"What are you? His mother?" Sierra asked flatly.

Joe opened one eye to see Cassie's face. Her smirk gave away the fact she wasn't really angry. "Okay. That's enough. The old ball and chain is flipping out," Joe joked, shaking his head to expel Sierra's fingers from his mane.

"Anyway, you were saying…" said Cassie.

Joe looked confused. "What was I saying?" he chuckled.

"You two are like old married people. You were probably talking about what coupon to use for dinner or figuring out what show to watch tonight. You two are sad. Wasting your young years. Let's go out tonight. Let's go to the city! C'mon. Whaddaya say?" Sierra's face was excited, color in her cheeks.

"Haha." Cassie laughed sarcastically. "We have school tonight."

Joe, who had been listening to Sierra with interest, said, "Cass, we could miss one night…"

"Really? Going into the city is expensive. Where are we going to get an extra hundred bucks to throw away?" asked Cassie.

Joe looked down and studied the crack in his Converse sneakers. "Cassie's right. We don't have any extra cash right now with our trip to Boston coming up."

"When are you guys going to Boston?" asked Sierra.

"We're not sure yet…" Cassie said quickly, giving Sierra a don't-go-there look.

"Probably next month…" said Joe at the same time. A look of annoyance crossed Joe's face.

Sierra looked from one to the other, picked up her feather duster and started to go over to the magazine rack. "Well, anyway, tonight we could drive into the city and go to this club I know. I'll drive and pay the tolls and pay for gas and the bouncer loves me, so he'll let us in for free. It'll only cost what you drink. You guys can come up with a few bucks for a beer or two, can't ya?"

Joe looked at Cassie. "It might be fun…"

"You guys talk it over. We have another hour before quitting time," said Sierra as she sauntered away.

Joe turned to Cassie. "Let's go, babe. Let's have some fun. We could dance!" Joe did a little dance move and smiled.

Cassie watched a mother and two daughters as they looked through the silver jewelry arrangement that had taken her two hours to set up the day before and hoped the girls wouldn't try on every bracelet, necklace, and ring. When she looked back at Joe, he was studying her intently. "I have to feed Gram. You know I do," said Cassie defensively.

Joe stuck his hands in his pockets with more force than necessary. "I'm sure Sierra will wait."

The girls had each chosen a necklace and seemed very happy with their selections as they approached the counter giggling and comparing their new treasures. Cassie tipped her head to the side to tell Joe to get out of the way as the mother got to the counter. The girls smiled when they saw Cassie's rainbow-colored hair, but their mother had a look of disapproval on her face. Cassie purposely reached up and put her hair behind her ear to show off her many earrings to the kids.

"Girls, give me the necklaces so the woman can ring them up. Go and wait by the door," said the mother. Cassie finished the transaction without talking to the woman, but as she handed her the change she said, "Thank you," with a big, innocent smile.

Joe started to laugh. The woman, looking flustered, took her change and her bag and hurried to the door.

"Well, you scared her away," said Joe. "Better be careful chasing away customers."

"Screw her. I hope both girls get ugly tattoos and a nose ring. Did you see the way she was judging me?"

Cassie watched Joe's mouth open to answer and then close again without speaking. She followed his eyes and saw Rick coming through the pharmacy door, his broad shoulders filling the doorway. Cassie's and Rick's eyes met across the store, and panic gripped Cassie's intestines. As if in slow motion, Rick stopped short and looked from Cassie to Joe. Cassie felt Joe tense up, his jaw jutting out and his eyes, usually jolly, glinting with something Cassie had never seen before. Anger? She had seen him angry before. Hatred? Yes, his face showed his hatred of Rick.

Rick's shoulders were rounded and his hands pitched away from his body. He looked ready for combat. Like in an old Western movie, he looked ready to grab his guns out of their holsters. His feet were spread apart and his eyes had finally come to rest on Joe's face. He was wearing a dirty green military jacket and camouflage pants, but Cassie noticed that his hair looked clean and combed. She had a stray thought that he had cleaned himself up to see Sierra.

No one moved until Sierra came down the deodorant aisle singing "Single Ladies" by Beyonce. *"Do da do da do put a ring on it, Wuh, oh, uh, uh, oh, oh, uh."* She stopped singing when she saw Rick. "Uh oh," she said. It took her a minute, but Cassie could see her quickly sizing up the situation. "Rick, you bastard, where have you been?" she asked, advancing toward Rick with an exaggerated wriggle and a suggestive gaze. Taking Rick completely off guard, she took his face in both her hands and kissed him on the lips. As she did, a pack of teenagers came flying through the door hooting and catcalling when they ran into the kissing pair. Sierra took Rick by the hand and pulled him toward the refrigerated section in the rear of the store.

Cassie exhaled for the first time in minutes. "Joe, go home and I'll meet you there," she said, fear shaking her voice.

Joe looked at Cassie as if he couldn't believe what she just said. "I'm not leaving. Do you really want me to run away while he's in the back with Sierra? Like a coward? I'm the one who beat the shit out of *him*. And I'm not leaving you while he's here."

Now Cassie wished she had told Joe about the guns and Rick's threats to hurt Sally. As her mind raced about what to do, she spotted one of the teenage boys pocketing a candy bar. Sorry to use the kid as an excuse, Cassie picked up the intercom and asked Mr. Ladinsky to come to the front of the store, knowing that he would call the police. Joe gave her a quizzical look, and Cassie mouthed that the kids were stealing candy.

Looking confused and angry, Mr. Ladinsky, in his starched white coat, walked purposefully toward Cassie, frowning when he noticed Joe standing off to the side. "What is it, Cassie?" he asked in a stern tone.

"I'm sorry to disturb you, Mr. Ladinsky," Cassie said, "but that boy over there, the one with the red coat? He just put a Snickers in his pocket."

Mr. Ladinsky drew air in through his nose and pivoted in his shiny black shoes toward the boy in the red coat. Walking briskly, he approached the boy. "Empty out your pockets!" he demanded.

The boy tried to run, but Mr. Ladinsky grabbed his hood and dragged him toward the counter where Cassie stood. "Cassie, call the police. I am sick and tired of these kids coming in here and stealing from me. It's time to make an example of one of them." When Cassie didn't move immediately, he snapped at her. "Do it Cassie! Make the call. Now, give me the candy bar. What else do you have?"

While the boy twisted and tried to get away, Cassie called 911, feeling like a fool to report the theft of one candy bar. "Hello, this is the Jenkins Pharmacy, and we have a shoplifter in the store. Yes, please send a car." Cassie put down the receiver as if it were burning her hand. She looked away from the boy, not wanting to meet his eyes.

By the time the cop car arrived, Mr. Ladinsky had made the boy empty his pockets to find one Snickers bar, fifty cents, and a condom. Cassie told the police what she had seen and then told Mr. Ladinsky she was leaving; her shift was over. Sierra and Rick had been out of sight somewhere in the back of the store, and Cassie wanted to leave with Joe and get in his car while the police were still on the premises. Grabbing her purse with one hand and Joe's hand with the other, she pulled Joe toward the door, hoping that Sierra had taken Rick in the back room for some action. Once outside, they headed toward Joe's car in the parking lot in the back of the store.

"Jeez, Cass, did you have to call the cops on that poor kid? I hope they just give him a warning," said Joe.

"Joe, there are things I haven't told you…about Rick…"

"Like what?" asked Joe, stopping and pulling Cassie around to face him.

"Let's go and I'll tell you everything. Please, let's just get in the car," pleaded Cassie. But as Joe took a step forward, the back door opened and Rick appeared in the doorway. Joe stopped walking and Cassie pulled on his arm. "Joe, just keep walking," she said urgently.

Joe and Cassie took a step toward the car as Rick called out, "Hey, half-breed. You better watch out. I'll be there when you least expect it."

Joe turned to confront Rick. Cassie looked to the front of the pharmacy to see if the police car was still there. She couldn't see the car, but she could see the flashing lights. "C'mon, Joe. Ignore him. Please." She pulled on Joe's arm to get him to move toward the car.

"Listen, asshole…" started Joe.

"Joe, no, please…" wailed Cassie. "Let's just go…"

Joe took a step toward Rick. "If you ever touch Cassie again…"

As Rick took a step toward Joe, the police car pulled into the parking lot. The light from the headlights shone on Joe, Cassie, and Rick as the car slowly approached. Rick put his head down and headed toward the street. The cop car pulled up to Joe and Cassie.

"Everything okay here?" asked the officer driving the patrol car, looking from Joe to Rick.

"Yeah. Everything's fine," said Joe.

"Then move along. We don't need any trouble. Go get in your car," said the cop.

"Yes, Joe, it's freezing," said Cassie, looping her arm through Joe's and turning him to his car.

"I'll wait till you're in," said the officer to their backs.

Cassie said a silent "thank you" to the policeman as she hurried Joe to the car.

Always Running Back

The wind was howling with the coming storm as Cassie and Joe hurried into Joe's apartment. Joe had insisted upon hearing the entire story about Rick and his threats, and even though Cassie knew that Sally was waiting to eat dinner, she agreed to go back to his apartment to talk. After hanging his leather jacket on the hook by the door, Joe started to pace the living room while Cassie went and sat on the couch. She tried to gather her thoughts, but Joe was making her so nervous she couldn't think straight.

Finally, Joe stopped in front of Cassie and said, "So tell me, and also tell me why you didn't tell me before." With both hands on his hips, he loomed over Cassie, his eyes glinting like shiny green gems.

"I was afraid to tell you. I thought you might go over there to Rick's apartment. He has guns. Guns that he's shown Sierra. Military guns from his days in the Marines…"

"I can't believe that guy's an ex-Marine," Joe said shaking his head. "That piece of shit?"

"Yeah, three tours in Afghanistan, according to Frank…"

"Great." Joe reached up to push his hair back from his face, his beautiful lips drawn down in a frown. "What else? Lots of people have guns."

"Well…one day he came over…"

Joe raised his eyebrows and his eyes grew wide. Slowly he repeated, "Came over...he came over to your apartment? You let him into your apartment?" His voice a few octaves higher than usual.

"No! No, I opened the back door and he stuck his foot in the doorjamb so I couldn't close it, and he wouldn't leave, and Frank happened by and chased him away, but before Frank came Rick offered to shoot Gram. He said I could be as 'free as a bird.' He put his finger like this." Cassie held her index finger to her temple and used her thumb to show the shooting of the gun.

Joe laughed. "He offered to shoot your grandmother? Why'd you stop him?"

"Joe!" Cassie cried. "Stop it with the jokes about Sally's death. I mean it!" Cassie was now on her feet, chin high, legs planted firmly.

"So let me recap. The crazy man has guns. That's bad. He obviously has the hots for you. That's bad. *He offered to shoot Sally.* I make jokes about getting rid of Sally, but he might really do it. No, seriously, Cassie, I think you need to move out of there. Even if you report him to the police they can't do anything. Restraining orders are useless." Joe took both of Cassie's hands in his and stared into her eyes. "Babe, you gotta get out of there. Move in here. Please. Please, Cassie, I won't let him hurt you. If you're not around he'll move on. What do you say?"

Cassie took her time answering. "Joe, that sounds great. I want to be with you. I love you. I want to move in here. I want to go to BU. I want to do all of these things, but—"

Joe dropped Cassie's hands and started to pace again. "I know. What are you supposed to do with Gram? Well, just leave her there, Cassie. We can take her food and visit her. You just won't live there. You'll live here with me."

"I already sleep here every night. What's the difference? Technically, I'm living here and living there."

He stopped pacing in front of Cassie. "But your things are there. You live there and sleep here. Quite frankly, it's unsettling how you have to run back and forth all the time and I know it must be worse for you than it is for me."

"It's complicated… Listen, I've been thinking a lot about this. If someone gets sick with a physical illness they go to the doctor and do whatever it takes to get better, but with a mental illness it's never-ending. It goes on and on, sometimes better, sometimes worse, but it never fully heals. And that's what I'm up against."

"And Rick? He's not going to leave you alone. He's just as sick as she is." Joe walked toward the kitchen, stopped, and turned around. "It's always gonna be like this. You'll always be running back there. Right? Are you really considering going up to Boston? Not for a weekend but to study? Is it even an option?"

Cassie closed her eyes and rubbed her temples, her mouth drawn in a sharp line, cheeks flushed. Saying a definite yes or no was impossible. She just couldn't choose. She was beginning to feel that Joe was not really trying to understand her predicament. "Joe, I'll be back. I'm taking the car." She went over to Joe's jacket and took his keys.

"You're not going home alone now. Rick will be furious. Cass, come on, don't go home tonight. If she gets hungry, she'll get herself something to eat. She will," Joe insisted, his eyes pleading with her. "You baby her."

"No, I have to feed her. I'm not letting her go hungry."

"Then I'm going with you." Joe grabbed his jacket.

As they left the apartment, sleet and rain stung their cheeks. They jogged to the car, got in, and drove to Cassie's in silence. They had to park down the street, so when they got to the apartment they were soaking wet. When Cassie reached out to put her key in the lock the door slid open—it was already unlocked. They hurried inside to get out of the storm and saw Sally asleep on the couch. On the coffee table in front of her was Bossy the cat, dead. Her neck had been snapped and twisted around so her face rested on her back, eyes wide open like glassy beads staring at Cassie as she came in the room.

We Don't Have Any Proof

"**G**ram! Wake up! Are you all right?" Cassie ran over to the couch and shook her grandmother until her eyes opened.

"Jillian! Go away!" moaned Sally, pushing Cassie away.

"Gram, it's Cassie. Cassie. Are you okay?"

Sally struggled to sit up. "Yes, I'm okay."

"What happened to Bossy?" Cassie asked, pointing to the cat. "Who did this to Bossy?" Tears streamed down Cassie's face as she reached out to pet the poor dead animal.

"Cass…we've got to call the police," said Joe, wiping the sleet and rain from his face.

Cassie put her cheek to Bossy's belly and let herself cry, stroking her poor twisted head. She hadn't done anything to anybody except rub their legs with her furry cheek and curl up to take a nap if they sat down on the couch. What had happened? Cassie got up and looked around the living room for any clues. Sally seemed groggy but fine. Panic set in, knowing that Sally couldn't have done it, the question was, who did? Cassie flew into the kitchen to make sure the back door was locked, and it was, the curtain pulled shut.

"Joe, go check the bedrooms. Maybe someone's still here," she said.

Joe went into the kitchen and grabbed a large knife from the butcher's block, walked back through the living room and down the hallway. Cassie followed along behind him. "Stay here," he said as he turned into Cassie's room and flipped on the light. Seeing no one, he returned to the hallway and made his way to Sally's room. "All clear," he said with a sigh of relief.

"Check the bathroom," Cassie croaked, her mouth so dry she couldn't even swallow. The hairs on the back of her neck stood on end.

Joe held the knife out in front of him as he reached into the bathroom to turn on the light. He took a step into the small room to look into the bathtub. "Ahh! No one!" He collapsed against the door, hand to his heart, and took a deep breath.

"Thank God!" gasped Cassie.

"Cassie, did I have dinner?" asked Sally, sounding confused.

Cassie and Joe exchanged a look. "What the hell went on here?" asked Joe.

"I don't know. I have to find a box to put Bossy in. I can't just leave her on the table," said Cassie, turning toward her bedroom.

"Cass, don't touch the cat," Joe said. "You've got to call the cops...we both know who did this." He reached out to take Cassie's arm, but she pulled it away and headed into her room. Joe followed along, begging her to call the police. He watched as she threw her coat on the bed and then went to the closet and pulled out the box covered in green foil, threw the lid on the bed, and dumped out a few years' worth of bank statements. On her way back to the living room she opened the linen closet and pulled out a clean dish towel.

"I'll put her in here while I figure out what to do with her," Cassie said, almost to herself.

Joe grabbed another towel out of the closet and dried his face and hair. Then he followed Cassie down the hall into the living room, put the knife on the table, and put his dripping coat on the back of a chair. He turned to watch Cassie move the cat.

Cassie lined the box with the dish towel and then turned to the cat. Her tiny shoulders were shaking and tears were streaming down her cheeks as she closed the cat's eyes, carefully picked her up, squeezed her into the box, and quickly closed the lid. She took a deep breath in through her nose, resting one hand on the top of the box.

Sally had sat silently watching Cassie put the cat in the box. "Cassie, what happened to the cat?" She pitifully looked from Cassie to Joe. "Did she die?"

"Yes, Gram. Bossy's dead. Did you see her die? Did you see anyone hurt her?" asked Cassie.

Sally stared straight ahead for a few minutes. "No, I didn't see anyone touch her. I feel really tired. I think I'll go to bed." Sally used the armrest to hoist herself up and out of the couch.

Cassie and Joe looked at each other. "Okay, Gram. Let me help you," said Cassie, putting her arm through Sally's to steady her as she walked to the bedroom.

Joe was pacing in the living room when Cassie got back. She could see how agitated he was. "Cass, I know this sounds crazy, but what if Rick came in, slipped Sally some kind of drug, Sally passed out, and Rick killed the cat and left?"

Cassie looked at the coffee table for a glass, something that Rick could have put drugs in and then made Sally drink it, but there was nothing there. She went into the kitchen to see if there was a glass on the counter or in the sink. Nothing.

Joe waited impatiently while Cassie searched for clues. "That doesn't mean that it didn't happen. He could have taken the glass with him or brought a paper cup in with him. We're not detectives, let's call the police and make a report."

Cassie plopped down in one of the chairs in front of the windows. "Have you seen Stripe?"

"What?"

"My other cat."

"No." Joe got out his cell phone. "I'm calling 911."

Cassie leaped out of the chair and grabbed his phone. "No! Joe, I don't want to involve the police."

"Cass, this was a warning. First the cat and then—"

"No, I can't afford to piss him off anymore." Cassie's tone was final.

Joe shook his head. "This is absurd. Maybe they'll lock him up."

"We don't have any proof. We can't just tell the police we think he did it. Based on what? A theory? Let's look around and see if he left any evidence. Have you seen Stripe? Stripe!" Cassie started to race around the apartment looking in all of Stripe's favorite places, making kissing sounds. Under the chairs, under the couch, back to her room, under the bed. "I want to find Stripe. What if she's dead too? What if he hid her somewhere?"

"So you think it's him too?" wailed Joe.

"Of course I do, but how do we accuse him when we have no evidence? I don't want the cops to make us face each other. I couldn't do it right now. I still have to live here. Sally still has to live here. I want to calm him down, not ratchet this up."

"Cassie, he killed your cat! He snapped her neck!"

"I know, Joe. I know." Cassie's mind was swirling. Rick had been in her apartment. Her knees grew weak when she thought about him prowling around, possibly drugging Sally. He could easily have snapped Sally's neck, just like the cat, but her gut told her to be more vigilant in protecting Sally and not to involve the police.

A Serious Threat

Rick watched out the window from his darkened living room as Cassie and Joe ran down the sidewalk toward her apartment, heads down to shield their faces from the sting of the sleet. He had folded back the end of one piece of the Venetian blind, exactly at eye level in order to watch the street. He smiled at the thought of what awaited them. The glassy eyes of the cat looking to heaven. Ha! He only wished he could see the scene.

He had learned the technique in his military training. It was meant to snap the neck of a man, so the cat had been a piece of cake. It was getting the bitch to drink the roofie without a scuffle that had been a little harder. He'd given her an extra dose to make sure she passed out and when she came to, she would be confused and would have forgotten that he had been there. He remembered standing over her and ordering her to drink it, but she wouldn't. She was a tough old broad. More spine than he thought she would have. He finally had to grab her by the hair and pour it down her throat. Holding her mouth shut to make sure she swallowed it.

He considered himself a pro when it came to using roofies to get what he wanted. Thoughts of the sergeant's wife, her long blonde hair flowing over the side of the bed. He had slipped the drug in her drink out on the porch and then waited until she went in the house, followed her in and up the stairs. Sarge had been entertaining his guests, oblivious to what was happening to his prized possession upstairs.

Damn, he itched to see their faces when they saw the cat. Head on backward, staring up to the ceiling. He laughed out loud. It was a dark demented sound. They would know he meant business. They would know he was a serious threat now. He didn't think Cassie would call the cops again. Twice in one day would be suspicious. They would brand her a nut job. She would be too scared to make him mad. He would use that to lure her, to have power over her, to hurt the bastard boyfriend. They had gone inside, nothing more to see.

As he moved away from the window, Stripe hissed at him from the shadows.

Waiting To Be Happy

It had been two weeks since they had found one cat dead and the other gone missing. Cassie had put out cat food on the back porch in hopes that Stripe would come home, but the cat had not reappeared. They suspected that Rick had killed her too, but Cassie was afraid to confront him. Joe had stayed with Cassie for the first week, and then he said he needed a break and went home to his apartment.

Everything had been quiet, no sign of Rick at all. After a few days of staying with Sally every minute that Cassie wasn't working or at school, life gradually started to go back to normal. Cassie started sleeping at Joe's again and going home in the morning. On Saturday she took Joe's car and spent the day doing her chores. By the time she was done, it was five o'clock and time to make Sally dinner. As she opened the door to the apartment she could see Sally asleep in her chair. Sally was almost childlike when she was sleeping. So thin and pale. Yet so wrinkled and unkempt. Tears rose to Cassie's eyes. She thought about packing her things, leaving the keys, and walking out of the apartment for the last time. *Do it, Cassie,* she prodded herself, but she stood frozen in place.

Sighing, she took off her hat, gloves, and coat, and threw them on the couch. She decided to wash the dishes before Sally woke up, so she went quietly to the kitchen. She wet the sponge and picked up the first dish, but she heard a noise in the living room. Turning off the water, she called, "Gram?"

"Jillian? Is that you?"

Jillian? What did that mean? Cassie never talked about her mother and neither did Sally. She hoped Sally was just dreaming. Cassie went into the living room and saw her grandmother was awake. She looked up at Cassie and wrinkled her nose. "You're not Jillian. Why are you here? Where's my daughter?" she said in a loud and angry voice.

"Gram, it's me. Cassie. Are you okay?" she asked, walking toward Sally.

Sally's eyes became large with rage and she put up a fist.

"What are you doing, Gram? It's Cassie. Jillian left years ago. Don't you remember? You're still dreaming. We've been here, just the two of us, for a long time. Years, we've been here together for years." Worried now, Cassie wondered if Sally had had a stroke or something. Did dementia happen overnight or was it a process? Was this the beginning of that process? Sally's eyes had a blank look, but her speech was fine. She seemed to be able to move her limbs. "I'll get you some water. Do you want some water?"

Sally continued to stare at her with an angry look as if Cassie was an intruder. She didn't answer her question.

Once in the kitchen, Cassie was trembling so hard that she had to grab the counter for support. Had things just gotten worse? She didn't think she could bear it. She found a clean glass and filled it with water from the tap. Taking a sip herself, she replenished the glass and went back into the living room.

She held out the glass and Sally took it. "Thanks, Cassie," she said.

"So now you know I'm Cassie?"

"Of course I know you're Cassie," said Sally between deep gulps of water. She finished the glass and held it out for more.

"Maybe you're just dehydrated," said Cassie, letting out a huge breath, feeling the danger of the moment pass. Back in the kitchen, she poured more water and brought it to Sally, whose face now had more color. "Here you go."

"Can you put on the TV? I'm hungry."

Cassie felt the stress pain between her shoulder blades relax. Back to normal. Whatever normal was. She went back into the kitchen and finished doing the dishes, then made dinner. Sitting to watch MTV with Sally as she ate her chicken nuggets and fries, Cassie felt relieved that something more serious wasn't wrong with Sally. But why had she been so confused?

After a few songs she went into the bathroom and took a long shower. She was almost feeling strong enough to battle Sally into the tub. She couldn't remember the last time Sally took a bath. She spent her own shower time thinking of ways to cajole Sally into the tub. Sometimes she used rewards. "If you take a bath I'll bring you ice cream tomorrow." Sally liked ice cream. Sometimes she had to sink to threats. "If you don't get in the bath I won't come home tomorrow. I'll stay at Joe's." This had been the advice of the last psychiatrist she had taken Sally to, but quite frankly, it didn't work. By the time she got dressed she had decided to go the reward route. She would be late getting back to Joe, but she'd deal with him. More rewards of a different kind.

She turned on the water in the tub and went to talk to Sally. When she walked into the living room Sally was trying, unsuccessfully, to get out of the chair. She had both hands on the armrests and she was trying to heave herself up to a standing position. Cassie went to help her.

"Need some help, Gram?" she asked, trying to grab Sally under one arm.

"No! Don't help me. I have to do it myself," said Sally, her small birdlike eyes bright with anger.

Cassie stopped and watched as Sally tried again and again to stand up. Fear crept back into Cassie's stomach as she watched Sally try to stand.

"Gram, did anything happen today? Did you fall down? Did you hit your head? Did you have a stroke?"

"No. I did not have a stroke. I just need a minute. Get out. Get out of here!" she suddenly yelled. "I can't do anything with you staring at me."

Cassie retreated to the kitchen and debated what to do. She knew she couldn't leave Sally if she couldn't stand up. She also knew that if she didn't go back to Joe tonight he would be pissed off. She looked at her phone. Almost nine o'clock. It was a wonder that Joe hadn't called already. Cassie stood in the small galley kitchen and the walls seemed to press in on her. Joe on one side, Sally on the other. She wanted to scream. To tell them both to take care of themselves.

As she waited for Sally to get out of the chair, she noticed a photograph that she had posted on the refrigerator of her and Joe. It had been taken at Joe's cousin's wedding. They had gone at the last minute after Joe's mother had called him for the fourth time and he felt that he had to go. That it was important to his mother. Cassie had sided with Julie, Joe's mother, and off they went to cousin Rose's wedding.

In the photo, Cassie was wearing a long red dress that she found at the Salvation Army for five dollars. She had told people it was vintage. She had piled her hair on top of her head with wispy tendrils framing her face. Joe wore a tie. It was the only time Cassie had seen him wear a shirt and tie. He looked hot! She stared at the photo, trying to bring back how happy she had felt at the wedding. Everyone was smiling and laughing and having a good time. She and Joe had danced and drank champagne, eaten pigs in a blanket and mini quiche. She had been carefree for one night.

Cassie had never gone to a wedding before. It was held at the local Knights of Columbus Hall that was right down the street from the Lutheran Church where the wedding took place. Cassie and Joe held hands as Rose walked up the aisle on her father's arm to meet Ron in front of the minister. Joe stood out in the white crowd, but everyone seemed to love him as he introduced her around outside the church, where they all threw birdseed at the couple as they led the procession down the street to the hall.

As Cassie stood in the dark kitchen remembering that fun day, she wondered if she would ever wear a long white dress and smile, looking deeply into Joe's eyes as his relatives watched them get married. Would it ever be her turn to be happy?

On His Side

Joe woke in a foul mood. After Cassie had called last night and told him that she couldn't leave Sally, he had thrown his phone across the room, cracking the glass. Now Sally couldn't get out of her chair. Cassie would never be able to leave her. Joe lay in bed hating Sally. There was nothing sympathetic about her. She was ugly, smelled like shit half the time—looked like the kind of old hag in a Shakespearean play—with a kerchief on her head, missing teeth, and facial hair. But the worst thing about her was that she was mean to Cassie sometimes and prone to these unexplainable outbursts. And now she couldn't even stand up. What would they do when she was incontinent? Joe grimaced.

Maybe he should just break up with Cassie, but as soon as he thought about not seeing her, he felt bad. *Damn, girl!* Why was this so complicated?

Unable to continue lying in bed, Joe got up and went into the kitchen to make coffee. He needed someone to talk to about his predicament. His mom? What would she say? *"Relationships are hard. You have to take the good with the bad. When you're with someone you're with their family."* Platitudes. The guys at school didn't know anything about Sally and he would have to try to explain the situation starting from the beginning. No, he wanted to talk to someone who knew about Sally, but who would be sympathetic to him. Someone who would be on his side. Sierra. He could talk freely to Sierra, and she would see things his way. Had to stay in public places with that one, but she would give him what he needed. She would reinforce his attitude. Justify his anger. Make him feel that it was okay to be unsympathetic toward Sally.

Seeing Sierra also had another benefit. It would piss off Cassie, and right now he wanted to piss her off. He was sick of being the understanding boyfriend. He wondered if Sierra was working today. Damn! He just remembered that Cassie had his car. Shit! Now he was also stranded at home. Maybe Sierra would pick him up. He knew she would. His conscience kicked in, telling him that this was a very bad idea, but he pushed the thought away and focused on needing to have a conversation with someone other than Cassie about his life, his needs, his future.

He looked at his broken phone—which he also blamed Sally for—and pushed the contacts icon. Sierra Kole. There she was. Sierra had made Cassie give her Joe's number on the night that Cassie was so drunk at the Dragger Inn. Cassie didn't even remember giving it to her so that she could text Joe. He pressed Sierra's number and she answered on the sixth ring.

"Heh-low," Sierra answered in a sleepy voice.

Joe looked at the clock. It was just nine thirty in the morning and he realized it was early for Sierra.

"Sierra? It's Joe."

"Hey there. She's not here. Must be with her other boyfriend."

"Very funny. I'm not looking for Cassie. I need to talk to you. Can you come and get me?"

"Sure, baby. Is this a booty call? Because I am all in if it is," Sierra purred.

"No. I need someone to talk to and I think you'll see my side."

"Oh. Too bad. I had planned on sleeping in today."

"Okay. Forget I called."

"I'll be there soon. Just give me a little bit and text me your address."

"Okay, thanks. See you soon." Joe tapped the red circle and the phone disconnected.

An hour later Joe saw Sierra's yellow Beetle drive up in front of his apartment. Grabbing his leather jacket, he went outside and hopped in the car.

Sierra's spicy perfume filled the air, and warning signals went off like firecrackers in Joe's brain.

"Where to, soldier?" Sierra said with a smile, her eyes hidden by oversized dark glasses.

"Wanna get some breakfast? How about Vicky's Diner on Route 1?"

"Sounds good." Sierra started driving toward Route 1. "So, what's the crisis? Did Cassie break up with you? Were you a bad boy?"

Joe laughed. "No, she didn't break up with me and I wasn't bad. It's much more boring…"

"Oh, that's disappointing," Sierra chuckled.

"It's Cassie's grandmother. She's ruining our life…"

Sierra grunted. "Well, that old woman has got to go. Life's too short to be changing bedpans and spoon-feeding that old hag."

"I knew you would see it my way," Joe said. "I have plans. Plans to go to Boston, and then around the world. I want to be a famous reporter. I can't be tied to Cassie's grandma." They had reached the diner. Sierra parked and they went inside. The hostess seated them in a booth in the back of the diner.

"My philosophy of life is it's all about me," said Sierra. "There's never been anybody in my life who has put me before themselves, so why should I? If I were you, I'd move on. I mean Cassie's nice, but really Joe…you could do better," Sierra said, looking up at Joe through her thick black bangs.

Joe laughed. He knew this was going to happen. He knew, with an opening, Sierra was going to make a play, but he wasn't interested. What he wanted was for Sierra to listen to him and to back him up. "The thing is, I love her. I love how fearless and independent she is. I love her feisty side, and she is loyal to a fault, which I guess could be considered a good thing. I just want her to put *us* first. To think about me and her before anyone else, and Cassie won't do that. It's like me and Sally are competing for Cassie's time and attention all the time. And now, the old lady is getting sicker. She couldn't stand up last night."

"Here's the solution. I'll take Cassie out, and while she's out of the way, you go over and put a pillow over her face while she's sleeping. She won't even be able to fight you!"

Joe put his hands up and rubbed his eyes. "I wish I could. I just really wish she would die of natural causes and we'd be free. Me and Cass. To go to college and then Europe."

Sierra smiled a wicked smile. "Just tell Cassie you went over for a little pillow talk and she was dead. I just noticed that your fingertip is gone. What happened?" Sierra reached out and gave the tip a caress.

"Lawn mower."

"Ouch! But it's appealing in a weird way."

"Sexy…yeah I know. I think it reminds women of a penis…"

"Yes!" Sierra opened her large brown eyes even bigger and smiled her most lascivious smile.

Joe withdrew his hand from the top of the table and put it in his lap. They ordered coffee and waffles. "The thing is…people leave people all the time. I'm not talking about couples breaking up. I'm talking about dads leaving their kids or moms leaving, which I guess happens less, but it does happen. Children leave their parents all the time. I don't live with my mom. In some ways Sally is Cassie's mom, and she should be able to move on with her life. Cassie's actual mom left in the middle of the night. Did you know that?"

"Yeah. I wouldn't spend one day with that smelly woman. I saw them once in ShopRite and she is so weird. Long nails. Dirty face. Insulted a woman standing in line. I'd be embarrassed to be seen with her," declared Sierra. "She's crazy. Belongs in the nut house."

The waitress brought their food and Joe poured maple syrup on his waffle. Sierra had whipped cream on hers.

"Cassie would never even consider putting her away in a hospital." Joe ate his waffle in four large bites. Sierra had one small bite and then picked at the whipped cream as she studied Joe's face. She didn't try to hide her stare.

"Why'd ya call me, Joe?" asked Sierra, raising her big brown eyes to his.

Joe looked at her as if just realizing she was there. "Needed someone to talk to. Someone who knows what I'm talking about. Knows Cassie, I mean."

"Well, here's what I know. Cassie is in for the long haul. She's not leaving that woman. She worries about her all the time. *What's Gram gonna eat? What's Gram gonna do when I'm late?* I mean, she's obsessive. *How do*

I take care of Gram and see Joe? The girl's young and shouldn't be worrying about all that. Let her go hungry one night and she'll find the food in the kitchen herself. I told Cassie that." Sierra shook her head.

Joe listened to Sierra and knew that she was right. Cassie would never leave Sally. "Cassie's different. She's not like you and me. She actually cares about other people more than herself. Sometimes I think she's just trying to *not* be her mom. If Jillian hadn't left, then Cassie would be free. I really think Sally has to die before Cassie lives her life."

"So, you're gonna kill her?" Sierra asked matter-of-factly.

Joe laughed when he saw the serious look on Sierra's face. "No! Of course not! But she does have to die at some point. Last night Cassie said she couldn't stand up. Maybe she's on her last leg, so to speak." Sierra laughed and Joe shrugged, trying to repress a little smile. Deep down Joe knew it was wrong to wish Sally dead, but she was standing in the way of all of his hopes and dreams.

"See? Now you're feeling better," said Sierra.

"Hey, did Cassie tell you about her cat?"

"Her cat?" Sierra looked very uninterested.

"Rick killed her cat…"

Sierra perked up. "Rick did? How do you know?"

"It was the day Cassie called the cops on the kid at the pharmacy—on Rick, really. Yeah, when we got to her apartment that night the cat was lying on the coffee table with her neck broke. He had strangled her and, we think, stole the other cat."

It was Sierra's turn to look glum now.

Joe considered Sierra's pretty face. "You didn't know? Sierra, you better stay away from that guy. I think he's dangerous."

"How do you know it was him?"

"We're pretty sure…"

Sierra pushed one side of her thick hair over her shoulder. "Well, you don't know. Maybe Granny had one of her tirades and killed her."

"Her neck was completely turned around."

"I don't know what to say." Sierra pushed pieces of waffle around her plate.

"What do you see in him? Honestly?"

"I thought we were here to talk about your love life, not mine."

Sierra looked at her phone for the time and signaled to the waitress. "I have to get to work. Sorry." Sierra glanced at Joe's unhappy face. "Cassie's lucky that you care so much about her. Most guys would just say enough is enough."

Joe tried to smile, but his momentary feeling of being understood was gone.

"Gotta go," said Sierra, pulling on her coat.

Joe paid the bill and they walked outside to Sierra's Beetle. Joe looked over the top of the bright yellow car and said, "Sierra? Thanks. I needed to vent. Thanks for listening."

"You're welcome, I'll be your sounding board anytime," Sierra said with a sultry smile.

Emergency

Joe had purposely turned off his phone when Sierra picked him up. It was like blocking Cassie out of his life for a brief time. For a therapy session. Sierra had agreed to drop Joe at Cassie's, but as the Beetle drove up Kensington Terrace Joe got a sick feeling in his stomach. There was Frank Jaworksi, standing on Cassie's small front porch, his club car parked on the sidewalk.

"Who's that?" asked Sierra.

"Frank, the groundskeeper," answered Joe with an edge. "I'm not his favorite guy. Doesn't like Cassie being with a black boy."

Sierra pulled to a stop and Joe rolled down his window. "Ambulance just left," Frank stated.

"What happened?" Joe asked.

"I'm not sure. I pulled up just as they were leaving," answered Frank.

"What hospital?" Joe asked.

"The driver said Sullivan Memorial," Frank answered with a tone of concern in his voice.

"Thanks." Joe rolled up the window. He could see his car up the road, but he didn't have the extra set of keys. He took out his phone and turned it on. Six calls from Cassie. Joe felt the blood drain from his face. He couldn't bear to listen to the messages, but when he checked his texts there was only one from Cassie: *Taking Gram to Sullivan Memorial. Please come.*

"They're going to Sullivan. Do you have time to drop me off?" Joe asked Sierra.

"You owe me," she said with a smile.

Sullivan Memorial Hospital was a fifteen-minute drive away down Route 1. Joe's guilt felt like a vise crushing his rib cage. If he had called Cassie this morning he would have been with her. Instead he was with Sierra, hoping for Sally's demise. What kind of a person was he? Cassie was too good for him—of that, he was sure.

"Next right." He pointed to a weathered sign.

They pulled into a parking lot marked "Emergency" and Joe jumped out of the car. He leaned down to talk to Sierra, and she lowered the window.

"Cheer up. Maybe your dreams have been answered. Maybe she died in her sleep," said Sierra.

Joe winced. He didn't like to think of himself as someone who would be happy if Cassie's grandmother died. He closed his eyes for a second.

"It was only talk. Blowing off steam," Joe said.

"You better go in." Sierra rolled up the electronic window and drove off.

Joe stood in the parking lot watching the bright yellow vehicle drive away. He had an urge to call her back. *"Take me with you!"* he wanted to yell. He had no idea what he was going to find inside. Was Sally dead? He felt like he had willed her to die. Had wanted her to die. But would they take her to the hospital if she was dead or the morgue? He didn't know.

He walked toward the doors marked "Emergency" and was afraid that Cassie would take one look at him and know that he had spent the morning plotting against her. Talking shit about Sally with Sierra. He felt like he had cheated on Cassie just by eating waffles with another woman. He worried that Sierra would lie about where they were and what they had done.

The parking lot was empty. No other emergencies this morning. Only the one. Only Cassie's emergency, and he hadn't been there for her. His feet felt heavy as he walked toward the sliding doors. He wondered randomly how they would get back to one of their apartments without a car. A problem for later. He couldn't help but think if Sally had died that they were free, but would Cassie blame him for not being there with her? He stopped in his tracks. Maybe Sally wasn't dead. Maybe he was getting ahead of himself.

The automatic sliding doors creaked as they opened and Joe walked through them into an empty waiting room. No one at the reception desk. Eerie. Creak. Another sliding door. Curtains and nurses' stations. A lone nurse in pink scrubs and white sneakers disappeared behind a curtain. Joe thought back to the day he lost the tip of his finger. His finger throbbed. He walked toward the curtain where the nurse in pink had disappeared.

"Cassie," he called. More a whisper than a shout.

The nurse pushed aside the curtain and came out to see Joe. "Can I help you?" she asked. She was young with curly dark hair and sculpted eyebrows.

"Yes, I'm looking for Sally Bishop. She came in in an ambulance with her granddaughter," said Joe.

"They took her upstairs to the third floor," said the nurse.

Joe looked around. "Is there an elevator?"

The nurse pointed down the hall. "Around the corner to your right."

"Thanks," said Joe as he slowly made his way down the hall and to the elevator.

As soon as the doors opened on the third floor he could hear Sally screaming. "Cassie, don't leave me here. I don't want to be in this place. I'm not coming back here."

Joe could hear Cassie trying to reason with Sally. "It's okay, Gram. We have to figure out what's going on with you. Why you can't stand up."

Disappointment planted itself in his gut. She was still alive.

Suddenly Cassie was running toward him down the hall in her skinny black jeans, her multi-colored hair flying loose around her face. He opened his arms and she jumped into his embrace, crying and glad to see him. No questions about where he was. That would come later, he was sure. It felt so good to have her in his arms. Smell her shampoo. Secure in the knowledge that she wanted him to be there.

"Babe, what happened?" he mumbled into her hair.

"I called you and called you. She couldn't get up. I didn't know what to do and finally I called 911 this morning. We slept in the living room because

I couldn't get her to the bed. I don't know what's wrong with her. Where were you?" Cassie looked up at Joe with bloodshot eyes.

Joe shook his head. "I turned off my phone. I needed a minute. I'm so sorry."

They stood hugging in the hallway for some time.

"So, is she staying here? What's wrong with her? Do they know?" Joe finally asked.

"They want to do some tests but she won't let them," Cassie said, pulling away from Joe's embrace. "They want to do an MRI, but she won't get in the machine. They want me to sign papers to let them drug her. Do you think I should? Sign the papers?" Cassie's sharp little face looked paper-thin. Joe wondered when she last ate, but knowing her, now was not the time to ask.

"Yes, sign the papers, Cass. We have to know what's wrong in order to help her," said Joe, feeling like the biggest hypocrite. He started the morning by wondering how to off the old lady, and now he was talking like he cared. His head began to swim. Did he care or did he not care? He didn't even know. He knew he cared that Cassie was upset.

As they stood in the old tiled hallway, Sally began to cause a scene. They heard something fall. Cassie rushed down the hall to Sally's room and Joe followed.

"I want to go home!" Sally yelled angrily, pulling at the intravenous tube taped to her scrawny arm. She had knocked over the tray table, which had landed on the visitor's chair. When Joe walked in she stopped yelling and stared at him with defiance. "It's you who wants me in here," she yelled, pointing at Joe. "You want to take Cassie away. It's you!"

Cassie turned to Joe. "Why don't you wait in the hall?"

"Should I get the nurse? Where are all the nurses? Doesn't anyone work here?" asked Joe.

"Let me try to calm her down," said Cassie.

Joe was glad to go find the waiting room. He didn't need Sally yelling at him like that. He wandered down the hall, trying not to look into the hospital rooms filled with old people, some tied to their beds. Many calling for family members who were not there. At the end of the hallway was a small room with four chairs and a coffee table. He sat down, put his head in his hands, closed his eyes, and promptly fell asleep. When he woke, Cassie was standing in front of him.

"Cass…how is she?" Joe reached out his hand to pull Cassie to sit with him.

"She's asleep. They're keeping her overnight. Let's go," said Cassie, taking Joe's hand but pulling him up instead of sitting with him. "I really need to get out of here."

They took the stairs to get out of the hospital as quickly as possible. Once outside, Joe remembered they had no car. "I'll call an Uber," he said.

Cassie looked at him quizzically. "How'd you get here?"

Joe was caught off guard. He hadn't worked out how to tell Cassie about Sierra. Not a good liar, he stared at Cassie with a blank look.

"What's wrong with you? How'd you get here?" Cassie asked again.

"Sierra drove me."

Cassie's eyes narrowed. "Sierra brought you here? Why?"

"We…we were having breakfast…and…"

"Wait." Cassie put her hand up and shook her head. "You were having breakfast with Sierra? And last night? Were you with Sierra last night?" Cassie's mouth began to twitch like she might cry.

Joe grabbed her shoulders and shook her. "Cassie, I was not with Sierra last night. This morning I was mad and I wanted someone to talk to. It was either my mom or Sierra and I chose Sierra. I'm sorry. All we did was get waffles and talk about you. I swear."

Cassie pulled the collar of her jacket closer around her neck. "I don't even know what to think." She rummaged in her purse and pulled out her phone.

"What are you doing? Who are you calling?" Joe asked desperately.

"Uber. I'm just getting an Uber. Unless you want to call Sierra," Cassie said with a glare.

"No, Uber," said Joe, looking down at his sneakers.

Right Next Door

C assie was happy to go to work. She needed to stop thinking about Sally and Sally's health and Joe and Joe's demands and Rick and the dead cat. As she ticked them off in her head, her legs felt weak. The hospital had decided to keep Sally for observation for a few more days. They had found a thyroid problem and they were trying to monitor her reaction to the medication. Cassie was staying at Joe's and letting him pamper her.

She had dropped Joe at Home Depot and then continued on to the pharmacy. She had decided not to press Joe about his breakfast with Sierra. Quite frankly, if Joe took off with Sierra, Cassie couldn't blame him. Cassie was laden down with so many problems, while Sierra was fun and sexy and rich and carefree. Who wouldn't choose Sierra over her? Sierra was prettier with big boobs and thick, fabulous hair. She had a fabulous apartment that Cassie hoped Joe had not seen. She even had her own car! Sierra was everything that Cassie wasn't. Cassie was smarter, but did men really care about how smart she was? Sure, they said they did, but Cassie wasn't convinced that it mattered much to them. Sierra would cheat on him, of that Cassie was sure. Cassie was loyal. That had to count for something.

Luckily, it was Sierra's day off, so Cassie had a few slow hours to think about nothing but shampoo and deodorant as she filled the vacant spaces on the shelves. Even Mr. Ladinsky was off today, so the pharmacy was very quiet. Cassie was in the front of the store and the part-time pharmacist, Mr.

Chen, was in the back. Cassie unlocked the front door, signed into the cash register, and went in the back to get a box of Pantene. When she came back into the main room, she saw Rick pretending to look for a greeting card. Immediately her palms started to sweat, the blood rushed out of her head, and her ears felt hot. She crept down the shampoo aisle, knowing that if he decided to buy something she would have to go to the cash register. She hoped he was just looking for Sierra and would leave when he realized she wasn't there.

She wanted to yell out, "What did you do to my cat? Did you drug Sally? And where's my other cat?" But she forced herself to keep as calm as possible. She felt very vulnerable with only Mr. Chen to help her.

Cassie took extra care to line up the bottles just right. Keeping her eyes on the shampoo and her ears perked for Rick's voice, she wished she could just disappear. She felt trapped and checked again to make sure that Mr. Chen was in the back. As she stood up and reached down to pick up the empty carton, Rick appeared at the end of the aisle.

Holding up a card, he said, "I need to check out."

Cassie quietly walked to the counter.

"Just buying this get-well card," he said with a smirk.

Cassie closed her eyes, summoning all her strength to look Rick in the eye. "Rick, leave me and Sally alone. Do you hear me?"

"I'm just worried about her, that's all. Kinda miss hearing her through the wall. You know, she calls for you when you're with that fairy guy. Yeah, calls for you, but you're not there. Thought I might get some flowers and go over to the hospital and bring her this card."

"Get out! Get out of here before I call the cops," Cassie seethed through bared teeth.

Rick put back his head and laughed. "What exactly would you say to the cops? There's a guy in here trying to buy a greeting card? The nice one with the embossed front. Doesn't seem like a crime to me," he said with a scowl. "How are the cats?" He looked at her and raised his eyebrows, a smirk forming on his face.

"Do you have Stripe?" Cassie blurted out.

Rick laughed, a low demented sound.

Cassie felt her cheeks grow hot. "I'm going in the back to get another box to stock the shelves and do my job. If you're not gone when I get back I will call 911 and tell them you're stealing from the store," Cassie said, trying to keep her voice steady.

"Okay. I'm going. Now. But I'll be around. That's the thing, Cassie. I'll always be right next door. I'm not going anywhere. Here's your card." He held the card out to her and when she wouldn't take it, he laid it down on the counter. "I'll see you around. Maybe when you're bringing Grandma home." Rick turned around on his heel and headed out of the pharmacy.

Cassie felt her knees go weak as she slumped to the ground, burying her head in her chest.

Well Enough

Sally had been pronounced "well" enough to go home. Of course, "well" was a relative term. She could stand up by herself and walk the length of the hallway with a walker. Yesterday, when the doctors were deciding if she could go home, she had put on quite a show, smiling and saying "hello" to the other patients as she walked down the hall. It had taken everything she had in her to make it back to the chair beside her bed, but it had worked. Wrinkled old Dr. Weiner had nodded his head and said the nurse should call Cassie and tell her to pick up Sally in the morning.

After a month in the hospital, Sally had been diagnosed with thyroid disease, dehydration, and PTSD. She was on Synthroid and had agreed to see Dr. Warren, a psychiatrist. Sally wondered how long it would take her to crack Dr. Warren. In the past Sally had been thrown out of therapy, asked to leave therapy, told she was too angry for group therapy, and told that therapy probably wouldn't help her. In Sally's opinion, psychiatrists were all the same—full of reasons why she couldn't be helped.

During her second week in the hospital, Sally had her first meeting with Dr. Emma Warren: *hair-in-a-bun, no-makeup, wrinkled-blouse Warren*, Sally had called her when telling Cassie about the appointment. Sally remembered thinking, *You might honestly want to help me, but you can't. The task is just too big for your weak shoulders. How do you put a person back together after other people have spent so much time and energy pulling them apart?*

After a life of crazy and being worked on by a master destroyer like her father, with an assist by her mother, Sally knew that no amount of talk therapy could ever fix her—it had been tried before. But if that was what it took to get out of here, yes, she was willing to have a chat with Dr. Warren. Sure, Dr. Warren could listen to her talk about what had happened to her when she was thirteen and fourteen and fifteen and sixteen, but nothing anyone said—herself included—could heal her. Add to that fifty years of dealing with her pain any way she could, and Sally looked crazy in other people's eyes, but she was really just doing the best she could. Navigating her pain; she had become adept at weaving a protective web around herself to avoid more pain. Walls had been built. Moats dug. The drawbridge had been secured.

She had to be careful not to let people get too close, except for Cassie. Cassie would never hurt her. Yeah, she yelled at her when Sally threw things and made a mess, but she knew Cassie would always be there. She had to admit that she had been surprised when Jillian had left without a word and then never came back. Ungrateful bitch. That's what Jillian was.

Jillian had always thought that the world existed only for her and that she was the leading lady. Everyone else was playing a supporting role. Sally knew that having her as a mother couldn't have been easy. She wasn't exactly the PTA president type, but Sally had kept food on the table until Jillian was old enough to work. At fourteen, Sally had told Jillian to go get a job and she had. She also kept every dime she ever earned for herself, but at least Sally didn't have to buy her things anymore.

But Cassie wasn't like Jillian. As soon as Jillian flew off to Australia, Sally and Cassie became a team, living in a world where no one else mattered. Relying on each other; understanding each other. They knew they needed each other to survive. Yes, Cassie did all of the work around the house, but it was Sally's apartment and her money that kept them going at first. Sally wanted to do more. She wanted to do the dishes, for instance, and help Cassie, but when she went over to the sink she got so confused. Should she put the soap on the sponge first or turn the water on first? Which way was the right way? Her mother used to yell at her if she didn't do things the right way. She couldn't decide which way was the right way, so after she stood at the sink, holding the sponge, unable to make a move for some time, she eventually just went and sat down on the couch.

Her couch at home was more comfortable than this hospital chair she was sitting in. She heard the nurses lingering, chatting outside her room. They always seemed so above all this sickness. As if they never got sick. Surely they did, but maybe, being around germs all the time, they were immune.

What time was it? She wanted to go home and watch her big-screen TV that Cassie had bought her. She missed MTV. They didn't have that station in the hospital.

She closed her eyes to rest and started to think of all the shrinks that had tried to heal her. The first one was Dr. Sylvia McThom. Her advice was simple but impossible. "Get out of that house! Get an apartment where you'll be safe." Ridiculous advice for a fourteen-year-old. When Sally told her mother Dr. McThom's advice, she canceled Sally's next session and they never saw her again.

Sally sat slumped in the hospital chair, remembering. Her next psychiatrist had been Dr. Norman Giametti. Sally took one look at him and was scared shitless. He would fold his soft, manicured hands on top of his crossed knee and watch Sally squirm. He never asked her a question to kick things off but just waited for her to start talking. What did he want her to say? Sally never knew. She nodded off counting the number of psychiatrists she had seen.

"Gram. Wake up." Cassie's voice woke Sally around noon. "Let's go home!" Cassie gently touched Sally's shoulder.

"Yes, let's go home," Sally said with a smile.

Maybe I Can Fix Her

The new shrink told Cassie that Sally suffered from PTSD. Post-traumatic stress disorder. This had been one of the diagnoses throughout the years, but Cassie hadn't really thought about what it meant. The words post-traumatic stress disorder actually made sense. Stress that was caused by trauma. That was something Cassie could understand. Those words meant something.

Cassie wanted to know more, to understand what was wrong with Sally. Maybe she could fix her. After class she headed to the college library and took out all the books on PTSD. Sally had been home for a week, so Cassie went first to her apartment to make Sally dinner and help her to bed, and then she went to Joe's to study together. Then back home in the gray light of dawn. Cassie had staked out the apartment for a few mornings to figure out what time Rick went to work. Luckily, he went early at six thirty. Cassie started going home from Joe's at six forty-five, circling the block to make sure that Rick's car was gone. When she felt it was safe, she parked and jogged to her door.

It was a lot of back and forth, but Cassie felt like she had arrived at a schedule that she could manage. She liked having Joe to discuss things with in the evening.

"Did you know that promiscuity can be caused by PTSD?" she asked Joe, who was working from his desk while Cassie was snuggled up on the leather couch.

"Caused by PTSD? How's that?" asked Joe, looking up from the article he was writing.

"Well, not caused by PTSD. Really caused by sexual abuse, which leads to PTSD," Cassie explained. "Sleeping with someone you barely know gives you short-term feelings of acceptance. It's a substitute for love. People who have been sexually abused can't trust that other people will actually love them."

"Why? Was Sally promiscuous?"

Cassie hesitated. "I was actually thinking of Sierra."

Joe's eyebrows went up in the way they did when a new concept had been introduced. He turned toward Cassie. "You know, I've always wondered why she didn't take better care of herself. Find a nice guy more her age. What's with all the married men? And what's with Rick? That is disgusting."

Cassie smiled a mischievous little grin.

"What?" Joe asked, also reflecting her smile.

"Sierra once told me she wanted to sleep with us."

"Us? Like, the two of us together?"

"Yeah."

Joe got up and walked over to Cassie and stood looking down at her. "And you said no? Without consulting me?"

"That's right. I don't like to share." Cassie reached up and pulled Joe down on top of her and kissed him. "I'm not sharing you with anyone, let alone Sierra. God only knows where her mouth has been."

"Yuck. That is a terrible thought. Maybe we could have made her gargle," Joe said with a chuckle.

Cassie slapped Joe playfully in the chest. "Joe!"

"Ow! I'm only kidding. But seriously, have you found out any helpful information about Sally? Why would Sally have PTSD?" Joe asked, rolling over to lie on his side.

Cassie twirled a piece of her blue hair before she began. "Sally's father was really mean. Verbal abuse, physical abuse, he also kissed her, not like a dad. Like a man, so I guess sexual abuse. He gave her a black eye once that I know of. She was sixteen and they got into a fight. He was a violent drunk and had been drinking. I don't know what they were fighting about, but it became physical and Sally's mom tried to get between them. They were in the doorway to Sally's bedroom and somehow, after he punched Sally in the eye, her mother's fingers got slammed in the doorjamb and she broke her finger. Sally and her mom ended up in the emergency room." Cassie took a deep breath before resuming. "After that Sally just cried all the time and the school kicked her out. Said she was disturbing the other kids and that they weren't equipped to help her."

Joe gave Cassie a long hug. "I'm so sorry you have to deal with this. It's a lot."

"The books talk about her having flashbacks, nightmares, and anxiety. It also talks about how people with PTSD can't do stuff. Like simple stuff—combing their hair, taking a shower, doing the dishes…"

"That explains a lot," said Joe. "What can we do for her? To make her better? Did the new shrink say she could be cured?" Joe looked hopeful.

"The word 'cured' has never been used in any of my discussions with any of her shrinks. But that's what I'm searching for. Ways I can fix her. Things I can do to make her better. But…"

"What?" Joe's look of concern touched Cassie, but deep in her mind she wondered if he was concerned for her or for Sally.

"I mean…maybe it's been too long. Maybe her mind can't let go of the bad things. Maybe she can't forget. I wonder how many times he punched her? I wonder if he…" Cassie couldn't say the words.

"Wouldn't her mom have left? Taken Sally and moved away?"

"Sally told me once that her mother never believed her. I don't really know. Probably she was in denial. Sally doesn't have many good things to say about her either. I only have the broken pieces of memories that Sally shares with me." Cassie sighed. "I have to wash my face and start writing my article for class tomorrow."

"I know, me too. I need to finish mine." Joe leaned down and gave her a soft kiss, rolled over her, and went back to his desk.

Flashback

Rick's nightmares had been getting worse. He would no sooner be asleep than the guns would start exploding, and he would be on his belly on the floor reaching for his rifle. When his alarm went off at six in the morning, he was already awake, sitting in the yard chair, holding his rifle, fully dressed, his boots tied and ready to see action.

As the number of sleepless nights started to add up, Rick had a harder and harder time keeping up at work. Framing was hard work, and he couldn't afford to nod off when he was on the roof or up on the fifth floor, where he had been working last week when he felt his boot start to slip on wet wood.

It was Monday and he hadn't slept all weekend. He was expected to be at the construction site by seven. Maybe if he ate something he could sleep for a half hour and take the edge off his exhaustion. Still holding his rifle, he walked into the filthy kitchen and opened the fridge. Three beers and an open can of half-eaten tuna was all there was on the shelf. Rick slammed the door and opened the cupboard over the sink, saw a box of Cheerios, and smiled. He knew they would be stale, but that was okay. He was used to stale food.

He rested the butt of the rifle in the inner curve of his boot and leaned the gun against his leg. Sticking his hand in the box of Cheerios, he pulled out a fistful and greedily ate the cereal. He didn't stop until the box was empty, then he washed it down with a glass of water. After belching, he went back into the bedroom and threw himself down on the bed. It felt good to shut his eyes.

A full stomach did the job, and when he opened his eyes again it was six forty-five. Fuck! Now he would be late. Dashing out of the apartment, he ran to his car, jumped in, and took off with screeching wheels. He just caught a glimpse of Frank in his club car at the corner and shot him the bird. *Fuck you! You old bastard*, he said under his breath as he sped by.

It was a half-hour drive to the construction site, but Rick made it in twenty minutes. He was still late but thought he might have a chance to slip in unnoticed, until he saw Tom Wendel, the foreman, standing by the chain-link fence, watching him jog to the gate. The look on Tom's face was unforgiving.

"Tom, man..." Rick started to make up an excuse for being late when Tom held up his hand and stuck it in Rick's face.

"I'm sick of excuses, Rick. You're fired," Tom said matter-of-factly and started to turn around and enter the gate.

"Tom, I'm sorry, man. It won't happen again. I'll be early every day this week." Rick started to follow Tom through the gate.

Tom turned around and squared his shoulders, his bulk filling up the entranceway. "No. We're done. You've been late every day for a month, and when you're here you suck. Half the time you're drunk. No, we're done. Get out of here. We'll send you your last paycheck." Tom turned around to walk away, but before he could close the gate Rick pushed him with all his might. Tom stumbled but recovered quickly. His face contorted in anger, he came at Rick and grabbed him hard by the neck and shoulder, turned him around, and threw him face-first toward the curb.

Rick felt the asphalt scrape the skin from his cheekbone as he fell into the gutter and slid about a foot before crashing into a dumpster. Stars floated before his closed eyes at the impact, and it took him a few minutes to come back to reality. He sat up slowly and rubbed the top of his head. Tom watched him for a second before slamming the gate shut behind him.

Suddenly Rick was on high alert, ready for incoming missiles. He pushed himself up and crouched on all fours, surveying the street. He was back in Afghanistan. He had dropped his rifle. Where was it? He had to try to make it back to his car. Staying low, he crossed the street, and got down behind the first parked car, then the next. His car was two vehicles up. He surveyed the construction site and, seeing no one, he bolted to his car and got in, slamming the door behind him.

He caught a glimpse of his dirty, bleeding face in the rearview mirror, his eyes bulging, his nose running, and laughed. He'd show them. He'd escape and get to safety. He turned the key in the ignition and pulled away from the curb. Breathing heavily, part of him tried to separate reality from flashback but couldn't. Everything was real; everything was surreal. The houses were barracks. The cars were military jeeps. His next mission was to get back to the apartment.

Steady, Rick, steady. It was almost like coming down from a high. Reality started to overtake the flashback. *Breathe. In through your nose. Out through your mouth. Repeat. You're at a stop sign. Put on your blinker. Slow. Breathe.*

He turned onto Kensington Terrace. Now a parking place. He knew where he was. The air was clearing. A space, not too far from his apartment. *Ease in. Shut the car off.* He scanned the street. No one in sight. Almost safe.

He got out of the car and walked purposefully to his apartment, climbed the three stairs. Opened the door and walked inside. Leaning back against the door, he started to cry.

Scarf

Every Tuesday, Cassie took Sally to see Dr. Warren. She had arranged to take time off from the pharmacy on Tuesdays and make it up on Saturdays. Joe was not happy, but Cassie was getting tired of Joe's complaints. If he wanted a carefree party girl, maybe Cassie was not the one for him. She didn't like the fact that working added to the time she spent doing all her chores on Saturday, but until she fixed Sally, this was just the way it had to be. She was hoping that Dr. Warren could get Sally to open up about her past and help her cope with all of the things that had happened when she was a girl.

"C'mon, Gram." Cassie went and got the walker out of the closet and stood by the chair waiting for Sally.

When Sally saw the walker, she grimaced. "I don't need that thing!" she said angrily.

"The doctor wants you to use it when you go outside. For support."

"I don't need it!" declared Sally, looking out the window. "Is it raining out? I don't think we should go if it's raining. It looks really gray," said Sally.

"It's not raining. No rain is in the forecast. We'll try it without the walker. C'mon, where's your coat? Let's go." Sighing in frustration, Cassie went to the closet and pulled out Sally's old purple coat. "Here. Let me help you," she said, holding out the coat so Sally could slip her arms in.

Obeying like a child, Sally allowed Cassie to help her into the coat. She had lost so much weight that the fabric engulfed Sally like a blanket. Cassie stood back and took a look at her. "We need to buy you a new winter coat."

"No, we don't. This one is fine. Let me look out the window and see if it's raining."

"We're going to be late." Cassie took Sally's hand and pulled her gently toward the door.

"All right. I'm coming. You're hurting me," complained Sally.

Cassie helped Sally out the door and down the stairs. Sally stopped to adjust her multicolored kerchief. Cassie reached out and retied it for her. When she was done she looked into Sally's eyes and smiled. Sally smiled back with her lopsided grin.

"Afterwards we'll get lunch. Okay? Wendy's?" asked Cassie, looping her arm through Sally's as they walked to Joe's car.

"I love Wendy's! Can we sit inside?"

"Okay."

Dr. Warren's office was in the basement of the Methodist Church, a dirty limestone building that had once been beautiful. Sally didn't like the fact that the office was in a church and said so every time they pulled into the parking lot.

"Why are we going to a church to see a doctor? Doctors should be in an office, not a church," complained Sally.

"Well, this is where her office is, so this is where we're going." Cassie parked the Honda as close to the door as she could.

"You always say that God doesn't exist," Sally said in an accusatory tone, as Cassie opened Sally's door and started to help her out. "I can do it! You don't need to help me."

Cassie waited for Sally to get out of the car, tapping her boot on the pavement. Sally looked up suspiciously. Cassie stopped tapping.

They entered through a heavy wooden door that had been painted red a long time ago. The smell of mold engulfed them as they stepped into the dark, dank hallway and made their way to the other end of the corridor, through a glass door, and into a makeshift set of offices where Dr. Warren met her patients out of the hospital. She was standing by the inner door to her counseling room as if she had been waiting for them for some time.

"Your blouse is wrinkled again." Sally greeted the therapist in a monotone voice.

"Gram…" groaned Cassie.

"Don't worry. How are you both?" asked Dr. Warren in a cheerful tone, ushering them both into the room.

"We're okay," said Cassie.

"I'm hungry," said Sally. "We're going to lunch at Wendy's."

"Sally, I thought I'd ask Cassie to sit in today. Is that okay with you?" asked Dr. Warren, taking her place in one of the largest of the mismatched chairs set up in a semicircle in the middle of the room. The chairs were evenly placed around a faded carpet with an oriental design.

"I don't care," said Sally, plopping herself down in one of the chairs.

"Cassie?"

"Oh. Okay…but I'm not prepared," Cassie stumbled. "I mean I don't know what to say. Haven't gathered my thoughts."

"Nothing to prepare for. You can just listen." Dr. Warren extended a hand toward the empty chair.

Cassie hesitated, but after a few moments took a seat.

Sally sat with her legs crossed at the knee, staring intently at Dr. Warren.

"So, how was the last week, Sally?" Dr. Warren sat with pad and pen in hand.

"Why are you always taking notes?" Sally's tiny eyes studied the psychiatrist intently.

"To help me remember what you say."

"To make sure I don't contradict myself?" Sally adjusted her scarf, which was slipping to one side of her head exposing her matted gray hair.

"No. So that I can help you make sense of what has happened to you in your life."

"So, what's happened to me? What do you know about what's happened to me? Nothing. That's what you know." Sally crossed and uncrossed her legs and then started to brush lint off her corduroy pants.

"Sally, tell me about your scarf. I've never seen you without it. Why do you wear a scarf all the time?" asked Dr. Warren.

The question seemed to surprise Sally; reaching up to her chin, she absent-mindedly twisted the polyester ends of the scarf. Cassie watched Sally and realized that Sally had never—as far back as she could remember—ventured out of the apartment without a scarf. It was like a protective shield keeping her safe from people's stares. That was always Cassie's understanding of Sally's scarf. They had never discussed it until now.

"It's my hair," Sally finally said.

Dr. Warren's mouth twitched uncomfortably before she said, "You don't like your hair?"

A smile broke out on Sally's face and she started to laugh, first a series of ha's, then a deeper belly laugh. "No. Because they used to like it too much."

Dr. Warren glanced at Cassie, who shrugged. This was new information to her. "Who used to like it too much?" the therapist asked.

Sally looked at Cassie and then at Dr. Warren before replying. "My father. He wanted to touch it. Long and gold; soft and flowing. It was like a beacon to his libido. I couldn't run away. I couldn't hide. Touching. Touching. Until I had to put it away."

Cassie was not prepared for this response. She had never thought much about Sally's hair. She remembered back to the photos of Sally as a young girl and her long golden hair and realized that Sally had decided, a long time ago, to hide one of the most beautiful things about herself. Cassie stole a look at Dr. Warren. She looked distressed, unsure of how to handle Sally's revelation.

Dr. Warren finally said, "So, you decided to hide your hair because your father touched it? Because it made you desirable?" asked Dr. Warren, sympathy in her eyes.

Sally looked scared and then defiant. "I didn't like him looking at me and then touching me. First my hair and then… My hair wasn't red like some girls. It was gold. It was beautiful." Sally smiled, but then her eyes flashed with anger. "But I took it away from him. He couldn't look at it anymore. If it was dull and dirty, he wouldn't want it." Sally stared at Dr. Warren. "Don't look at me that way. I don't need your pity."

"Of course not. I'm just sorry that you were treated that way… We'll talk more next week when you come. I'm proud of you, Sally, for having the courage to be so honest," said the doctor.

"I'm always honest, and who are you to be *proud* of me? Cassie, let's go." Sally hoisted herself out of the chair and headed toward the door.

Dr. Warren and Cassie were slower to pry themselves from their chairs. "Wait, Gram," Cassie called as the doctor reached out to touch her arm.

"I just want to say how nice it is for Sally to have you. To be there for her. To advocate for her. I know it's not easy." Dr. Warren gave Cassie's arm a squeeze.

"I help her because I can, because I love her. She's always been in my life. When my mother left, it was just the two of us. It's been the two of us for a long time. My mother…" Cassie's voice trailed off.

"Where is your mother?"

Cassie felt tears rise up unexpectedly and gush down her cheeks. "She ran off with her boyfriend. They went to Australia when I was fourteen. Haven't seen her since."

Dr. Warren shifted Sally's chart from one hand to the other. "Some people can't take the pain."

"Some people just want to take care of themselves," said Cassie. "Thanks, Dr. Warren. We'll see you next week."

"Cassie…did you know…know…why she wears the scarf?"

"No, I didn't know." The doctor and Cassie looked at each other. "But from what I've been reading it makes sense. I've been reading a lot about PTSD."

"I think that's a good idea. It may help you to understand her. Talking about why she hides parts of herself may help her."

"I hope so. Ah, Dr. Warren, do you think she might ever get to a point where she could take care of herself?" Cassie felt her chest tighten as she watched Dr. Warren's face and waited for her to answer.

Dr. Warren adjusted the collar of her shirt while she gathered her thoughts. "Cassie, I want to be honest with you and the answer is, I don't know. She's had a lifetime of pain and she's erected barriers to deal with that pain. She's also very dependent on you. I can see that. But we can work toward that."

"Okay. Yes, let's work toward that. We'll see you next week." Cassie walked out of the office and caught up with Sally, who was slowly making her way to the car.

"I'm getting a double cheeseburger and fries," said Sally with a smile on her face. "Cassie, get it for me without the bun. I can't eat the bun."

"I always do," said Cassie.

"Yes, you always do," said Sally.

Faux Shopping

Sierra sometimes found her married men at the mall. Usually confused about what to buy their wives for a special occasion, Sierra would find her new victim in the fine jewelry department at the pricier department stores: she'd pretend to be looking at the jewelry as she scrutinized the men. She would make herself available to comment on their selection, and that would lead to a conversation.

Her process started with their haircut. Was it a two-hundred-dollar cut or a fifteen-dollar barbershop special? Next, the clothes. Tailor-made or off the rack? Casual clothes were okay off the rack, but no GAP or Old Navy. She liked Theory or Ralph Lauren. Shirt tucked. No socks and loafers.

Wedding ring—check. It had been two weeks since her latest conquest, Doug, had said goodbye at the end of a long weekend in Bermuda. He had teared up as he took the ring box out of his jacket pocket and placed it on the white tablecloth at the expensive restaurant where they were just finishing dinner. A three-carat ruby encircled by diamonds. She would add it to her collection of breakup jewelry. He'd called two or three times after they got back, but she hadn't picked up or returned the calls. She really hadn't been invested enough in the relationship to care one way or the other if she ever saw him again. He wasn't worth her time.

Anyway, onward and upward, she always said. She needed to offset the tawdry nights she had been spending with Rick with some glamour. A girl needed more than sex, she needed a fancy restaurant and a new bauble or two to make her feel special. Now that she knew Rick had lost his job, she needed to wean herself off that dirty affair. Now he was a total loser. His apartment had also started to smell like cat piss, which was gross. The whole apartment was disgusting. Sierra frowned. Maybe one more roll before he was surely evicted. She didn't want him showing up at her apartment looking to move in. Yes, one more night of debauchery and that would be the end.

Rick was one person who Sierra could be herself with. It was thrilling to just show up at his dirty nest and start fucking without all the preamble. She didn't put on any airs with Rick. She liked it rough and she didn't give a shit what he thought of her. Isn't that what her father had done when he would slip into her bed and just start touching her and then leave once he was done? Hadn't he been her first sexual teacher? No need for talk, no wooing or asking for consent. Just the smell of the exertion when she woke up the next morning. Had it really happened? She could smell that it had.

Pulling into the Nordstrom parking lot, she looked around for a new sports car to park next to. Men looking to break out of their lives usually started with a new car to make them feel young again, sexy. She made two loops around the lot but didn't see any Porsches or Mercedes. She parked next to an Audi, grabbed her Prada bag, and hurried into the store. Jewelry was on the first floor, so she took the escalator down one flight and entered the fine jewelry department. She had worn the ruby Doug gave her so that the store clerks would know she had the money to buy fine jewelry. They treated you differently if they thought you might buy something and weren't just wasting their time.

Glancing around the department, she immediately saw two targets. A tall black man, late forties, nice coat, bald, made it hard to judge his barber, but his skin looked like he had recently had a facial. The other man was white, also forty-five-ish, with nice shoulders and thick, wavy dark hair. Gray at the temples and sideburns. Expensive loafers, creased jeans. Hard to choose.

Sierra walked over to the counter where the black guy was being shown a necklace. A solitaire diamond. One carat. Too small? Sierra looked over at the necklace, but the man kept talking to the saleswoman. Usually they would ask her a question like, "Do you like it? It's for my wife."

Sierra continued her faux shopping, moving from counter to counter until she ended up at the counter with the other man. He was looking at a sapphire ring. Probably two carats, surrounded by diamonds set in platinum. Could be an engagement ring for his next trophy wife, but could also be a birthday gift or an anniversary present for wife number one. Sierra looked at the ring as if she was admiring it, and then up at the man's face, confident that he would see her interest and look over at her. Instead, when Sierra looked from the ring to the man's face, he was still staring at the ring. She watched him perch it on the tip of his pinkie and stick his arm out to see it from a distance.

"Can I show you something?" asked a petite blonde saleswoman.

Sierra, startled, looked at the woman with blank eyes, but recovered quickly and said the first lie that came to her mind. "Oh, yes, I'm looking for a gift for my sister."

"Are you looking for a sapphire? I can show you a selection of nice pieces."

Even the conversation had not turned the man's head. "She likes pearls. Show me some pearl earrings, please," said Sierra. She felt stunned. Off her game. How did she look? She took a peek in the large mirror behind the counter as she and the saleswoman walked over to the pearl counter. She looked gorgeous. Satin-smooth hair. Large, luscious lips. What was wrong with these men? Their wives must be shopping in the store and they didn't want to get caught admiring her. Yes, that was it. But if their wives were in the store, then why were they buying jewelry for them? Usually jewelry like this was a surprise. Why was she so invisible to them?

They had arrived at the pearls. Donna, the saleswoman, took a keychain out of her pocket and opened the cabinet. Sierra busily pointed out three or four pairs of earrings to look at closer. She knew that she was laughing a little too loud, smiling a little too brightly, flipping her hair too many times, but a feeling of desperation was pressing on her chest. She thought of going over to the black guy and being more aggressive. Commenting on the necklace he was considering and starting a conversation, but she felt herself losing her nerve. Her confidence, her greatest strength, had melted and lay in a puddle at her feet.

Donna carpeted the counter with velvet and brought Sierra's choices out of the cabinet. Sierra had never had to buy jewelry for herself, so she was shocked at the prices of the earrings. Two hundred dollars for the plain ones. Three hundred and eighty dollars for the ones with a little diamond. The drop earrings were four hundred and sixty dollars. Her imaginary sister definitely wasn't getting those. Sierra knew she could walk out of the store without buying anything, but she was reeling from the imagined rejection of these two men. Had she lost her appeal? She quickly decided on the plain ones and paid Donna with her debit card.

Feeling dizzy she went and sat in one of the fancy seating areas in the mall. Holding the small Nordstrom bag with the tissue sticking out, she sat and tried to collect herself. *Breathe in through your nose. Keep it together, Sierra. Two men engrossed in their purchases doesn't mean anything.* She would come back tomorrow and try again. She looked down at her leggings and thought for the first time they might be too working class. Maybe a nice pink—*barf*—little dress. No, pink just wasn't her color. Red. Yes, red could work. She looked around the mall at the women coming and going and tried to study them.

Many were wearing jeans with rips in them and colored shirts. Blue, checkered, pink, yellow, flowered. She had never worn a flower pattern in her life. She was strictly a monochrome girl. When did all this color become fashionable? *Next,* she thought with a sneer, *I'll have to wear something with a cat on it.*

Maybe she should just go shopping instead of trying to pick someone up. Maybe it was just her wardrobe that needed fixing. She felt panicked. Where should she shop? Where did all these Waspy women shop? She wasn't Waspy. That had always been her appeal. She suddenly felt fat, underdressed, large of hip, whorish, slutty. Was this Rick's effect? Could the men sense that she had been sleeping with that lowlife? That she had joined the ranks of the unwashed?

Desperation filled her. She looked around the mall at her options. Banana Republic. Anthropologie. Lucky Brand. Madewell. She usually shopped online. *Let's see.* Lucky had ripped jeans, so she decided to start there. As she was getting ready to get up, a young man about her age, with a toothy grin and a mop of unruly hair, plopped himself down in the chair next to her. He smelled like transmission fluid. Sierra wrinkled her nose.

"Hey, beautiful. Why so sad?" he asked.

"You wouldn't understand."

"Try me."

Sierra noticed that his eyes were a vivid blue and his fingernails dirty. Sierra closed her eyes and tried to compose herself. This was the kind of man who was attracted to her now. What could he possibly offer her? She was sure that her apartment was nicer than his. Her car newer and more expensive. Her clothes, she had decided, were her problem. A problem she needed to fix immediately.

"I need to meet my fiancé," she said with finality. Her tone closed down the pick-up.

"Too bad. He's a lucky man," said the stranger, pulling a toothpick out of his shirt pocket and putting it in his mouth.

Sierra got up to leave. Looking down at him she said, "Thanks. That's really nice of you to say." As she walked slowly to the Lucky store, she realized that that was the most honest sentence she had ever said to a man.

Trigger

After Cassie and Sally had lunch at Wendy's, and Cassie had gone to work, Sally settled into the couch, so comfy, for an afternoon of MTV. She aimed the remote at the TV, pressed the button, and nothing happened. She stared at the blank screen and didn't know what to do. Why wasn't the TV going on? Sally pressed the button again and again, but the screen remained blank. She banged the remote on the coffee table, tried again. Nothing.

Suddenly exhausted from the effort and the therapy session, she put her head back on the soft couch and closed her eyes. Doc Warren came to mind. No other psychiatrist over all the years she had been dragged to therapy had asked her about the scarf—that was pretty smart of Doc Warren. *Maybe there's more to her than a wrinkled blouse.* Sally always thought of herself as a puzzle that no one could figure out. She didn't want them to figure her out. She had carefully and purposely made herself offensive and repulsive. Her natural beauty had brought her nothing but pain. *It had to go.* She had a message for everyone. *Stay away! I'm ugly. You don't want to be near me. I smell bad. I'm dirty.* The other shrinks never bothered to look for clues, but Doc Warren had looked at Sally and seen a clue that had been staring all the others in the face. Would she ask about her teeth next? Her teeth that she had purposely let rot out of her head? No one wanted to kiss a mouth without teeth.

The thought of a kiss triggered terror in Sally's innards. Full body tremors. When Sally thought of two sets of lips coming together, her intestines started to contract. She could feel the weakness in her lower abdomen and the need to relieve herself. Because it had all started with a kiss the summer she was thirteen. That summer was the last time Sally had felt happy. She had a friend, Susan, and she and Susan loved to be together. They walked around the neighborhood together, they ate pizza, they listened to the radio, they wondered about boys together. Susan was her best friend. They told each other everything. Sally conjured up Susan's face and smiled. She always thought that she was probably with Susan the last time she was happy.

Sally's mother, Agnes, worked nights as a nurse at the local hospital and left the apartment every evening at six to begin her twelve-hour shift. Her father, Greg, a high school social studies teacher, usually made her dinner, answered any questions she had about her homework, and then they watched TV together until her bedtime. While they watched *Gunsmoke* and *The Man from U.N.C.L.E.* her father drank a steady stream of red wine. Once in a while, usually on Fridays, it was vodka. When he drank vodka, he got foul-tempered and angry, and Sally knew to go to bed early.

On the last night of her childhood, a Friday night, she had noted the clear liquid in his glass and had gone to bed early and right to sleep, but sometime later she woke up to find something being shoved in her mouth. She clamped her mouth shut, but his tongue was strong, pressing against her soft lips to try to force them apart, and he had cradled her head in the crux of his arm to keep it still. She opened her eyes to find him kneeling by the side of her bed. The new growth of his mustache was sharp and cut into her top lip as he tried to force her to open her mouth. She didn't, she wouldn't open her mouth. He stroked her hair. *Your hair is so beautiful,* he murmured. She felt his fingers in her hair, smoothing it, feeling its silky weight. She remembered lying there like an opossum. Her fear of his closeness and what might happen next had caused her to involuntarily shut down.

That first time, he had gotten up and left. Sally couldn't go back to sleep. It was hard to feel safe in her bed anymore. She started to sleep during lunchtime at school in the back of the vacant auditorium so she could try to stay awake at night. Susan kept asking her what was wrong, but even responding was too much for Sally. She told Susan to go away.

The next week nothing happened. She tried to pretend everything was okay. *He was just drunk. It wouldn't happen again.* Then, it was another Friday night, and she stayed awake as long as she could, but sometime early in the morning she felt the blankets peeled back and a warm body smelling like alcohol and Old Spice slipping between the sheets. Kissing was the least of her fears from that night forward.

Sally remembered her mother asking her why she was losing weight. *I've lost my appetite,* she had said. Her mother also asked her why she wasn't hanging out with Susan. She told her Susan was busy. After telling Susan everything for years, how could she tell her best friend that her father was raping her? At school now, she felt transparent. Like everyone knew what was happening. She wanted to hide. She started to stay by herself. Her grades slipped. She knew Susan didn't understand why she wouldn't go out for ice cream or pizza after school. She felt years older than Susan. What did they have in common now? She couldn't giggle; she couldn't pretend to wonder how it would feel to kiss a boy.

Sally worried that her mother wouldn't believe her. That she would blame her for what was happening. She worried about the fight that would naturally happen when her mother confronted her father. Well, it turned out that she didn't have to worry about that confrontation. When Sally finally gathered the courage and confided in her mother that her father had kissed her, suggesting there had been more, her mother said nothing at first, giving her a penetrating stare.

"Oh, c'mon now. I'm sure that's an exaggeration. He was probably drunk," she finally said.

"That's not all that happened," said Sally, her hands clammy, her mouth dry.

"Don't be ridiculous. Don't make up these lies." Her mother's small brown eyes were hard. She was getting ready for work. She pulled the crisp white nurse's uniform over her head and smoothed her hair.

"I'm not lying. Why don't you believe me?" Sally yelled.

"I have to go to work."

Sally had no one else to turn to. She had to protect herself by making herself undesirable: it was the only way. She stopped showering. Stopped combing her long golden hair that her father loved so much, and it grew matted and dull. The school guidance counselor called her parents in and they decided that Sally should get counseling, which started the string of psychiatrists, psychologists and counselors who tried to unlock the secret that was Sally.

As the years went by and the abuse continued, Sally resorted to crying, screaming, and jumping up and down. Her pain just couldn't stay inside anymore. The school finally said that they were not equipped to educate her; she was upsetting the other students. She was expelled and came home to stay. TV became her friend and she spent most of her time in her room. The second psychiatrist they brought her to, Dr. Giametti, helped them get Social Security Disability for Sally. That was probably the best thing any psychiatrist ever did for her.

Then, God heard her prayers and her parents were killed in a car crash when she was twenty. She felt they had gotten what they deserved and that they would be together in hell, doing penance for what they had done to her. She was glad that they died. She smiled now and leaned back into the couch, remembering the day that the two police officers had come to the door and very solemnly told her that her parents were dead. She had to fight the urge to hug them. The torture was over. They could never hurt her again.

The local priest, Father Coughlin, helped her bury them. As Sally stood by their graves and watched the dirt spill onto the coffins, she wished that the three of them could start over in a new life where they would love and protect her the way good parents should. She cried and Father Coughlin tried to comfort her, but he didn't understand that she was crying for something she never had, not for what she had lost.

After her parents died, Father Coughlin also helped her move from the house they had rented to Kensington Apartments. Sally tried to heal herself. She cut off all her hair and let it grow out again. She tried to eat and gain a little weight. But she had lost the ability to trust people. That was impossible to get back after seven years of abuse. Sometimes the sadness, fear, and anger would well up in her chest, and she would scream and break things to open a valve and let out the pain. She was plagued by flashbacks. Snippets of abuse that made her palms sweat, her mouth run dry, her limbs shake.

Sally shifted positions on the couch. She tried the remote again. Maybe the batteries were dead. She tried to think where Cassie might keep extra batteries. She was tired and didn't feel like looking through the kitchen drawers. She closed her eyes again. She couldn't stop the images leaping into her brain. It was a few years later when Ernie Bishop entered the picture.

Ernie was a drifter who was trying to settle down. He had been born and raised in Seattle, but some problems with the law had forced him to leave town. He aimlessly traveled across the country for a year, doing odd jobs, and landed in Tinden, New Jersey where he had an uncle. Ernie had long blond hair that he was very proud of and that he would leave loose, flowing down his back.

Sally shuddered when she thought of Ernie. Even though she had told everyone—including Jillian and Cassie—that she had married Ernie Bishop, it was a lie. They had met twice. The first time was at the dumpster in the courtyard. Sally had been throwing out her trash when Ernie came over to hold the lid of the dumpster for her. She had been terrified and threw in her trash quickly, then started heading back to her apartment.

"Hi, I'm Ernie Bishop," he called after her. "Moved in with my uncle in 14B. Come from Seattle."

"Thank you," she remembered muttering, needing to get back to the safety of her apartment. Once inside, she tried to quiet her racing heart. She put the safety lock on the door. When she ran out of food a few days later, she was forced to go to the store. It was pouring rain. Looking out the window, she saw the drops, like bullets, falling hard in the puddles. The wind blew it in sheets against the cars parked out front. Having no choice, she summoned her courage, bundled up in her yellow hooded rain jacket, and walked around the corner to 7-Eleven. On her way home, she felt his presence behind her as he jogged up to join her.

"Hey, wait up. I'm not going to hurt you," he said with a smile. His long hair was drenched from the storm.

Sally hugged the bag of groceries; when she looked up at him the rain beat on her cheeks. "Hi," she said. She put her head down and tried to sink back into the large hood on her rain jacket.

When they got to her apartment he followed her up to the door. She could hear her heartbeat thrashing in her ears. She fumbled with the key. She was torn, maybe it was safer out here, but panic took over and urged her to get inside, out of the rain. Dizziness overwhelmed her, fearful thoughts ran through her mind, and she dropped the grocery bag. He picked it up for her. After she opened the door, she turned around to get the bag from him, but he pushed her inside and closed the door behind them.

They stood looking at each other; the rain dripping from their coats and shoes formed puddles around their feet. Without warning, he reached out and picked her up; the groceries fell into the puddle of water. He carried her to the bedroom. Her worst nightmare. She kicked and scratched him, desperately fighting him. His eyes were bright and his teeth bared when she looked at him. She screamed for help, but he threw her down on the bed, held his huge hand over her mouth, and brutally raped her. Sally never saw him again and never told a soul what happened. Who was there to tell? No one would believe her. Her own mother hadn't believed her before.

After that miserable, slate-gray day, pouring with rain, the clouds never lifted for Sally again. Even when the sun was bright and spread its warmth on everyone else, Sally felt the gray, cold rain lurking around the corner, waiting to catch her off guard. In her mind, dread and wariness were constantly being tossed and caught in the wind of her thoughts rushing through her brain. Fear always quivered just beneath the surface and she was always on high alert. She knew she would always be living in the rain after that day. The sun would never come out for her again.

She regressed. Any progress she had made since her parents died was undone. She stopped eating, stopped washing herself, stopped throwing out the trash. She was afraid to go outside. It was Frank Jaworksi who saved her. After a while he noticed that he hadn't seen her for some time. He bought her groceries and left them outside on her stoop. She saw him through the blinds but was afraid to open the door. She finally left him a note taped to the front door to say thank you.

Then, of course, the unspeakable became apparent. She was pregnant. She noticed the nausea first, couldn't hold anything down. Then her boobs grew tender and she was even more temperamental than usual. Crying all the time. She remembered thinking that she was the unluckiest girl in the world, but there it was. She was having Ernie Bishop's baby. *That fucker! That bastard! Unbelievable!*

She knew she couldn't rely on Frank forever, and she was right—after the first three months she was hungry. Hungrier than she had ever been in her life. She started watching out all of her windows to see if Ernie was still around, but she never saw him. Slowly, she began chancing quick walks to the store for groceries. She went to the bank and withdrew three hundred dollars for Frank. She had no idea how much he had spent on her, but she hoped this was enough. He never asked her for more and when he would see her on the street, he never mentioned the food he had left her. Sally would smile shyly at him, but she never got too close. She wouldn't allow herself to trust him. She would never trust any man.

The pain started early one morning. Sally knew it was time. She didn't have a doctor; she never had any pre-natal care. She just called a taxi and went over to Sullivan Memorial Hospital. Showed up at the emergency room and said that her baby was on the way. She wasn't even scared; she just wanted the baby out. The doctor asked her if she wanted any drugs to ease the pain, but Sally said she wanted the birth to be as quick as possible. She didn't care how much it hurt. In some weird way the pain felt good. It was all-consuming. The pain overshadowed all of her demons. There was no thinking about nights past when her guts were being ripped out. And then it was over. Jillian Bishop came into the world at 4:23 that afternoon, and Sally checked herself out of the hospital the next morning.

Sally was tired of all these unwelcome memories and the pain that came with them. As if it all happened yesterday. She wanted to watch MTV so badly. When would Cassie come home? The afternoon had become evening as she sat on the couch, the remote nestled in her lap. She wrapped her arms around herself in a hug and squeezed tight. MTV was her escape and she needed a dose now. Although she hadn't cried in years, she felt the tears welling up in her eyes. She gave in to the urge and cried herself to sleep.

Letter to the Editor

The assignment was to find an interesting article in the news and write a letter to the editor in response. Not long—150 words—that clearly laid out your reaction to the piece and added to the public debate of the topic.

Cassie felt that she had been doing the least amount of work possible in her classes. This assessment was backed up by her professor, Dr. Katz, who had written at the top of her last assignment, "I am deeply disappointed by your work of late. Please put more effort into your writing." Cassie was so used to gold stars and top grades that this assessment of her work, though true, hurt. She decided that she needed to move her schoolwork up on the to-do list.

Opening her browser, Cassie went to the *Tinden Record* and started to scroll down the headlines. "Overdose Deaths Rise to 89 this Year, A Record High," "Early Signs of Rheumatoid Arthritis," "Starbucks Opens New Location, Giving Out Free Lattes," "Homeless Woman Found Dead in Warrior's Park."

Scrolling down, Cassie read the story of Jane Doe, who was found dead sitting on a park bench on Friday. The police were asking anyone who knew the woman or knew if she had relatives to call their hotline. It was a short article with a photo of the park bench tied up with yellow tape.

Cassie stared at the photo and tried to imagine the woman's final hours. It had been cold on Friday. She closed her eyes and thought of the woman, too sick to get up, welcoming death to take her from the life she had been living. Maybe she wasn't even sick. Maybe she had just willed herself to die. Would this be Sally if Cassie left her? If there was no one to write the check to pay the rent on her apartment, she would be evicted. Cassie knew she had to write an open letter to the family of this woman. This would be her letter to the editor.

❀ ❀ ❀

Hours later, Joe found Cassie asleep on the couch. Crumpled paper scattered around the apartment. He picked one up and read it to himself:

To the Editor:

The family of the homeless woman who died on a park bench last week should be ashamed of themselves. No one, no matter what their problems, deserves to die outside, alone, cold, wet, and hungry. I guess it's possible that she was an orphan with no parents, siblings, husband, or children, but somehow, I doubt it. To the family: were you afraid that your lives would be negatively impacted by the shame of being seen with her? Was she mentally ill? Were her transgressions so monumental that she was cast out of your family and shown no compassion? Was your fear of association with her so great that you cut all ties? Washed away all memories? Possibly sought absolution for this abandonment in the confession booth?

I know firsthand what it's like to take care of a person who is mentally ill. It's hard. But I would never leave a family member to die in a public park.

You should come forward now and claim her and give her a proper burial. That is all that can be asked of you now. Do you have the courage to come forward? If so, call the police hotline.

Sincerely,

Cassie Pennebaker

Joe rubbed his eyes and fell into a chair. He hoped that Cassie was just handing in the letter as an assignment at school and not sending it to the *Record*. They would print it. They were always looking for copy. He looked to see if Cassie was awake. Sound asleep. She looked so young and vulnerable when she was sleeping.

He tried to imagine the kind of future Cassie had suggested, one going to Rutgers, staying local, but it just didn't excite him. He didn't want to compromise and stay in Tinden. He wanted a change. He wanted to live in a real city that had museums, restaurants, concerts, and history. He wanted a bigger life than Tinden or Rutgers had to offer.

Joe got up, went to the kitchen, and opened the fridge. Letter or no letter, he needed to eat. He looked at his options. Waffles. Frozen pizza. Pasta. He pivoted and put on the oven to preheat. Pizza was the winner. Leaning on the counter, he ran a hand through his thick hair and sighed.

Why did he care if Cassie published the letter? It just didn't seem right to judge other people in that public way. She didn't know this family or even if there was a family. She didn't know their circumstances. Once in a while Cassie could be self-righteous, morally superior to everyone. Her own choice wasn't right for everyone.

"Joe?" he heard Cassie call.

"Hey, babe. You were really zonked out. I'm making pizza," Joe said, coming back into the living room. He bent down to kiss Cassie.

"Pizza sounds good," she said with a smile.

"What's all this?" Joe pointed to the balls of crumpled paper.

Cassie looked at the debris and shrugged. "It's my homework. I have to write a letter to the editor. Dr. Katz has been 'disappointed' in my work of late, so I'm trying to do something real. Something I really care about that hopefully shows off my writing. Want to read it?"

Joe was on his way back to the kitchen. He needed time to think of what to say about Cassie's letter. "I'd love to read it after I eat. I'm starving."

❈❈❈

They ate in silence. Cassie remained quiet because she was editing the letter in her head. She wanted to say that family mattered, but was she being too hard on the family? Would the family ever read it? Would they know that the woman on the park bench was theirs? She hoped that more details about the woman would come out—approximate age, maybe a birthmark, eye color. She thought of calling the police and pretending to be a reporter to ask more questions.

"Okay. Let's see the letter," Joe said, wiping his mouth after wolfing down four slices of pizza.

Cassie printed out the latest copy and handed it to Joe, who sat back on the couch and studied it. Cassie watched his beautiful face and knew that he had his answer as to whether she would leave Sally. Her heart started to race.

"It's good. Really good," he said, handing her the paper. He leaned his head on the back of the couch and closed his eyes.

She fought the urge to climb on top of him and kiss him, but his lips looked so soft that she couldn't help herself. As she leaned down to kiss him, she saw the tears gathering in the corners of his eyes and watched as one tear rolled down the soft curve of his cheek.

"You'll never leave her," he whispered.

"No," she said as her lips touched his.

Gun for Hire

I t was now the middle of the month, and that meant Rick had another three weeks to figure out what he was going to do. In two weeks, he wouldn't be able to pay the rent, and then there would be a ten-day grace period. Maybe by then he could figure out something. Another construction gig. Maybe move south, where it was warmer. Start over.

Then there was Sierra's ruby ring. He had noticed it the last time he saw her, when she had shown up unexpectedly in the middle of the night. It made him hard just to think of her knock on the door, *rap rapraprap rap*; doing it on the floor because they couldn't wait until they walked twenty feet to the bedroom.

He knew she was just using him, as he was using her, but he was glad she was so fucked up that she kept coming over. He didn't ask why. He didn't really give a shit, but now she might help him out. That ring alone must be worth $3,000. How could he get it off her? He could just knock her out and take it. Maybe use his last roofie on Sierra. Be gone by the time she came around. She was so crazy that she might just give it to him. She said some old dude who she was seeing had given it to her as a parting gift. She said she had a whole jewelry box full of them. Her breakup jewelry, she said. He chuckled to himself. What would he give her the final time he saw her? He scanned his room—beer cap or bullet—were the only options. He laughed.

Rick lay on his mattress wearing only his boxers. He had finally wrung the neck of the other cat and thrown it in the dumpster, but the place still reeked of cat piss. He got up and cracked the window as he thought about options to stealing Sierra's ring. He plopped back on the mattress. What could he do to get rent money? He stared at his rifle, then at his Beretta and realized that lots of people wanted other people dead. He could kill someone for money. He just didn't know how to go about finding someone who was looking for a gun for hire.

Jumping up off the mattress like a cat, he snatched up his Beretta and rubbed the barrel. It glinted in the dull light, and he pulled it slowly under his nose, breathing in the faint fumes of oil and gunpowder. He hadn't shot her in a while, but he was a master marksman. He could easily shoot someone's spouse, boss, ex-lover, mother, whoever, and walk away without batting an eye.

Rick felt smug and proud of himself—in less than an hour he had come up with two plans. Steal the ring, be a gun for hire. Scratching his balls and smiling confidently, he went into the kitchen to get a beer.

Is It Raining?

t was like the light in Cassie and Joe's relationship had burned out, and neither one could summon the strength to replace the bulb. So when Cassie got her letter to the editor back from her professor with an A+ plastered at the top, she had to fight the urge to text Joe. The letter had outed her. Her honesty in the letter had made it clear to Joe that Cassie would never leave Sally. She hadn't meant to be dishonest with Joe, but she had been. She had known for some time that she was not going to BU. And yet she had given Joe hope that she might. Easier to move the confrontation down the road than to flat out be brutal and tell him she couldn't—or wouldn't—go, but now the letter had done the heavy lifting.

She had gone to her apartment after work to feed Sally when she got the email from her professor. A+. *Heartfelt, daring, and honest. You should submit it to the* Record. *Well done! Dr. Katz*

"What are you smiling about?" asked Sally, absently touching the buttons on her shirt. Cassie could tell that Sally was asking God questions and counting her buttons for answers.

Cassie looked up, her smile bright. "I just got an A+ on my homework, Gram!"

Sally looked unimpressed. "You always get an A+. Are you still in school? Aren't you too old to be in school? I left school when I was sixteen. They threw me out—"

"Gram, I know the story—"

"My parents never liked me—"

Cassie closed her eyes and shook her head. "Gram, you know, I was actually feeling happy for a minute there. You always have to ruin it. I don't want to hear it!" she yelled angrily, springing out of the chair. She grabbed her jacket from the closet. "I'm going out."

"Is it raining?"

"No, it is NOT raining!" Cassie screamed as she slammed the front door. "Every fucking time," Cassie mumbled under her breath. She realized she had nowhere to go. For a brief moment she regretted the fact that she didn't have any girlfriends. This would have been the perfect time to call a friend and say "Hey, can you pick me up? Wanna get a drink?" She thought of calling Sierra, but something stopped her. She didn't want to only call Sierra when she needed her. That didn't feel right. They weren't really friends. She didn't want to confide in Sierra knowing she couldn't care less.

Even though it was almost April, the night air was still brisk. Turning up her collar, she started to walk down the street, noting that there were no lights on in Rick's apartment. It made her nervous to think she might meet him walking on the street. She picked up her pace and decided to head toward the Tinden diner. It was just a short walk and it felt good to be out by herself. Once she got to the diner, the warm air inside smelled like onions and pie crust. It smelled inviting. It was past dinner hour and the diner was quiet. She just wanted a table in the back where she could be alone for an hour or so.

"Sit anywhere," yelled Irma, the owner of and part-time waitress at the diner, as she washed the counter. She smiled as Cassie waved to her and headed to the back, where she climbed into a booth. Finally alone with her thoughts, she texted Joe and told him she wasn't coming over tonight. Usually this would result in a phone call to make her change her mind, but tonight he just texted back: *K*.

Taking out her phone, she reread the email from Dr. Katz. Did she dare submit the letter to the *Record*? Did she have the authority to call out the homeless woman's family? As she pondered the answer, the waitress came over to get her order.

"How are ya, Cassie? What can I getcha?" asked Irma. She still wore the iconic teal waitress dress with its white collar.

"I'm good, Irma. Thanks. I'll have a cup of tea, milk and sugar, and a piece of cherry pie," answered Cassie.

"How's your grandmother?" asked Irma.

"She's okay."

"You still living over there in Kensington Apartments? You still living with her?" Irma asked with a slight hesitation.

"Yeah. Still living there. Still taking care of her," Cassie said with a shrug.

"You're a good girl, Cassie...not...like your mother," Irma said and walked off, not waiting for a reply.

"Not like my mother," Cassie repeated under her breath. *If I ever write a memoir that will be the title. Not Like My Mother. No, I am not like her. Not like that bitch.* Cassie turned back to her phone and brought up her letter to the editor, read it again, made a few minor edits, and saved it. Irma came back and delivered the tea and pie.

"Thanks, Irma," Cassie said.

"Pie's on me."

Cassie smiled.

While she ate the pie, she googled how to submit a letter to the editor of the *Tinden Record.* Pretty simple. Submit name, address, phone, email, and letter to a specified email. The thought of publicly taking a stand like this made her feel nervous, and she started to sweat. The hot tea wasn't helping. She decided to search the *Record* for any other articles about the homeless woman. There, on page 47, right before the Sports section, was a tiny update:

Homeless Woman Died of Heart Failure

Tinden Chief Medical Examiner, Dr. Michael Grassley, reported that the woman found dead in Warrior's Park last Friday died of heart failure. She was found with no identification and is currently referred to as Jane Doe. She was approximately 65 years old, 5 feet 6 inches tall, with blue eyes and gray

hair. She was not known to the staff of the Tinden Homeless Shelter. The police
are again urging residents to call the hotline if they can identify her.

Cassie stared at her pie, cherries oozing out of the buttery crust. It made
her angry to think of this woman taking her final breath outside in the dark,
her only companions the leaves rustling around her feet. She felt something
stirring in her chest. She wanted to call attention to people who were discarded
and to the causes of their mental illness. Why should people die alone in parks
and alleyways and abandoned buildings? A serious look had to be taken at the
way people treated each other, especially within families.

Taking a deep breath, Cassie copied and pasted her letter into the body
of an email along with the other requested information. Exhale. Send. She hit
the button. A stillness came over her and she couldn't move. She was numb.

"Will that be all?" asked Irma, approaching Cassie from behind.

Cassie jumped and let out a little yelp.

"Did I scare ya, honey?" Irma chuckled.

Cassie laughed. "A little, I guess. Yeah, just the check."

After paying the bill and leaving Irma a generous tip, Cassie went out
into the dark night. She tried to light a cigarette, but the wind kept blowing
her lighter out. With nowhere else to go, she decided to go back to the
apartment and watch TV with Sally. Collar raised and shoulders hunched, she
hurried down the main road and turned onto the side road that led to
Kensington Terrace. She noted a car had also turned onto the road behind her.
The headlights lit the street. As Cassie got to the corner, the car pulled up,
blocking her from crossing the street. When the window powered down, she
saw Rick's ugly grin come out of the shadow.

"Can I give you a lift?" he asked, leaning over in the car to look up at
her.

"No. Thank you," Cassie said, quickly looking around to see if anyone
else was in sight. The street was empty. Only one streetlight had a working
bulb, halfway down the block.

"C'mon. Hop in," he said with a menacing tone.

"Leave me alone, Rick," Cassie said with authority and took a step, but Rick drove up to block her. Panicked now, Cassie couldn't decide which way to run. She was all alone, no one in sight. If he picked her up and threw her in the car she would be defenseless. He could do anything to her. As she heard Rick's demonic laughter emanating from the car, another vehicle turned onto the narrow road, forcing Rick to move out of the way and onto Kensington Terrace. Cassie wasted no time in sprinting down the block to her apartment, struggling with the key, and finally slamming the door behind her.

Breathing heavily, heart thumping, Cassie locked the door and pulled down the shade. Safe inside, she turned and tried to steady her breath.

Sally hadn't moved from where Cassie had left her more than an hour ago. "Is it raining, Cassie?" asked Gram.

Rinse and repeat, thought Cassie. *Rinse and repeat.* She stumbled over to one of the chairs and slumped down into its cozy softness. "Clear skies, Gram. Only clear skies."

Uncharted Waters

Joe, who was a stringer for the *Tinden Record*, was the first to see the letter online. Seeing Cassie's name at the end of the letter made Joe feel sick. Ever since she had left his apartment the other night, Joe had been walking around with a hollow pit in his stomach, unable to concentrate at work or at school. It was over between them. Over, yet the words had not been spoken. There had been no fight. No breakup text, no breakup sex. That might be nice.

They were in uncharted waters. He knew now she wasn't going to BU. What were their options? He wasn't interested in a long-distance relationship. He had no intention of getting in his car every Friday night, getting on I-95, and tearing down to New Jersey just to leave again on Sunday night. No, Boston was where his new life would begin with a new apartment, new friends, new favorite bar to hang out in—something he didn't have now because Cassie was only twenty—maybe a part-time job, a new girlfriend.

A new girlfriend—that was not an idea he had entertained in a long time. He had always had a girlfriend ever since he was fourteen years old and had kissed Lois behind the school. He had dated Lois for a few years, and then there was Sheila, Corey, Sue—he couldn't even remember. His friends called him a serial monogamist in high school. He only dated one girl at a time, but there was always a girl. Then he had met Cassie and he had thought she was *the one*.

Funny, really, she wasn't beautiful or sexy in a Victoria Secret model kind of way. But she was so sure of herself, comfortable in her own skin, that it was hard not to think she had all the answers, was right all the time. She always took the moral high road—it was just the way she was built. Where did it come from? She had no role model, maybe a reverse role model: she did try to do exactly the opposite of what Jillian would do. No, Cassie was honest, forthright, and trustworthy, but there was always drama and turmoil around Sally. Jeez, maybe he was ready for a little intrigue that didn't involve mentally unstable grandmothers. Maybe just a simple girl with normal faults, mundane problems.

The problem was he loved Cassie. Really loved her. Like she was part of him. He couldn't imagine life without her. He always wanted to know what she thought about everything. A thing didn't happen until he told her about it. Like now, he wanted to talk to her about the letter. How was she feeling about it? Did she regret it? That he doubted. Cassie didn't do regret. He went back to the letter on his computer and saw that there were already eleven comments.

Clicking the comment bar, he pulled up the responses to the letter.

Hockey Mom Who the hell does Cassie Pennebaker think she is? The dead woman's family probably went through enough. Probably drugs, fights, cops, who knows? Pennebaker should mind her own business.

Kirk Mind your own business!

Dorothy I think Pennebaker is right. Everyone deserves to be properly buried, but if they wouldn't help her while she was alive, I doubt they'll come forward now. But they should.

Sal She was probably a drunk!

Willis Pennebaker's a drunk!

FKL The poor woman. I am praying for her.

And so it went down the line. Joe counted two critical comments to every one in support. Cassie was strong. She wouldn't care about the comments. Probably wouldn't even read them. Joe clapped his laptop closed. He had more important things to think about. Grabbing his coffee cup from the coffee table, he took it into the kitchen and rinsed it out. He decided to go for a run and clear his mind before going to Home Depot to work.

He looked around for his running sneakers, a present from Cassie for his last birthday. Black Addidas ZX 2K 4D. Had cost her $200, which made him feel guilty, but he did love the way they made him feel when he was running. He sat down on the bed to put them on, picked up Cassie's old T-shirt that she wore to sleep in sometimes, and couldn't resist the urge to bury his face in it. The soft cloth smelling like her made him want to curl up in bed, which was just what he did. Two hours later, he woke up to find her standing over him.

Not Exactly Friends

Time was running out with every passing hour. Rick was sleeping all day and drinking all night with the last few dollars he had. Drunk or hungover, he hadn't been able to implement either of his plans. Sierra had not come over and he still couldn't quite figure out how to get a hitman job. He thought of talking to his drug dealer, Quentin, but Quentin was a man of few words. He operated out of the back of his vehicle, an old white van that said "Oasis Church – We are always there for you." Rick would text him when he wanted to score some weed and they would meet, usually in Warrior's Park. There was a parking lot all the way down by the pond that was off the beaten track.

Rick knew Quentin was a lowlife drug dealer, but that didn't necessarily mean he knew anything about being a hitman. Rick felt a little leery of putting himself out there as a gun for hire. Not that Quentin was going to call the cops on him. Rick laughed at the thought of Quentin with his dreads and tats and truck full of drugs calling the cops to report that some other lowlife was looking to kill somebody for money. He could see the cop taking Quentin's statement, smirking, and wondering what fight these two hooligans had gotten into to make one give up the other.

Well, he could use a bag of weed, so he texted Quentin and set up a time to meet. He pushed himself out of his yard chair and headed into the bedroom to sleep a few hours so he was sober enough to drive his car without getting pulled over. As he nodded off to sleep, he had a vague recollection of trying to get Cassie in his car. Just to give her a ride. Wasn't sure if it was a dream or if it had really happened.

Waking a few hours later, his throat was parched, and he coughed and felt pain shoot through his brain behind his eyes. He rolled off the mattress and into the kitchen, poured himself a glass of water, and drank greedily. The bulb over the sink had gone out earlier in the week and he didn't want to spend any of his precious last dollars to replace it, but while he drank another glass of water his eyes adjusted to the dim light. He drifted over to the back door and peered out into the courtyard, where one dim bulb on the back porch illuminated the black night. He broke into a grin as he watched Cassie bound out of her apartment, bag of trash in her arms, run to the dumpster, and throw the bag inside.

He thought about opening his door and scaring her, but he didn't have the energy and he had to get to the park to meet Quentin. What was it about her that made him want her? No boobs—and he liked big, sweaty boobs—no ass to speak of. It was something in her attitude. She was really just an innocent and there were things he could teach her.

He stumbled back into the bedroom to find his pants. He couldn't stop thinking about Cassie. She was a girl who needed a hitman. One bullet to the head would put that old bag away for good. Of course, Cassie would never do that. He could tell she loved the old woman, always doting on her, asking if she could make it to the car. He would watch out the window as Cassie helped the old woman down the stairs, never rushing her, and then getting her into the car. Always careful, always fussing over her so she didn't fall or get hurt. Made him want to go out there and push the old bitch down the stairs.

He bet the boyfriend wanted to get rid of her. Rick's eyes opened wide. That was it! He leered. Maybe the boyfriend would pay him a few thou to off the old bag. He didn't look like he had a lot of money, but he could probably come up with two or three thou to blow her away. Problem was, they weren't exactly friends, he and Joe. How could he approach him without the guy going to the cops? He would have to think on that after he got his weed.

He smiled his devilish grin as he pulled on his pants.

Awakening

"Wake up, sleeping beauty," said Cassie as she looked down at Joe in the bed with her T-shirt wrapped around his neck. "I think you're late for work."

"Mmm. I was going for a run," said Joe sleepily.

"Mmm. And my T-shirt got wrapped around your throat, choking you and making you pass out?"

"Something like that. C'mere." Joe reached up, grabbed Cassie by the arm, and pulled her into bed, cuddling up with his face in her neck and closing his eyes.

Cassie allowed herself to be cuddled, but after a few minutes said, "Joe, guess what? They published my letter! It's crazy. There are over a hundred comments."

That was a caffeine jolt for Joe, who was now wide awake. Rolling on his back, he exclaimed, "Over a hundred?"

"Yup." Cassie reached into her jacket pocket and took out her phone to check for more comments. "And the police are getting calls. Mostly crackpots, but one could turn out to be her family. And there's more, Joe," Cassie's eyes were bright with excitement, "the *Tinden Record* called me and they want me to go in tomorrow for an interview. To be a reporter."

"Cass, wow, that's amazing," Joe said with a tone of disappointment.

Cassie looked over at Joe and their noses touched. "What?" she asked, with a frown. She thought Joe would be happy for her, but instead she felt like he had let the air out of her party balloon.

"Nothing."

"What?"

Joe kissed Cassie and said, "No, it's just that I've been stringing there for months now and they didn't ask me. And also…" Joe turned and sat up. "Cass, forget it, that's great. What are the comments saying?"

Turning on her back, her lips pressed tight, Cassie started to scroll through the comments. "Mostly how I should mind my own business. Here's one from someone named Joshua: *Who the f..k is Pennebaker to make this family feel bad? My brother was a drug addict and my mom went through hell with him. You don't know what other family members have to endure.* No feelings for the dead woman at all." Cassie's face lit up with purpose. "Joe, I want to write a whole series of articles about keeping mentally ill people in your life. You know how hard it is, but think of all the poor people who have been cast out and could instead get help, or at least keep a roof over their heads and food in their stomachs if their families helped them."

Joe groaned.

"What? Why are you groaning?"

"You sound like you're going through a religious awakening or something." Joe sat up at the edge of the bed, unwrapped Cassie's T-shirt from his neck, and put it beside her on the bed.

Cassie's face looked serious. "I hope not." She bit her bottom lip. "That would be weird for an atheist to have a religious awakening. No, I just think I found something I'm passionate about, that's all. I thought you would support me," she said, feeling deflated.

"I do support you, but it's like we're on two different tracks. Veering away from each other. I'm taking a shower," said Joe, and he went into the bathroom. Cassie followed him in and sat on the toilet as he ran the water. As he got into the shower, Cassie studied Joe's beautiful back.

"You are hot, though. Just like Sierra always says," giggled Cassie, trying to lighten the mood.

Pushing aside the shower curtain, Joe stuck his head out of the shower, dripping water on Cassie's legs. "Sierra always says that? Not you?"

"Not as much as her," Cassie teased.

Joe finished washing himself, turned off the water, snapped back the shower curtain, and grabbed his towel from the rack. Cassie admired his beautiful body. As she stared at him, she noticed he was getting aroused.

"Happy to see me?" she asked, looking up at him with a little smile.

Joe wrapped the towel around his waist and walked past Cassie to the bedroom. "Not as happy as I would be if Sierra was here," he said over his shoulder.

Cassie walked through the bedroom to the hallway and turned around. "At some point we need to talk, Joe."

Joe zipped up his jeans. "I know."

There For Each Other

Who was calling Cassie now at work? Mr. Ladinsky had forbidden cell phone usage while his employees were working. Of course, all of his employees still checked their texts, Facebook, Instagram, Twitter and email when they were working, but they tried not to actually take calls unless absolutely necessary. He had threatened to take their phones during work hours. "I'll make you check your phones in when you get here if I see you talking on them. Our customers have to come first," he had bellowed.

Cassie took her phone out of her back pocket to see who it was. Frank Jaworski. Frank would only call her for one reason—Sally. She answered the call, her heart pounding.

"Frank?" she whispered.

"Cassie? I can hardly hear you."

"I'm at work. What's wrong?"

"It's Sally. She fell in the courtyard. I picked her up and took her home, but she's in pain. Can you come?"

"Yes, yes. Of course, I'll be right there." Cassie hung up the phone and looked around the pharmacy. Mr. and Mrs. Ladinsky were behind the pharmacist's counter. They would not be happy.

Cassie grabbed her purse from the shelf under the cash register, took a deep fortifying breath, and walked to the back of the store. "Ah, Mr.

Ladinsky?" she asked tentatively. "Mr. Ladinsky, my grandmother fell down and she's in a lot of pain. I have to go."

Both Mr. and Mrs. Ladinsky looked up from measuring out pills and pouring them into the small orange bottles. Mr. Ladinsky was the first to speak. "When is Sierra scheduled to come in?"

"Not for two hours," said Cassie feeling the look of irritation coming at her from Mrs. Ladinsky. She hated working the register. "I have to go."

"Go," said Mr. Ladinsky, and he waved his hand at her as if she was a pest.

Cassie turned on her heel, the anger rising up to her cheeks. She didn't appreciate Mr. Ladinsky dismissing her like that. She was a model employee, and it was not her fault that Sally had fallen. Sierra was late, called in sick, and left early all the time, and Mr. Ladinsky just seemed happy that she agreed to work for him. Cassie was now even more determined to get the reporter job at the *Record. To hell with you, Mr. Ladinsky, you old perv.*

She realized as she left the pharmacy that she had to walk home because Joe had not offered her his car and she didn't dare ask him for it. She knew he was hurting. He was gray and overcast, not the sunny guy she loved. She hated herself for ruining what they had, but if he really loved her, wouldn't he find a way to make it work? Couldn't they find a way to make it work together without going to Boston?

Once she got outside the sun was shining. It was that wonderful time of year, on the cusp of spring, when there was a hint of warmth in the breeze. Her scarf flew out behind her in the gentle wind. Rounding the corner on Kensington, she could see Frank's club car parked outside her apartment. *Frank, dear Frank.* She teared up when she thought about him. He was one of the few people who had always been there for her and Sally. She jogged the rest of the way to the apartment.

Frank opened the door before she could get her key in the lock. "I'm sorry to call you, Cassie, but she was outside, without a coat, and slipped near the dumpster. Mrs. Ramos called the office and I came right over."

Cassie looked over at Sally sitting on the couch, wrapped in a blanket. Her face was ashen and she looked dazed. "Gram! Gram, how are you? Are you okay?" Cassie sat down next to Sally on the couch, reaching out to take her hand. "Gram, what were you doing outside? Where are you hurt?"

"I wasn't outside," Sally yelled. "He pushed me down!"

Frank started to object. "Cassie, I did no such—"

"I know, Frank, she's probably talking about her father. She slips back in time."

"He threw me down! Pulling my hair," exclaimed Sally. Her eyes now bright with anger.

"Gram, where are you hurt?" pleaded Cassie.

"She couldn't walk very well. I think she hurt her leg," said Frank.

Cassie lifted the blanket, reached inside, and pressed on Sally's right leg. No response. Then she tried the left thigh, and Sally howled in pain. "Get away! Don't touch me!" she growled, tears from the pain forming in her eyes.

"I think she might have broken her hip," said Frank.

Cassie felt dizzy and sat back down on the couch. She wanted to call Joe, but she knew she couldn't. Back in the ambulance. Back to the hospital. Her head was spinning, vision blurred, the room seemed to go out of focus. She never had a minute to gain her ground. To feel that everything was okay.

"Cassie, are *you* all right?" She opened her eyes and saw Frank standing over her, a concerned look on his weathered face.

"I…yes…I'm okay. I need to call the ambulance," said Cassie blankly.

"I will do it. You stay put a minute. You look pale." Frank took his cell phone out to call 911 and give the operator the address. Within minutes they heard the wail of the sirens, and Cassie's stomach churned. She quickly went into Sally's room and grabbed her Medicare card, her shoes, and a sweater.

Five minutes later there was a knock on the door. When Cassie opened it, she recognized the two EMS paramedics from the last time Sally had gone to the hospital. She could tell they remembered how difficult Sally had been on that occasion by the way they asked what the problem was without greeting her.

"What happened?" asked the older paramedic.

"My grandmother fell. I think she hurt her left hip," said Cassie and went to sit down.

The younger paramedic walked over to Sally. "Mrs. Bishop, my name is Tom. Remember me?"

Sally looked at him suspiciously, her eyes bright with pain, and wrapped the blanket tighter around her shoulders.

"I need to take a look at your leg. Okay? Should I call you Sally?" asked Tom.

"No, it's not okay," said Sally, gripping the blanket still tighter.

"Gram, they have to look at your leg. Let go of the blanket." Cassie, still feeling a little light-headed, got up slowly, went over to the couch, and pulled the blanket away from Sally's hurt leg.

Tom moved in and applied pressure to Sally's hip. Sally squealed in pain and started to cry. "Yup, it's broken," said Tom. "Harry, let's load her up." The paramedics exited the apartment to get the gurney. Cassie sat by Sally and held her hand, trying to reassure her that she would be all right. When Cassie glanced up at Frank, she was surprised by how distraught he looked. His mouth was puckered, and Cassie could tell he was holding back tears as he watched Sally cry.

"Gram, let me have the blanket and I'll help you put on your sweater and your shoes."

But Sally held tight. When Tom and Harry returned, Sally was still wrapped in the blanket.

"It's okay, we'll just take her, blanket and all. Be easier," said Tom.

As Tom and Harry stood over Sally she suddenly started to scream. "You keep your fucking hands off me, you bastards!" She screamed with a scowl. "Cassie, don't let them touch me!"

"Gram, they're here to help you. You need to go to the hospital," pleaded Cassie. "I'll go in the ambulance with you. We'll go together."

"These sons of bitches are *not* going to touch me. Do you hear me?" wailed Sally.

"Harry, wrap her arms in the blanket so she can't scratch us," said Tom.

"I'll scratch your eyes out! Do you hear me?"

And on it went until Sally started to get tired. Her screams turned to whispers and finally she closed her eyes. Tom and Harry took this opportunity to pick her up, place her on the gurney, and pull the protective belts tight.

"Should I put on her shoes?" Cassie asked.

"Don't need them," said Harry as he and Tom started to roll the gurney toward the door. Sally lay back against the pillow, exhausted.

"You can ride in back," said Tom to Cassie.

As Cassie and Frank followed the gurney down to the street, Cassie felt compelled to turn and hug Frank. "Thank you. You've always been there for her." She gave him a brief hug.

"No, Cassie. *You* are the one who is always there for her," said Frank.

Their eyes met. "Yes, we've always been there for each other," she said. "I know."

She's Back

In the morning, when Sierra opened her closet, it still took her a minute to get used to all the color. For years, every garment had been black, but now the middle section of the large walk-in closet was filled with color. Red. Emerald. Magenta. Turquoise. Some color called spice. Silk shirts, sweaters, and blazers. She was finding that it took her a lot longer to get dressed than it had in the past. Now she had to make decisions. What color did she feel like wearing? The answer was always the same—black. After excessively shopping for three days at the mall, Sierra felt that she had a fine collection of clothes covering most of the spectrum. She couldn't bring herself to buy anything pink or orange, but she had to admit she looked great in bright colors with her dark hair and eyes.

After she had bombed out that day in the mall, she had seriously reassessed her clothing options. She was maturing—she would be twenty-three in a few months—and the men she wanted to attract were looking for a bit more sophistication than a girl dressed in black leggings and a low-cut black sweater.

The week after her tragic trip to the mall, she had visited all the department stores and some of the smaller high-end shops to try on clothes that she had never looked at before. Once the saleswomen knew that price was not a consideration, she just stayed in the dressing rooms and they brought her outfit after outfit. She had to have curbside pickup at each store to get all the bags into her car.

But the new threads were working. When she felt that she had shopped enough, she tried out her new look. Dressed in a flaming-red silk popover top, slim ivory jeans, a tan suede jacket, and matching tan suede boots, she had gone back to the fine jewelry counter at Nordstrom. There she quickly met Thurston. *Were real people actually named Thurston?* Thurston Smythe, Jr. was black, forty-four, tall, and handsome with skin that shone from care. The kind of skin that looked polished, not a pore to be seen. She had helped him pick out an opal and diamond necklace for his wife—for their twentieth anniversary—and then they had headed into the city, where he kept a little six-room *pied-a-terre* for a catered dinner and a long night of sweaty sex.

He had told her that red was her color, and because she had not had time to pack an overnight bag, he took her to Saks the next morning, where he bought her a red silk dress to wear that day. She had apologized that she would also need shoes and a matching bag. "Not a problem," he had said. He took her to the Frick Museum, where he forced her to look at boring art, but a nice lunch followed at the Tribeca Grill, a restaurant owned by Robert De Niro, a friend of Thurston's.

Sierra was in a great mood, smiling, hanging on Thurston's every word, but by four o'clock in the afternoon, she was tired and her face muscles hurt. Sierra was used to listening to her rich boyfriends talk about themselves nonstop, and she liked it that way. She always directed the conversation back to them. She didn't have a lot of accomplishments or dreams to talk about and her childhood, in particular, was off-limits to everybody.

They headed back to New Jersey in his Jag. She could tell he would be back for more as he dropped her off at her apartment. He had handed her his phone for her to enter her number. She asked what name to put it under, and he had said, "Stephen Sierra." She had laughed and told him to have a great anniversary.

While purchasing the new handbag she had thrown in a tote to carry her clothes back from the city. She had told him that she would only use it with him. That seemed to make him happy. The bag and tote had cost $1,200. A small price to pay for her company if she said so herself.

Now, in her apartment, she hung up her new dress in the color section of her closet, emptied the tote, and slipped into her old comfy pj's. Plopping down on the couch, she turned on the news and fell asleep. A little smile on her face. She was back.

Admitted

Everything in Joe's life was uncertain. Up in the air. Waiting for next steps. It gave him an unsettled feeling, like he was driving the car but he couldn't see the road. Joe realized he had never really made a serious life decision before. Growing up with just him and his mom, life had been easy. They weren't rich, but he grew up in a house—the same house his mom had grown up in and inherited when her mom passed—and he had always had whatever he needed. Teachers had described him as happy-go-lucky. Friendships came easily, he liked to have a good time, always had a smile on his face.

After his father left when he was ten, the air in the house settled. His parents had fought in the end, but then it was over. His father had told his mother he wasn't coming back to visit. She said that worked for her. No one asked Joe where he stood. His father was gone and that was that. Like he never existed. A figment of Joe's imagination, one that he rarely conjured up. His feelings toward his father didn't rise to the level of anger. He had never been that important to the family.

Julie, his mom, had given him a lot of love but not a lot of direction. She had kept him on a straight path to high school graduation, but then she had told him to get a job with benefits. Never anything about college or a career. She wanted him to be self-sufficient as soon as possible. The only decision he had made was to get his own apartment after he had been working and saving money for a few years after high school. He couldn't tell how his mom felt about his moving out; she hadn't said one way or the other. His mother loved him, but she was undemanding in her love. She had never set any expectations of when she wanted to see him. There was no set time every week when he was expected to call or come by. He knew he was always welcome at her house, but it was *her* house. She had turned his room into a study when he moved out.

He couldn't remember ever fighting with his mom. To say their relationship was laid back was an understatement. He never rebelled. She never laid down the law. They were easy-peasy, unruffled, relaxed, and their relationship bordered on unemotional. It was almost as if after his father left, neither he nor his mother wanted to feel that much again. Keep calm and carry on. Move ahead. Don't take life too seriously.

He had signed up for the creative writing course at the community college on a lark. He liked to write and was bored in the evenings. When he met Cassie he was going through the only time in his life when he didn't have a girlfriend. A six-month dry spell. He had always met girls at school, so he signed up for the class and the rest was history. They had bonded immediately. It was like they were both waiting for each other. After that first day when they had gone to Dunkin' Donuts, they were rarely apart, except for Cassie constantly running home to Sally.

When he met Cassie something in her intensity stoked a newfound ambition in him. He had never been driven until he had Cassie by his side. She had encouraged him to take more courses. She was taking two courses per semester, so he started taking two courses, and if he had to be honest with himself, there had been a sense of competition fostered. Totally on his part, she never competed, she just was…brilliant, motivated, driven, focused. That was just her nature. She had kick-started his own motivation, his ambition, his dreams, and now she was pulling the plug. Refusing to help him achieve his goals.

Now he knew what he wanted. He wanted to be a celebrated journalist. He craved adventure. He wanted to see the world outside of Union County, New Jersey. There had to be more. For some reason, Cassie had made more seem possible. But could he do it without her? If he left Cassie, would his ambition fizzle? Could he be competitive without her riding shotgun? She had allowed him to dream big dreams, to want to go to Jerusalem, Normandy, Venezuela, Moscow, to see mountains, deserts, palm trees, rivers, to meet influencers, leaders, heroes, and scoundrels, and to tell their stories. If he tried to go alone, would he go at all? He knew he wanted to.

Which reminded him, maybe he got the email from BU. For the millionth time since he sent in his application, he opened his computer to check his email.

There it was! He couldn't believe it. The email that might change his life. Boston University. He cracked his knuckles, then rubbed the back of his neck. He wished Cassie was here to read it for him. His knees bounced, his finger hovered over the email. He closed his eyes and clicked it open.

We are pleased to inform you...full scholarship...

Joe jumped up, grabbed Weezer, and spun him around. The cat, taken by surprise, meowed in protest. Joe brought the cat close to his chest, grabbed a paw, and started to waltz. Weezer reached down and bit him on the thumb, causing Joe to drop him. *Woohoo! We're in, Weezer!* The cat slunk under the couch.

"I'm in. I got a full ride!" Joe exclaimed to the empty room. Grinning ear to ear, he pulled his phone out of his pocket but didn't know who to call. A call to Cassie would be complicated. Ditto his mother, who would want to know why he was going to college when he had a good job at Home Depot. He could call one of the guys, but he didn't really want to tell them. He wanted to tell Cassie and have her be excited for him. The trouble was he didn't think she would be.

Swoon

Cassie spent all night at the hospital with Sally. The ortho doctor wandered in around seven the next morning and pronounced that Sally needed surgery to implant a steel rod into her hip. No time to debate, he had said. They were prepping the OR now.

Was this her choice, Cassie asked herself, or the ortho guy's, who seemed so sure of himself? Was he asking her or merely informing her? Cassie didn't know. Her sleep-deprived brain felt blunt and unsure. She decided to trust in the haughty demeanor of the broad-shouldered ortho doctor. Cassie looked at her phone for the time and remembered that today was the day of her interview with the *Record*. She desperately wanted to go to that interview and get the reporting job.

"How long will the operation take?" she asked the ortho doc.

"Two, two and half hours, and then recoup time. You can see her again around noon, one o'clock." He barely looked up from the computer that was stationed in the hallway on a rolling platform outside Sally's room. Cassie looked down the hall and saw an army of nurses and doctors entering data into the computers. Medicine had become all about covering your ass and billing codes.

Cassie peered into Sally's room and saw that, mercifully, Sally had nodded off. Taking this quiet moment to brace herself, Cassie decided to run home, take a shower, go to the interview, and get back to the hospital before one o'clock. Turning back to the ortho doc, she told him that she had an urgent matter to attend to and that she would be back. When he nodded his agreement, Cassie sprinted down the hallway and took the stairs to the main floor.

Standing in the parking lot, she called an Uber. The tiny map on her phone told her that Abdul in his Hyundai Elantra would arrive in three minutes. Cassie exhaled. It was all too much. The inside of her mouth felt dry and fuzzy after spending part of the night trying to sleep in the hard, plastic-cushioned chair beside Sally's bed. She lit up a cigarette to get the bad taste out of her mouth. They had given Sally some morphine for the pain around midnight, and Cassie had taken that opportunity to find the family waiting room and stretch out on the tired-looking couch beside the plastic palm tree. As she fell asleep, she wondered who had decided that a dusty plastic palm tree would bring comfort to distraught family members.

As she thought about the palm tree again, Abdul arrived. Cassie stamped out the cigarette and settled into the back seat for the short ride back to the apartment. She made a mental list of all the things she needed to do once she got there: make coffee, take shower, print out articles she had written at school...was there a loose-leaf binder in her closet that she could use as a portfolio? She would check. She would be meeting with Luke Miller, editor of the *Tinden Record*. If she had time she would google him. Her palms were sweating. So much to do. She would not think of Sally.

In an hour's time she was back out on the street calling for another Uber to take her to the paper. This time Sam would arrive in his Chevrolet Malibu in four minutes. She had not had time to google Miller, and she was too nervous to do it now. She hoped that her wild-colored hair wouldn't be a deal breaker. To offset her bright hair she had opted to wear jeans and a white shirt, plain but neat. She hoped that Miller wasn't sixty and stodgy and wouldn't judge her instantly by the way she looked. Obviously, he liked her writing or her nerve, since he had reached out to her after her letter.

She briefly wondered what was happening with Jane Doe and her burial. Had anyone come forward? After her interview she would call the police station to inquire. Thoughts of Sally now on the operating table stormed her brain. Blood. Scalpels. Masks on faces. Hot tingles ran up her spine, and she tried with all her might to thrust these thoughts out. She tried to focus on her breathing.

A car horn blared in front of her. Cassie startled and saw that her Uber ride was right in front of her in the street, waiting. She wondered how long Sam had been watching her. She jogged down the steps and got in the car.

"Sorry," she said.

"No prob," Sam replied, checked his GPS, and pulled away from the curb.

The *Record* was located on the top floor of a two-story yellow brick building in the center of Tinden. Downstairs there was a yoga studio and a hamburger joint. As Cassie got out of the Uber and saw the restaurant, she realized she hadn't eaten anything since the day before. She couldn't even remember the last thing she ate. *After. After the interview,* she told herself.

She went through the door marked *Tinden Record* and walked up an ancient stairway with worn maroon carpeting. Framed covers of the *Record* hung on the wall, yellowed with age. Once upstairs, the décor improved, and the space was light and airy with large palladium windows flooding the newsroom with bright sunshine. Cassie drank in the room of reporters with bowed heads and hunched backs furiously tapping away at their laptops. She had this feeling that she belonged here. Tapping away. It felt like home.

The receptionist told her to take a seat and pointed to three wooden chairs against the wall. Editions of the *Record* spilled out all over a rickety coffee table, and she picked up today's paper. Scanning the headlines. "Tinden Board of Ed Discusses New Social Studies Curriculum." "Town Council OK's Community Development Application." "Library Plans Book Discussion."

Someone moved in front of Cassie and stood watching her. She looked up to find a gorgeous man with wavy black hair, thick brows, and a pointed chin. He was around thirty, tall and slim, and staring at her as if she was very amusing, a little smile crossing his lips.

"Wow! I wish all of our readers were so intrigued by the school board and the town council." He held out his hand. "Hi! I'm Luke."

Cassie, aware that it was her turn to say something, placed the paper on top of the pile and stood up. "Hi, I'm Cassie," she said, taking his hand.

"Nice to meet you. Let's talk in my office," he said, gesturing for her to follow before heading down the hall to his office. Cassie trailed after him. Once inside, Cassie took a minute to look around the office. She had read somewhere that it was a good idea to comment on something in an interviewer's office. It created an opportunity to engage in small talk before the interview really got going. The office was full of books, newspapers, and on one wall was a glass case full of model ships. Cassie paused in front of the case and looked over the boats. There was a sailboat, a schooner, a sloop, and a dhow, all marked with little tags.

"Are you a sailor?" she asked, taking a seat in front of Luke's desk.

"Yeah. All the Millers are two things—reporters and sailors. The *Record* is our family business, and our hobby is sailing." Luke smiled and Cassie felt her stomach fall through the floor.

Luke studied her for a minute too long. "I know I'm not supposed to ask this, but how old are you?"

"If you're not supposed to ask, why are you asking?" Cassie's nerves were making it hard to filter what she said.

"I'm a reporter. I like to know things." He leaned back in his chair and played absent-mindedly with a paper clip.

"Your title on the door is editor." Her voice sounded much more confident than she felt.

"I'm always a reporter first." He tipped his head for emphasis and his dark wavy hair fell over his forehead.

"Well, I'm almost twenty-one, but if I don't get the job now, I am going to sue you." Cassie grinned. She had no idea where that came from.

Luke howled with laughter. "Okay, I guess this interview is over and you're hired."

Cassie laughed. "Maybe we should start over."

"Yeah, so, what prompted you to write that letter? It was really good and heartfelt."

"Well, I don't want to bore you with all the details of my life, but I have a mentally ill grandmother who I take care of, and when I saw the article about the homeless woman, it made me think of her. And how it could be her outside

194

alone if I wasn't there for her. Have you heard anything from the police? Has anyone come forward?"

"No, I haven't heard anything. So, do you want to be a reporter?"

"Yes, definitely. I've been taking some classes at Kent Community and have some clips for you to look at." Cassie handed Luke her makeshift portfolio. The pages were stuck in a Hello Kitty binder and she hadn't had a hole punch, so she had poked holes in the pages with the binder rings.

Luke smiled as he looked at the cover of the binder, but he didn't say anything. He took a good ten minutes to read her stories. Cassie fought the urge to chew on her fingernails. Finally, he gently tossed the binder on his desk. "So, what do you want to write about?"

"Well, I'll start anywhere you need me, but eventually I want to write about services for the poor, the homeless, survivors of abuse, and the mentally ill. Human interest stories that also give readers practical information on where they can go for help." Cassie had been practicing that line, and she thought that Luke liked what he heard.

"So you want to save the world?" Luke's eyes were the color of the sky on the most beautiful summer day. Cassie swooned.

"No, just help a little if I can," said Cassie.

"Well, the position I have open is an entry level position covering local stories. One day it might be the homeless lady dying in the park and the next day it might be some kids who made a lot of money for a cause by selling lemonade. You would have to go where the news is. Do you have a car?"

"Ah, no, but I've been thinking about getting one. I usually borrow a friend's car, but I don't think I can do that anymore. Does the paper have a car?" Cassie's hands had started to sweat and she rubbed them on her jeans.

Luke chuckled, and when Cassie noticed he had deep dimples, her stomach took another plunge. Jeez, this wasn't even fair. "No, the paper does not have a car," he said nicely. "You would have to find a way to get around."

"Okay, that won't be a problem," said Cassie with conviction, silently wondering what time it was.

"The way we work here is first you'll be on general assignment, as I said, then you might trade up to a beat—board of ed, town council, sports…"

When Cassie wrinkled her nose, Luke paused, then said, "Not a sports fan, eh?"

"I can cover sports," Cassie shot back.

"Your nose says otherwise. Doesn't matter. We have reporters lining up to cover sports. Every middle-aged man wants to relive his time on the field and watch their own kids who are playing now. We don't have a social services beat, per se, but I like the idea. People need services. Might even bring in advertising. Who knows?"

Cassie's face lit up. Luke's blue eyes twinkled. *Ugh,* thought Cassie, *how am I supposed to deal with this feeling in my stomach every day?*

"So, can you start Monday? Do you have any questions?"

Cassie's smile faded. "Umm, right now I work at Jenkins Pharmacy. I'd like to give them two weeks' notice. Aren't you supposed to do that? I've never actually quit a job before."

"It is customary. Don't you want to know how much you'll make?"

"Oh, yes! What is the salary and the hours?"

They worked out the details and agreed that she would start in two weeks. As he walked her out to the lobby door and they shook hands on the job, Cassie wondered if he was married; he didn't have a wedding ring. Immediately she felt guilty for the thought.

Sizzle and Pop

assie left the *Record* with her mind buzzing, flitting around in every direction. She had gotten a new job, she was a reporter! Her new boss was hot! Sally would be out of surgery by now. She was hungry. She needed a car. She felt like her brain might sizzle and pop and stop working because it was so full. She pulled out her phone to call another Uber, realizing how dependent she had become on Joe's car. While she was waiting for the Uber she googled car deals. She definitely needed a car now.

Once she got to the hospital, light-headed from lack of sleep and food but happy, Cassie asked the receptionist in the lobby of the hospital where she could find Sally Bishop. Sally Bishop was out of surgery and in the ICU—the Intensive Care Unit. Cassie didn't like the sound of that, but the receptionist said it was routine after surgery. She was handed a visitor's pass and told to go to the eleventh floor.

Once in the elevator, Cassie noticed that her excitement had morphed into fear. She had never seen anyone right after surgery. She wished Joe was there with her, but she knew she had to learn to handle Sally by herself once Joe went to Boston. They were in a funny place. She couldn't see a path forward for them if he went to Boston. She didn't like to think about breaking up with Joe. Anyway, September was months away. Maybe they could figure something out.

The elevator doors opened and the smell of bleach and Lysol filled her nostrils. Cautiously, she exited the elevator. There were three glass doors on each side of the vestibule with more doors behind them. She tried the center doors, but they were locked. Right side. Locked. As she tried the left side, a nurse in teal scrubs exited the door and Cassie snuck through.

The room was large and dark. Patients lay behind curtains hooked up to monitors and bags of saline. Efficient-looking nurses in soft-soled shoes checked the numbers on the screens beside each bed and adjusted dials. Cassie started to wander down the center of the room looking for Sally. She felt like she was intruding on the other patients and wished that someone would tell her where to find Sally.

Halfway down the center of the room a nurse in pink scrubs asked her who she was looking for, and when Cassie said "Sally Bishop," she pointed to the last bed on the left.

Cassie tried to ask, "How is she?" but the nurse had already scurried across the room into another curtained alcove. Cassie walked down to the last bed. The curtain was drawn around it and Cassie had to pull it aside to see Sally. She was still asleep with tubes running into both arms and some kind of monitor hooked up to her chest. Cassie assumed it was monitoring her heart. She looked gray and shrunken, and Cassie thought for a minute that she might be dead.

With tears streaming down her face, she wondered if she was crying because she might be dead or because a part of her wanted Sally to be dead. Wanted the continuous nightmare to be over.

As Cassie stood there staring at her grandmother, a nurse breezed in. "Oh, hi, are you family?" she asked, looking intently at Cassie.

"Yes, I'm her granddaughter. Her only family," said Cassie, wiping her nose on her scarf. The nurse held out a tissue box so Cassie could take one.

"It's taking more time than usual for her to come out of the anesthetic, but she's okay. The operation went well. I'd suggest you come back in an hour. Go to the cafeteria and get yourself some coffee. It's on the main floor." She gave Cassie a sympathetic smile. "Go ahead. She's going to be fine."

Cassie nodded and left the ICU. She took the elevator back down to the main floor and followed the signs for the cafeteria. Upon entering the cafeteria and smelling pizza, she realized she was starving and bought herself two slices and a Coke.

She thought about calling Joe but didn't know what to say. She didn't want him to come running to the hospital. Part of her felt like he didn't owe her that anymore. She tried to think about her new job. *I'm going to be a reporter!* That was amazing. But immediately she thought about how she had to give Mr. Ladinsky notice the next day. She shuddered when she thought of telling him. He could be so gruff and ornery. Oh well, he was the least of her problems.

After eating her pizza she went back up to the eleventh floor and found a family waiting room. There was no one else there so she lay down on the couch, and as soon as her head touched the soft cushion she was sound asleep.

Self-Pity

Joe checked his phone again and, seeing no calls, was pissed that Cassie hadn't at least tried to contact him. As he left work at Home Depot he couldn't decide whether to just call her and act like everything was okay and tell her his news about BU or wait for her to call him. *Damn,* he muttered. Life was taking him in one direction and her in another.

Once in the car, Joe ran his hands through his mop of curls and decided that if she wanted to be with him she could call him. He was going to nurse his anger and self-pity a little bit longer. Frowning now, he punched the dashboard and hurt his hand. *God almighty!* He decided to go to school early and find some friends to grab a burger with at the University Center. On the way, his phone rang, but when he looked at the caller ID, he cursed again. Sierra Kole. What did she want?

He answered the phone via Bluetooth. "Hello?"

"Hi, lover. It's me. Sierra."

No good could come of this. "What's up?"

"I thought you might have the night off since Cassie is at the hospital with the wicked witch."

There was his answer. That was why Cassie hadn't called. Joe breathed a sigh of relief. "She is? What happened?"

"You didn't know?" Sierra sounded genuinely surprised.

"No, I just got out of work."

"But it happened yesterday afternoon. Interesting, what's going on?"

"Sierra, what happened to Sally?"

"Apparently, she fell and broke her hip. Cassie had to leave work, and old Ladinsky was not happy. I had to sweet talk him down."

"And she never called me. I can't believe it." Joe pulled over to the curb. "Where's she now?"

"I don't know, lover. I assume at the hospital… Since you seem to be free, do you want to get a drink?"

"I was just on my way to school, but now I don't know what I'm doing."

"Meet me at the Dragger Inn for a cocktail," Sierra purred.

"I don't know if that's a good idea," Joe said, his voice low with uncertainty.

Sierra huffed. "So when you called me to talk, I came and had breakfast with you, and now you're not sure if it's a good idea to have a drink with me?" Sierra asked with an edge in her voice.

Joe closed his eyes and leaned his head back on the seat of the car. "Okay. One drink. I'll see you there in fifteen minutes." Joe hung up without waiting for an answer. Something was clearly going on with Cassie. She didn't even need him anymore. He turned the car around and headed to the Dragger Inn.

Joe arrived at the bar feeling guilty—guilty that he was at the bar and not on his way to the hospital to find Cassie. He couldn't really explain it, but it felt like even one more episode with Sally would make him choke. He could feel Cassie's anguish, worry, fear, panic, and dread over Sally. It filled his throat and made him want to cough. Simply put, he had just had enough. He couldn't take one more hour sitting in a waiting room while Cassie bit her nails and tried to make decisions about Sally. Still, he could feel Cassie's pain, and it was calling him.

He entered the dark bar and waited a moment for his eyes to adjust. Sierra was sitting at the middle of the bar in a bright green shirt that shimmered when she moved. She was surrounded by three guys, all standing, beers in hand, trying to amuse her. All wondering if one would win her, if only for the night.

As he walked toward the group, she spotted him and gave him a huge smile. Her eyes twinkled and she was clearly enjoying herself.

Holding out her hand to Joe, she said to the other men, "And here's my boyfriend, Joe. Hello, baby, you're late." She smiled at Joe and pulled him toward her. The other men mumbled hello and started to drift away.

"Now I'm your boyfriend?" asked Joe, taking the seat next to Sierra.

"It was an easy way to get rid of them," she replied, reaching out to push a stray curl from Joe's forehead. "You look blue, baby. What's the matter?"

Joe looked at Sierra and wondered what he had gotten himself into. She was pretty, and tonight she looked especially sexy in that green shirt.

"What's the matter?" she asked again, but now she seemed a bit irritated.

"No, it's just that, I don't think I've ever seen you wear a color before. You're always dressed in black. You look...nice," Joe stammered.

A slow smile started to form on Sierra's face. There was caution linked with excitement in the beautiful way her lips turned up at the corners. "Joe, that's so sweet of you. Thanks. I've been shopping. Branching out. Trying new colors. It's fun." She was clearly happy with Joe's compliment.

The bartender came over and Joe ordered a beer. There was a moment of awkward silence while they waited for Joe's drink.

"So, tell me what's going on with you and Cassie," Sierra said.

Joe hesitated. The bartender delivered his beer. Could he trust her? He knew he couldn't, but he needed to tell someone. "So, the good news is I got into BU, and the bad news is Cassie's not coming with me," he said flatly.

Sierra took a swig of her Corona. She took a minute to study a ring on her finger to buy a little time. "Well, I am very happy for you. Congratulations!" She held out her drink to toast him. "Well done!"

Joe touched his bottle to hers and tried to smile. "Thanks. You're the first person I've told. I haven't even told Cassie."

Sierra's face lit up. "I feel honored. I really thought she would go with you in the end. Find a way to take care of the old lady. Put her in a home or something." Sierra sounded genuinely disappointed for him.

Joe downed his beer and ordered himself and Sierra another round. A little high was taking the edge off his anger and his pain. A quick look around the bar told him that he was the envy of quite a few men right now. That never happened with Cassie. He shifted on his barstool so that he was facing Sierra.

Joe didn't want to say a lot of things that Sierra would repeat to Cassie. "Anyway, enough about me," Joe said. "Tell me about you. What's your story? Why do you work at the pharmacy when you clearly have money?"

"A girl's gotta work," said Sierra with a smile.

"Yeah, but why the pharmacy? Why don't you work at a high-end cosmetics store or something? Make commercials? You know you're hot." Joe was clearly already feeling the effects from chugging the second beer. He didn't care; he ordered another round.

"I'm too short. Five foot four, and my tits are too big," she said innocently.

They both laughed. "I hadn't noticed," said Joe with a guffaw.

"I didn't think you'd noticed with the collar so tight around your neck and the leash pulled taut," Sierra said with a glint in her eye.

"Nice," he said curtly. Joe realized he needed to slow down. He grabbed a handful of nuts from the bowl on the bar. Confusion over why he was here with Sierra overwhelmed him all of a sudden. "You know what, Sierra? I gotta go. Thanks for the invite. I'll see you around."

"No, Joe, don't go." Sierra put her manicured hand on his arm. "I won't mention Cassie again. I won't tease you. Please stay," she pleaded with a wide-eyed, innocent look.

"Nope. Gotta go while the going's good," he said. He started to put on his coat.

"It's just that…I gotta be honest, I've never met a man I couldn't have," Sierra said slowly, staring at Joe, her eyes intense under thick black lashes.

Taking a deep breath, Joe said, "I gotta go," and headed out of the bar. Once outside, the cold rush of cool air felt good on his face. He checked the time on his phone. It was late. Eight forty-five. Getting into his car, he knew he had to see Cassie. Assuming she would be home from the hospital by now, he drove over to her apartment.

Parking down the block, Joe walked to Cassie's apartment, noted that there were no lights on, and rang the bell. He tried to look in the window, but the shades were drawn. He glanced at Rick's apartment, all dark. He hoped Rick was out for the night or sleeping it off already. He decided to go around the back to see if any lights were on in the kitchen or Sally's room. To get to the back of the building and into the courtyard, Joe had to walk around all of the attached apartments. He had lost his buzz now and just felt hungry.

When he reached the back, he walked over to Cassie's porch and skipped up the few steps to her back door. He knocked loudly, "Cassie!" He knocked again, longer this time. "Cassie, are you there?" He swore under his breath that he did not want to go to the hospital when he felt a hand slap down on his shoulder.

Exclaiming and swinging around, his fists ready to fly, he came face to face with Rick. Their noses were ten inches apart.

"Jesus! Fuck man, you scared the shit out of me. Rick, I don't want any trouble." Joe took a step back, adrenaline coursing through his veins, fists high, ready to fight.

Rick laughed. A low awful sound. Joe noticed how bloodshot his eyes were as he slowly said, "I don't wanna fight. I think we can help each other."

Gun for Hire

Gun for hire? Did he really say that? Joe laughed as he drove away from Kensington Apartments to McDonald's. Now, blinded by hunger and only able to think clearly about a Big Mac and fries, he pulled through the drive-through and ordered. He could already taste the ketchup and pickles and the salty goodness of the fries. He hadn't eaten since lunchtime, and now it was going on ten o'clock.

After paying the girl at the window, he pulled into one of the spots in the parking lot and ate the first Big Mac with his eyes closed. He took a giant pull on his Coke and exhaled. Okay. Now, he could slow down and think about what had just happened. Rick had offered to shoot Sally in the head or hold a pillow over her face and smother her for $3,000. "All your problems gone. Poof. Like magic," he had said.

It made Joe feel like a criminal just to have listened to the offer. Rick must be desperate for money. He looked desperate. Dark circles under his eyes, sunken cheeks, a wretched look on his face. He sounded like he needed Joe to agree, his words punctuated with odd high-pitched cackles. Joe was so startled by the offer that he couldn't even remember exactly what he'd said. Something about Rick being crazy and then telling him to leave Cassie alone.

"You know where to find me," Rick had shouted across the courtyard as Joe walked away. Joe felt like he was in an episode of *Blue Bloods*. Was he supposed to report the offer? As Joe enjoyed his fries, he realized that if Rick was making this offer, that meant he did have a loaded gun. Maybe he was testing Joe. Just wanted to see what he would say, and then turn Cassie against him.

Feeling better now, after his fat-filled burgers and fries, he wondered what Cassie was doing right now. Sleeping at the hospital, he assumed. He knew it would be the right thing to go to her, but he couldn't. He couldn't take the scene at the hospital: Sally sick in the bed, Cassie distraught and crying. Maybe tomorrow he could muster the courage to go see her, but tonight he was depleted, exhausted. He needed to go home.

After throwing his trash in the can in the lot, he pulled out of the parking lot and started to go home. When he got stuck at a red light, he had a pang of guilt. He thought about Cassie all alone making life and death decisions. He should be there for her. The light turned green, but he just sat there, not moving. Red again. Good.

He thought about Rick's offer. "You take Cassie out to dinner, slip me the key, come back. All taken care of. Bam. All gone. Just like the cat," he had said. Rick said Cassie would get over it. Would she? Especially if Rick smothered Sally. Shooting her seemed like overkill. He chuckled at his own little joke. Overkill! The light turned green again. Good thing there was no traffic at this time of night in Tinden.

Joe, man, you are flipping out. Are you really thinking about this? He did want her dead, he admitted to himself, but he preferred a more natural demise. Maybe she was dying right now. He hoped that she was. It was hard to hate a vulnerable, sick old woman, but he did. His whole life was blowing up because of her. He couldn't be with the woman he loved because of her. When he first met Cassie he didn't realize the impact that her grandmother would have on his life.

Joe was so deep in thought, that it took him a minute to realize someone was furiously honking behind him because the light had turned green. He drove the car forward blindly and barely missed a stray dog that ran in front of him. It spooked him and he decided he had had enough for the day. He pushed thoughts of Rick and Sally and Cassie out of his mind and concentrated on driving home. He just wanted to get into his bed and pull the covers over his head. What could have been the best day of his life when he was accepted to college with a full scholarship was a swirl of pain, flirtation, intrigue, and angst.

Buttons

Cassie woke up with one foot on the floor and one arm flung over the back of the couch. When she opened her eyes, she was staring into the faces of three sad-looking people huddled together on the couch across from her. What looked like father, mother, and son stared back at her.

"Sorry," she mumbled as she sat up.

"No problem," said the father with a nod.

Noticing that it was dark outside the window, Cassie grabbed her phone from her pocket and looked at the time. Nine thirty at night. She had just slept for seven and a half hours. She wondered how long the family had been watching her. Had she been snoring? A wave of embarrassment propelled her up off the couch and toward the door.

Because they were all watching her every move, she said, "Take care," as she left the waiting room.

"God bless," said the man. His wife gave her a little smile.

Cassie headed back to the ICU and had to wait again for a nurse to come out in order to sneak in. She wondered if there was another door for visitors. There was a flurry of activity in the room. Doctors and nurses rushing around a bed on the other side of the room. Cassie was happy that it wasn't Sally's bed, and then immediately felt guilty.

As she got closer to Sally's bed she could hear her distinctive voice. High-pitched and throaty at the same time. "I can't answer any questions without the buttons," she was saying over and over again.

Cassie could tell by the sound of frustration in the nurse's voice that this had been going on for some time. "Try to relax. Are you in pain?"

Cassie entered through the curtain. "Gram, how are you?"

"Cassie, let's get out of here. I need my green shirt with the big buttons. Did you bring it?" asked Sally.

"Are you family?" asked the nurse.

"Yes, I'm Cassie. Her granddaughter. How is she?"

"She's full of fire and fury. Never saw someone go from being unconscious to furious so quickly, so I'd say that's a good sign…in a way. She's on pain meds, so she can't feel her hip pain yet. I'm Zena, her nurse." The elegant woman had large brown eyes and long slender fingers.

"Well, I guess that's good then. How long do you think she'll be here?" asked Cassie.

"Cassie, where's my green shirt?" interjected Sally.

"I'll bring it tomorrow, Gram. It's late and you need to get some sleep."

"She'll be here in the ICU through tomorrow, and then we'll move her to a regular bed," said Zena. "You can sit with her for a few minutes if you want. I'll be back." Zena walked out of the curtained area.

Cassie pulled up a chair next to the bed. "How do you feel, Gram?"

"I feel fine. Why am I here?" Sally looked up at Cassie and put out her scrawny hand for Cassie to hold.

"You broke your hip. You were out in the courtyard and Frank found you."

"Frank found me?"

"Yeah, and then he called me and we came to the hospital. You just had an operation on your hip."

"Frank has always been good to me."

"Yes, he has," agreed Cassie. "Guess what, Gram? I got a new job. I'm going to be a reporter with the *Tinden Record*. I start in two weeks."

"I never got to have a career." Sally closed her eyes for a minute. "Cassie, is it raining? I don't think I have my boots."

Cassie sighed. *Why do I try?* "It's not raining, Gram, and it's nice and warm in here." Cassie noticed that Sally was drifting off to sleep.

Cassie sat studying Sally's face. Withered and worn, it was a face that showed the pain Sally had felt. The furrowed brow. The deep frown lines. But it was a face that Cassie loved. She didn't see the ugliness when she looked at Sally. She saw her family.

She would try to remember Sally's green shirt when she came back tomorrow.

Secrets

On the way out of the hospital Cassie checked her phone. There was a text from Joe: *Went to your apartment.*

Suddenly, she was desperate to see Joe and lose herself in his arms. She called an Uber, typing in his address. She couldn't wait to tell him about her new job. She hoped he would be happy for her. His response when she had told him about the interview had been all about his stringing for the paper, but she could help him. She could introduce him to Luke. *Luke.* She hadn't been attracted to anyone like that since she saw Joe sitting in class working on his writing prompt.

She hoped that her feelings toward Luke were a product of her stress from the night before. She wasn't thinking clearly when he looked at her with those amazing blue eyes. She must have been delusional. He couldn't be *that* good-looking. At least, that was what she told herself.

Anyway, enough about Luke. Here was the Uber to take her to Joe. Whatever their future, together or apart, they still loved each other and were still together now. She couldn't imagine life without telling Joe what was happening. Except for their fights about Sally, she and Joe were almost always on the same page. Whether the topic was politics, religion, recycling, or writing, they were sympatico, supportive, in sync. He completed her.

As the driver pulled up to Joe's apartment, Cassie saw that the windows were all dark. She searched in the bottom of her backpack for her keyring, happy that Joe had given her a key a few months ago. Entering the apartment like a thief, she quietly dropped her jacket on the couch in the living room and snuck down the hall to Joe's bedroom. She could see his outline lying in the bed and could imagine how soft and warm she would be beside him in a few minutes. Taking off all her clothes, she slithered between the sheets and wrapped herself around him.

Drowsy with sleep, he embraced her and they kissed, hungry for the familiar touch of each other's bodies, they made love without a word. Afterward, Joe said, "I love you, Cassie."

"I love you, too," she replied, now half-asleep.

When they woke up the next morning, Cassie wanted to tell Joe about her new job but she felt unsure about his reaction. They made love again, and then Joe went to the kitchen to make coffee. Cassie lay in bed a minute to think; she decided she was too excited and had to share her news. She threw on one of Joe's sweatshirts and her jeans. She was nervous about betraying her attraction to Luke, so she decided to leave him out of the story as much as possible.

"Hey," he said as she walked into the kitchen.

She walked over and put her arms around his waist. "Hey yourself. Guess what?" She hadn't wanted to just blurt it out, but she couldn't help herself.

"Sally's in the hospital," said Joe.

Cassie frowned. She didn't know he knew. She started to ask why he hadn't reached out to her if he knew, but she decided not to let Sally ruin her moment. "Yes, but that's not what I want to tell you."

"What do you want to tell me?"

Her eyes were dancing. "I got that job at the *Record*. I'm their new general assignment reporter. I start in two weeks." Cassie looked up at Joe with a wide smile.

"No way! Cass, that's amazing. Congrats! When did that happen?"

"Yesterday. Yesterday was both awful and fantastic. Sally had to have an operation, which was awful, but while she was in the OR, I went over to the *Record* and they offered me the job on the spot." Cassie could feel her face beaming.

"Wow! Right there? Based solely on your letter to the editor?"

"That and a makeshift portfolio I threw together in a Hello Kitty binder," Cassie said with a laugh. "I could tell they were impressed by the presentation."

Joe chuckled. "Want coffee?" Without waiting for an answer, he poured two cups and handed her one. "Cass, that's so great. So, what will you be writing?" He walked into the living room and got under the afghan on the couch, holding up the side for her to crawl under.

She sat down carefully with the hot coffee and Joe placed the afghan over her lap before she answered. "Whatever's happening that day. It might be a car crash, or the example he used was kids selling lemonade for a cause and collecting a lot of money, but I told him I really wanted to cover social services. He said he wouldn't rule it out even though they don't cover it now." Cassie knew the words were tumbling out of her but she couldn't stop.

"Who's 'he'?" asked Joe.

"The editor."

"Luke. Luke Miller?"

"Yeah, Luke, do you know him?"

"I've met him a few times. Tried to get him to read my stuff, but he always said he didn't have an opening. I guess you were just in the right place at the right time," said Joe.

"Yeah, I guess I was. I start in two weeks. I have to tell Mr. Ladinsky today that I'm leaving the pharmacy. I have to give notice, which is kind of scary for some reason."

Joe stared out the window.

"Joe, earth to Joe. Did you hear me?" Cassie wondered why Joe spaced out when she mentioned the pharmacy.

"You'll be fine," Joe reassured her. "You've done a great job for Ladinsky. So, what happened to Sally?"

That was weird. Now he's deflecting. "She fell in the courtyard behind the apartment and broke her hip. Frank—the caretaker guy—found her and called me at work. She had to have an operation, but she's all right. She'll probably be in the hospital for a week, and then rehab. Joe…"

"Yeah?"

"I gotta get a car. I can't rely on yours all the time. They said I'll need one to go out and cover my assignments. I've been Ubering around the last couple of days and it's too expensive. Will you help me? How much do you pay a month?"

"You can use my car, babe. You don't need your own." Joe pushed a lock of hair out of Cassie's eye.

"Like today, for instance, I have to go home, go to the hospital, go to the pharmacy, go back to the hospital, and then come here. I can't always rely on you."

"Which leads me to my news. I was accepted to BU with a full ride!" Joe's green eyes sparkled.

Cassie smacked Joe's arm. "Talk about burying the lead. Oh my God! Joe that's amazing. Congratulations!" Cassie threw her arms around Joe's neck and kissed him. "I am so proud of you."

"Thanks, babe. Sounds like we both had success yesterday. Success that takes us in opposite directions, but success nonetheless."

Cassie's smile faded. "This is so hard."

"I know."

"The pieces of our lives just don't fit."

After a pause, he repeated softer, "I know."

They sat on the couch for a long time without saying anything. Cassie felt bereft of a solution to their conflicting needs, his dreams versus her responsibilities. She yearned for a way to put their lives back together again, but the situation felt hopeless.

Laundry

Time was running out. The end of the month was almost here. Rick thought he had made a mistake by approaching Joe. That sissy boy with his curls and his white teeth didn't have the balls to hire someone to take care of his problems. Rick turned to Plan B. He needed to steal Sierra's ruby ring and anything else she had in her "breakup box" and head down to the pawnshop. To do that he needed to clean himself up. Once upon a time he had been considered good-looking, handsome even, some had said. He needed to take a shower and give himself a haircut. He also needed some clean clothes if he was going to go to the Dragger Inn and somehow convince Sierra to take him back to her apartment.

He also needed some cash. He had stolen money at the laundromat before. Women would get sloppy, leaving their purses open on the folding table or on a chair while they emptied the washer or dryer. Men sometimes came in with bags of change for the machines. If that didn't work, he would try the upscale supermarket on Walnut. Rich women in an upscale store felt more comfortable leaving their purses unattended while they perused the meat or the produce.

Turning on the water in the shower, he hoped that there was a drop of shampoo left and that the dime-sized soap could get the stink off him. If not, he'd have to shower again after he stole some money and bought some soap.

After the shower, he still felt dirty, especially since he had no clean towel and he had to put his filthy clothes back on. He examined himself in the mirror and knew he also had to eat a decent meal to get the desperate look out of his eye. He rummaged around in the bottom of his closet and finally found his canvas bag, which he filled with a load of wash and headed out to the laundromat.

He parked in the lot and was happy to see that the place was filled with women doing their wash. He threw his laundry in the machine and went to sit in one of the chairs by the window. When lifting a wallet from a purse, timing was everything. The key was to wait until his laundry was almost dry, lift the wallet, get his clothes, and then get out as soon as he could.

While he waited for his laundry, he sized up the prospects. There was a young woman with earphones in her ears, dancing to music no one else could hear, but he didn't see a purse. An older woman was folding already. She would be done before he was ready. As he pretended to read the paper that someone had left on the seat next to him, a haggard-looking middle-aged woman entered the laundromat dragging three big bags of wash. She looked promising.

He watched her load five washers, and then she came to sit next to him. She smiled as she sat down. Rick smiled his most neighborly smile.

"Got a lot of laundry there," he commented.

"Five boys," she said.

"Is that right?" Rick beamed.

"Yeah, never caught a break with a girl." The woman smiled a shy smile.

"God bless," said Rick, ready to retch.

The woman laughed, and Rick could see that at one point this woman had been as beautiful as he had been handsome. Life had been hard on both of them and was just about to get harder on her.

"You live around here?" he ventured.

"Just around the corner," she said, smoothing her hair.

"Your husband work around here?" he asked, putting on his best shy grin.

"Haven't seen him in years," she volunteered.

"Sorry to hear that," he said, looking down to avoid her embarrassment.

"Actually, we're better off without him."

"Yeah," said Rick. "I think my wash is done." He went to move his laundry from the washer to the dryer.

He only had enough coins for ten minutes. He knew he had to make his move. She was his only hope. His palms were sweating, waiting for her to transfer her wash to the dryers. She had so many loads, he would have time. He sat and read the paper, waiting for her wash to finish. When her washers stopped, he went to pile his laundry into his canvas bag. She left her purse open on the folding table. He brought his laundry over to the table to fold, but he only folded one shirt. While she emptied another washer, he grabbed her wallet, stuck it in his bag, and went over to say goodbye.

"Nice talking to you," he said. *Stupid bitch.*

She smiled, a tragic, grateful smile. "Yeah, nice talking to you."

Rick steadied his pace leaving the laundromat. *Don't run. She has three more washers to empty. Don't cause alarm.* Once outside he moved quickly to his car, got in, and drove out of the parking lot. He drove to a supermarket on the other side of town and parked in the back. Heart thumping in his chest. Leaning his head back against the headrest, he closed his eyes and took a deep breath, getting ready to look in her wallet. Had he chosen a winner?

When he opened his eyes, he surveyed the parking lot. No police. No sirens. He pulled the old brown wallet out of his bag. There was a thick section of glassine photo sleeves with various photos of her five boys, overweight and pimply.

In the back pocket of the wallet, Rick found forty-two dollars. In the change section, thirty-seven cents. No credit cards. Not the stash he had hoped for, but enough to get him what he needed for the night. Shampoo, soap, a meal, and a twenty for the bar. Yeah, he was disappointed, but it would do. He stuffed the bills in his back pocket and shoved the wallet back into the bag with his clean clothes, making sure it was well hidden. In the store, he bought toiletries, a whole roasted chicken, a can of green beans, and a can of white potatoes.

His mouth was watering so badly that he thought a river of saliva would flow down his chin if he had to talk to anyone. It had been days since he had eaten an actual meal. Now, suddenly blinded by the prospect of eating, he hurriedly purchased his groceries and headed to the door. Outside, his eyes swept the lot for police cars, but seeing none, he jogged to his car and quickly drove home.

As he ran up his steps with the groceries and the laundry, he noted that Cassie's apartment was still dark. Damn, maybe the old woman would die without his help. Setting everything down on the kitchen counter, he tore open the plastic box with the chicken, tore off a leg, and took a huge bite. It tasted so delicious that he stood there chewing with his eyes closed. He didn't have a table to sit at, so he just stood at the counter, gorging himself on first the chicken, then the beans, and finally a few potatoes. He washed it all down with a full glass of water. He realized he couldn't remember the last time he drank a glass of water. Immediately he felt better than he had in weeks.

The greasy clock in the oven read six o'clock. Now for his makeover. His jeans and black T-shirt were still damp, so he draped them over the lawn chair to dry near the radiator. He headed to the bathroom with his soap, shampoo, and toothpaste, where he took a long, hot shower, washing his hair twice and soaping up his entire body. Might as well do it right, didn't know when he'd do it again.

His clean towel was still wet, but at least it soaked up some of the water. Now for a haircut. He went to find his scissors and a comb. Amazingly, they were both in the medicine closet where they belonged. He had learned to cut his own hair in the Marines, so he quickly gave his thick hair an adequate short cut. To shave or not to shave? He didn't want Sierra to get suspicious. Maybe just a trim to clean it up.

He put on his clean clothes once they were dry and grabbed his wallet from his other pair of pants. As he leaned down to pick them up from the floor he saw the stolen wallet, which he had dumped out of the bag with his clean clothes. He picked it up and threw it in the back of the coat closet. Tomorrow he would bag it and throw it in the dumpster, but tonight he had more important things to do.

Death is Clean

"Death is clean, Cassie," said Sally from the hospital bed. "All the shit, all the stink, the worry, the pain, gone in an instant. At least that's the way I see it. God told me so, and now I have my shirt and my buttons to make sure."

Sally had squealed with delight—or was it pain?—when Cassie had helped her into the shirt. The corduroy was worn and soft, and Sally had waited patiently while Cassie did up the buttons. Just three, like Sally told her. As soon as Sally had the shirt on, she closed her eyes and asked her deity some questions, which had been answered. Cassie could tell by the small smile that had started on Sally's lips.

"Dr. Warren's coming," said Cassie as she sat beside Sally, who was still in the ICU because her heart rate had been a little too slow after the operation.

"Who?"

"Your shrink."

Sally scrunched up her face, and Cassie winced when she saw that Sally had lost another tooth, widening the gap in the front of her mouth.

"I wonder if they have a dentist here that you can see before you come home," said Cassie.

"Death may be better than life. Hopefully there are no other people in death. No one to hurt you." Sally stopped and looked at Cassie, who felt almost ready to cry. "Not you, Cassie, you've never hurt me, but they never liked me. My parents never liked me."

"I'm going to talk to the nurse for a minute." Cassie got up and walked into the hallway. Biting her thumbnail to the quick, she leaned against the wall. She wanted to stay until Dr. Warren came, but Sally was hard to take today with all her talk of death, and Cassie had to get over to the pharmacy to give notice to Mr. Ladinsky. As sick as she was, Sally had never talked about death before. She always referred to herself as a survivor, which Cassie had to respect. Taking a deep breath, she went back into Sally's room.

Sally gave her a blank stare, and Cassie went to sit in the orange plastic chair by the window. A few minutes later, Dr. Warren walked briskly into the room. "Good morning. How is everyone?"

"Oh Jesus. How are people supposed to take you seriously when your clothes are always so wrinkled?" Sally complained. "Send your shirts to the cleaners if you don't have time to iron. I can't take you seriously."

Dr. Warren stood looking at Sally, a hard expression in her eyes. "How are you, Sally?"

"How do I look?" Sally said with a sneer.

"Good morning, Cassie," said Dr. Warren with a weak smile.

"Good morning," said Cassie sheepishly.

"We're not having a session, so you can cheer up, Sally. I just stopped in to see how you are, and I can see that you are fine. The broken hip has not broken your spirit."

"Your broken hip has not broken your spirit," Sally mimicked, curling her lip and swaying her head side to side.

"She's been talking a lot about death this morning. That's new," said Cassie.

"Are you thinking about death, Sally?" asked the doctor.

"I'm beginning to think it might be better than life, but don't worry, I'll never off myself. If I haven't done it yet, I won't do it," said Sally.

"That's probably true, but are you worrying about death?"

"Are you worrying about death?" Sally mimicked the doctor again.

Cassie felt sorry for Dr. Warren. Just trying to do her job, and she did look pathetic in her wrinkled blouse and dirty lab coat. She checked her phone for the time. She had to get going.

Standing up, she said, "Gram, I've got to go. Remember I told you I got a new job? And I have to go to the pharmacy and give notice? Remember?"

Sally gave her a dirty look. As Cassie turned to Dr. Warren to say goodbye, Joe appeared in the doorway.

"Oh God, now he's here," said Sally, regarding Joe angrily.

"Gram!" said Cassie.

"Don't worry, Cassie. I just came to give you a ride to work. I'll wait in the hall," Joe said, turning around and walking out of the room.

"Gram, I want you to be nicer to Joe. What is wrong with you?" Cassie scowled at Sally.

Sally crossed her arms over her chest and looked away from Cassie.

"I'm going." Cassie turned her back on Sally and said goodbye to Dr. Warren. "I'll let you know when she gets out so we can continue our appointments. If that's okay."

"Yes, let me know," said the doctor.

Cassie started to walk out of the room.

"Cassie? Are you coming back later?" asked Sally meekly.

Cassie stopped, glared at Sally, and then just walked out of the room. She found Joe looking glum leaning on the wall at the end of the hallway. "Sorry," she said.

"It's not your fault," Joe said, but his eyes looked pained. "She sees me as the enemy, and I guess I am."

"I know, I'm sorry. I never know what she's going to say…thanks for coming to give me a ride."

"I try to do the right thing by you. I really do," said Joe.

"I know. Let's get out of here." She took Joe's hand and walked to the elevator.

"Next time I'll meet you in the car," said Joe.

"Probably a good idea," said Cassie, stepping into the elevator.

Down a Notch

When Cassie arrived at the pharmacy she could hear Mr. Ladinsky spouting off to Sierra, who was in the greeting card aisle. "It's important to have a work ethic, Sierra. I usually look the other way when you're late, but you've been late the last three days and I want it to stop. Now Cassie's late too. How am I supposed to run a profitable shop when my employees are always late? And while I'm getting everything off my chest, you also left early yesterday. It's got to stop, Sierra. Do you hear me?" Mr. Ladinsky had worked up a sweat. Tiny beads of perspiration dotted his upper lip.

As Cassie approached them, she saw Sierra standing before him like a naughty little girl, looking genuinely surprised that old Mr. Ladinsky had the nerve to ream her out. She seemed to have been caught off guard and was deciding how to react when Cassie came barreling into the store.

Trying to catch her breath, Cassie said, "I'm so sorry, Mr. Ladinsky. I had to wait until Sally's psychiatrist came to see her before I could leave the hospital."

"She always has the good excuses," Sierra quipped.

"I know your grandmother is in the hospital and I'm sorry, but that does not mean that it's all right for you to be late. I was just telling Sierra that a good work ethic is important. Now that's it. Back to work." Mr. Ladinsky started to walk back to the pharmacy counter.

"Mr. Ladinsky? Before you go…" started Cassie.

Mr. Ladinsky turned back. "Yes," he said, clearly irritated.

"Um, I got a new job, so I'm giving notice," Cassie blurted out. "Two weeks' notice. I'm going to be a reporter at the *Record.* I'm…I'm sorry."

Mr. Ladinsky was speechless for a moment. "Oh. Well, I see. That's a real loss for the pharmacy. Congratulations, but a real loss. Real loss." Mr. Ladinsky continued to mumble as he turned back toward the pharmacy counter again and walked away.

❀❀❀

Sierra gestured for Cassie to follow her to the cash register. "You're leaving? Now I have to be here all alone?" she whispered.

"Sierra, I didn't realize that we were such great friends," Cassie said, dripping with sarcasm. "I didn't know you'd miss me."

"I kinda thought we were friends," said Sierra glumly. She went back to the greeting card aisle and started to restock the section. *Cassie always thinks she's better than everybody else. Wonder if she knows that Joe met me for a drink. Bet she doesn't know. Might be time for her to find out. Bring her down a notch.*

Sierra took her time with the greeting cards, carefully planning how she could tell Cassie about the drinks with Joe in a way that would suggest there might have been more. As the afternoon wore on, Sierra stoked her indignation. *Smug little bitch. Screw her. Always putting on airs. What is she—too good to be friends with me?*

When she saw Cassie closing up her textbook and checking the time on her phone, Sierra walked over to the cash register. "Time to go already? I was surprised the other night when I was having drinks with Joe at the Dragger Inn that he didn't know about your grandmother. Didn't know that she was in the hospital."

Cassie stared at Sierra as if she was speaking another language. "What?"

"Oh yeah. He didn't tell you? We met for a drink, but we got to talking and one drink led to another. You know how it is." Sierra smiled innocently. "And then I mentioned your grandmother and he had no idea what I was talking about. I thought Joe would be your first call, seeing that you're a couple and all. Or maybe you're not anymore."

"We are definitely a couple," was all Cassie said as she shoved her book in her backpack and went to the employee closet to get her coat.

"See you tomorrow…friend," said Sierra when Cassie brushed past her on the way out.

Where's Iowa?

Rick felt pretty good about himself as he stepped into the Dragger Inn. He hadn't been this clean or smelled this good in months, maybe years. He was betting on Sierra going to the Dragger Inn because he knew she hung out there sometimes before she showed up at his place. Taking a seat in the middle of the bar, he ordered a beer and knew he had to nurse it for a few hours. The first sip was so cold and tasted so good that he cursed the woman in the laundromat for not having more money in her wallet.

It was a Thursday night and the bar was hopping. With the prospect of one more workday until the weekend, the Dragger Inn's clientele was already starting to relax and blow off steam. If people were a little hungover at work on Friday—who cared?

A few good-looking ladies had been checking Rick out, but he didn't want to get involved and have to buy them a drink. He only had fifteen dollars left, and he wanted to buy Sierra at least one drink. He hoped that she would offer to get the second round, but you could never be sure. Even if a woman called herself a feminist, she usually still wanted the man to pick up the tab.

The night wore on. Rick's beer was gone. Feeling dejected, he was getting really pissed that he had gone to all this effort to clean himself up.

"What the fuck are you doing here?" Rick turned at the sound of Sierra's voice. She smiled, and Rick noticed how young she was for the first time.

"Well, hello to you too," he said with a grin.

"Gonna buy a girl a drink?" she asked, slurring her words ever so slightly. He got down from the barstool and motioned for her to sit. "How gallant," she said, taking the seat and putting her expensive leather jacket on the back. She was wearing a tight turquoise sweater and dangly silver earrings. Rick scanned her fingers for the ring. Her fingers were bare except for long black fake nails.

Rick nodded his approval. "Bright color for you. Bright blue! Whatcha drinkin'?"

"It's turquoise, and I'll have a mojito. Thanks. So, what brings you out of your cave?"

Rick shrugged. "Just felt like gettin' out." He motioned to the bartender, who came right over. Rick ordered her drink and another beer.

"You look...different...cleaned up...good." Sierra looked him up and down.

"I know you like to go slumming when you drop by, but I've been told I clean up nice," said Rick, giving her his best smile.

Their drinks arrived, and they clinked glasses and took a sip. Rick watched as the bartender took all of his money from the bar.

Conversation was not what usually brought them together, so both of them struggled to think of something to say.

Finally, in desperation, Rick asked, "So, you grow up around here?"

"Yeah, lived around here all my life. What about you? Where'd you grow up?"

"Iowa. Lived there until I joined the Marines."

"Where's Iowa?" asked Sierra, holding back a yawn.

Rick laughed. "Small talk's not your thing, is it?"

Sierra laughed too. "No. Seriously, baby, I don't give a shit where you grew up. Let's just say what we are—we're fuck buddies, no more and no less." She drained her mojito.

That was Rick's cue. He couldn't buy her another one. "Well, I'm glad you brought that up. We always go to my place. Let's go to your place tonight. Change it up a bit. See how creative we can be. Do you have a kitchen table?"

Sierra stood up, put on her jacket, and started to walk out of the bar. Rick, stunned by his success, grabbed his jacket and followed her out into the parking lot. Her yellow Beetle was parked in the back of the lot by a tall wooden fence. A dumpster was situated on one side of the car and a Suburban was parked on the other side. Sierra got in on the driver's side and motioned for Rick to get in on the passenger side. Rick got in eagerly, congratulating himself on his charm and persuasive personality. It hadn't taken much. *Smollett, man, you still got it.*

As he got in he saw that Sierra was throwing her bag and her jacket in the back seat. "Put your seat back. Let's do it in the car. I haven't done that in years." She smiled as she pulled her sweater over her head.

Rick tried to object. "This car's a little small. Don't you want…" Sierra shed her bra, climbed on top of him, and stuck her nipple in his mouth. Moving to the side she started to undo the zipper on his pants. He hadn't put on any boxers.

"Commando. Nice. Makes it easier." She flopped back into her seat to take off her own pants. "It's exciting. Someone might come and watch us." Her eyes lit up with excitement. She bent over and sucked long and hard on his penis, and then she was riding him, and he gave in to it.

They both came in an instant, but Rick knew she was good for a few rounds. Maybe he still had a chance to get into her apartment. As she wrestled with putting her clothes back on, he desperately searched his brain for a reason for her to bring him back to her apartment.

"Hey, Sierra…"

"Yeah? Get dressed, will you?" she said in an annoyed tone.

"Hey, I'm a little strapped for cash. Can we just go back to your place for the night? Do you have any beer?"

"Did you get evicted? Is that what this little visit is all about? Because I'll tell you one thing straight out—you are not moving into my apartment. I have a whole life that does not involve you. And cover yourself up." She threw a tissue from her purse in his lap.

"I did not get evicted. I just want to change it up a little," said Rick, wiping himself and pulling on his pants.

"Just throw that out the window. I don't want it in my car," said Sierra, pointing to the tissue.

Rick put down his window and tossed the tissue out. The cold air felt good.

"Well, go back into the bar and pick up someone else. That will change things up a bit for you. I don't bring guys like you home to my place. Now, let's go. I'm going back into the bar. I'll buy you a drink." Sierra wriggled into her jacket and grabbed her purse.

Fighting back the urge to punch her in the mouth, Rick put his jacket on and got out of the car. Sierra got out too, locked the doors, and started back into the bar. As he followed her inside, his head was swirling. He decided to have the drink she offered, leave the bar, and wait in the parking lot to follow her home. By the time they were back in the bar Rick had gotten control of himself. If the Marines had taught him one thing, it was to hurry up and wait.

There's a Difference

Cassie knew that after today she might not have Joe's car again, so after going to the hospital to visit Sally after work, she got out her to-do list and started her errands. She was trying, rather unsuccessfully, to keep her anger in check. She couldn't wait to confront Joe about the drinks he had with Sierra without mentioning it to her. From Sierra's description, they hadn't accidentally met at the Dragger Inn. They had agreed to meet there. Wasn't that technically a date? Two people agreeing to meet each other for drinks? It wasn't like Sierra and Joe were childhood friends and, having grown up together, thought of each other as brother and sister. No, sexy Sierra—who hit on every man she met, who said that she wanted to *do* Joe, who had even proposed a threesome with them—had sat with Joe at a bar, smiling, flirting, laughing. And Joe had not mentioned it to her.

Cassie pulled into the ShopRite parking lot and parked Joe's car in a slanted fashion across two spaces, slamming the door behind her. As she stormed across the parking lot she was aching for someone to call her out for taking up two spaces, but luckily for them, there was no one around. She grabbed a cart, pushed on the automatic door because it was opening too slowly, headed to the soap aisle and tossed in two jugs of Tide. Joe said Tide gave him a rash, and how she hoped that it would. She also needed Mr. Clean, Lysol bathroom cleaner, and Fantastik. With Sally out of the apartment, she wanted to do a thorough cleaning. She had also been planning on cleaning Joe's apartment, but now the chances of that looked slim to none.

Leaving ShopRite, she drove to her apartment and started cleaning in a whirl of motion, scrubbing the toilet, the tub, and the sink. Her anger grew as she collected the laundry strewn about the floor in her room and Sally's room and squashed it into the laundry basket. She grabbed the small plastic bag of quarters she collected for laundry and stormed out the back door and across the courtyard to the laundry room. For once, she didn't even care if Rick came out to hit on her because she was in the mood for a good fight.

As she came back across the courtyard after starting three loads of wash, she saw two girls she knew from high school leisurely walking together, giggling, their high-pitched laughter floating on the wind over Cassie's head. They each held a Victoria's Secret bag, and Cassie could tell they were excited about something. Cassie, usually not prone to self-pity, envied the girls as she watched them. Nothing to do but shop and laugh and plan the fun times they would have later tonight.

The girls noticed Cassie, and they smiled and waved. Cassie felt herself blush, like she had been spying on them. She waved back and hurriedly returned to her apartment, grinding her teeth on the way.

As she put the dishes in the sink to soak, suddenly she felt like she couldn't keep going. She went into the living room and sat down in one of the chairs, and tears started to flow down her cheeks. She let the tears flow and they turned into loud sobs that made her shoulders shake and her chest hurt. Cassie felt her guts twisting with frustration. She was so sick of being caught between Sally and Joe. Couldn't they see how much pain she was in? They both only thought about and cared about themselves.

Drying her eyes, Cassie went in the kitchen and finished the dishes and then went back to the laundry room. She transferred the wash from the washers to the dryers. When she came back in the back door, she found Joe in the living room. Joe looked at her tear-stained cheeks and swollen eyes and moved toward her to hug her, but when he opened his arms she punched him in the chest. "What the hell?" he asked, taking a step back.

"Are we dating other people now, Joe? Is that it? Without even breaking up, without a conversation, you went out with Sierra—"

"What? I did not," he said. "We were at the Dragger Inn and we had a drink."

"And now you're going to lie about it, too? You didn't just meet her there. You went to meet her there. There's a difference. A big difference," Cassie screamed.

"Cassie, you know, you're always the victim. Nothing you do could ever lead someone else to do something for themselves…"

"What do you mean? What did I do?"

"Well, if you remember, the night before I met Sierra you admitted that you'll never leave Sally. That if I go to Boston you're not coming with me. How do you think that made me feel? Huh? You think that made me feel good? All of our plans up in smoke…"

"You know, Joe, why does it have to be BU? Why can't we try to go to school in New Jersey? Work it out so I don't have to abandon Sally. Huh? You tell me that," she demanded.

"I want to plan a life together. I don't want Sally to be the deciding factor in all of our decisions. Sometimes I want to come first."

"You want to come first? I don't have the luxury of putting someone first. But don't you see you're right up there with her. You're both first. Neck and neck. You're first. She's first. And I'm somewhere below. You're getting as much of me as there is to get. Some people have choices that I don't have. I have responsibilities. I have an obligation. I'm not free to do only what I want to do. And you're right that I'm not going to leave her to die. I won't, I can't do it."

"What if I said it's me or her?" Joe yelled.

"If I have to make a choice, if you force me to make a choice, it has to be her. You're not depending on me for your survival. She is. Now get out." Cassie reached into her pocket, found Joe's car keys, and threw them at him. They hit his stomach and fell to the floor. "Take your car."

Joe leaned down and picked up the keys. His face was torn by anger, his nostrils flaring. Cassie stood across the room with her little fists clenched and her eyes ablaze. He shook his head. He was hunched over; she could see his lips trembling. It would be easy for them to hug, to kiss and make up. Push the decision-making down the road. But Cassie felt betrayed. He had let Sierra into their lives and she couldn't forgive him for that.

"I don't know what to say, Cassie," he said in a low voice.

"Then just get out," she said, exhausted. "Just leave."

His cheeks reddened. He turned and walked out the door.

As the door closed, Cassie felt the same way she had felt the night Jillian had left. It was done. It was over. She was on her own. Alone, with the burden of Sally to contend with. Another piece of her heart torn off. She felt ragged and tossed. Her rock, Joe, had succumbed to Sierra. Not even a worthy adversary, but a vapid, morally bankrupt simpleton. She was crushed.

I'll Take It

The next week passed in a blur. With all the money Cassie was spending on Uber she wouldn't be able to afford to get a car. She needed to lease the cheapest car available as soon as she could, and it had already been a long day. She had started at the hospital, where Sally was giving the physical therapist a hard time; then work at the pharmacy, where she spent her time avoiding Sierra; then school, where she avoided Joe; and then chores like paying the rent and cable bill. The Honda dealer was open until ten at night out on Route 1, and Cassie had seen an ad to lease a Honda Civic for $119 a month. Unlike most twenty-year-olds, Cassie had been paying bills for years and had a great credit score.

She arrived at the car dealership at eight thirty and was quickly greeted by Juan Sanchez. Cassie had planned on bringing Joe with her because she knew nothing about cars, but she was on her own now and would have to make her own decisions.

"Good evening. How can I help you tonight?" asked Juan as he approached Cassie.

She looked up at Juan, toothpick sticking out of the side of his mouth, as if she had forgotten where she was. "Hi. I need your cheapest car. Tonight. I saw an ad for a Civic," she said nervously.

"Why? You need to get out of town?" Juan laughed, a good-natured, slightly sleazy guffaw.

"No, I need it for my new job," said Cassie, looking around the showroom.

"Well, for you, pretty lady, we have one Civic left. Come, let's go look at her." Juan threw on his jacket and led her out to the parking lot.

Cassie knew there were questions about gas mileage and cruise control, but all she really cared about was having an automatic transmission. Juan assured her that the car they were heading toward was an automatic. They walked through the main lot, crossed a street, and entered a second lot where the cars were smaller and covered with dust and leaves.

"Don't worry. We'll run her through the car wash before you leave," said Juan, expertly shifting the toothpick to the other side of his mouth with his tongue.

Cassie was suddenly aware of the darkness of the night, the lonely parking lot with only one streetlamp. "Can we drive it over to the showroom where there's more light? So I can see it?" asked Cassie.

"Yes, yes, pretty lady, here's the remote. No key. You keep the remote in your purse or your pocket. That way you can quickly get into your car," said Juan. The light made the gel in Juan's hair shine.

The car was a weird green color—somewhere between forest and pistachio—but that didn't really matter to Cassie. The plastic smell of the new car hit Cassie in the face as she opened the door and got in. Juan quickly jumped into the passenger seat and showed her which button to hit to turn on the car. "Step on the brake and hit this button," he told her. Cassie adjusted the mirrors and drove the car over to the main lot.

When she stopped in front of the main door to the showroom, she said, "I'll take it."

Juan broke into a wide smile. "Awesome, pretty lady. I love a decisive woman. Let's get inside and do the paperwork."

It was too late to contact the leasing office or the insurance company, but Cassie wrote Juan a check for the down payment on her new car. She would come back in the morning and finish the paperwork. As she waited for an Uber to pick her up, she smiled. *Wow! I own a car.* That had been easier than she thought.

The Trap

Sierra liked a challenge—not too much of a challenge—but a little resistance so that she could feel like she had made a conquest. Rick? No challenge there. Thurston, her current married man, had actually said that he was thinking of leaving his wife. Since his wife was his main appeal, Sierra had not taken the news the way he had hoped. No, it was Joe who Sierra set her sights on. That would be a real conquest.

How would she get Joe to her apartment? That was the question Sierra pondered as she stocked the shelves at the pharmacy. Now that Cassie wasn't talking to her anymore after Sierra told her that she and Joe had had a drink at the Dragger Inn, the hours at the pharmacy seemed longer. Cassie would say hello and talk about the functioning of the pharmacy, but no friendly banter about life outside the job. Cassie didn't even update Sierra on her grandmother. She had noticed that Cassie now had her own car. A hideous green Honda.

As the hours wore on, Sierra started to hatch a plan. She would text Joe that she was having a small party at her apartment and he was invited. He wouldn't know until he got there that he was the only guest. Sierra knew it was a risky plot, better if she knew for sure that Cassie and Joe had broken up. Maybe she'd get a chance to ask Cassie.

After work she went home to compose the text. She poured herself a glass of red wine and sat down on one of the stools at the kitchen island. Her hands were sweating as she fished her phone out of her purse. She wanted to sound casual: *Hi! Having a small get-together tomorrow night at my place. Hope to see you there. Text me back for details.* This way she would know if he was coming. She stared at the text. Why was she so nervous? If he came, he came. If he didn't, to hell with him.

Later that night, as she got ready for bed, she started thinking about Rick. Why had he come to the bar and why did he all of sudden want to go to her apartment? And why was he all clean and combed? Well, one thing was for sure, she was never bringing him back to her apartment. She liked the squalor of his place because she knew that it would kill her father if he ever knew. Since he was dead, she hoped he was looking down—no, he would be looking up—and that it pissed him off.

She finished undressing, and while she was brushing her teeth, her phone dinged with a new text. Quickly spitting toothpaste out of her mouth, she went to find her phone. The message was from Joe. She smiled. *Time and address* was all it said. Sierra hooked up her phone to the charger for the night. She didn't want to answer him right away. *Don't look overeager,* she advised herself.

The next day at the pharmacy she thought of ways to find out if they were still together. Cassie was still avoiding her at every turn in the store. After lunch, Sierra went outside to sit in her car. It was time to text Joe back: *8 pm. Bring a bottle of wine,* she wrote. Immediately she was hit back: *Sounds good!*

As she went back into the store, Cassie was coming out. Sierra couldn't control herself. "New car?" she asked.

"Yeah. Need it for the new job," said Cassie.

"Can't use Joe's car anymore?" Sierra asked with a grin.

"Good to have my own," said Cassie, eyeing her suspiciously. "What are you smiling about?"

Sierra rolled her eyes and shook her head. "Nothin'," she finally said.

"Okay. See you tomorrow," Cassie said.

"Going to Joe's?" Sierra asked.

"Bye," Cassie called, making her way to her car.

Sierra went back to work, taking over the cash register now that Cassie had left. There were only a few customers, so Sierra went over to the food aisle and took a large bag of chips and a can of onion dip and put them under the register where she would bag them and walk out of the pharmacy with them when she left. She felt that she gave so much to the pharmacy that it was only right that she should have a few perks. She was worth it.

Turning her attention to Joe, she fantasized about how the evening would go. Joe would come in and notice that no one else was there. *They must be fashionably late,* she would say. They would have a drink, then another. Then she would seduce him.

This was a conquest that would piss off dear ol' Dad. Growing up, Sierra was not allowed to have black friends. Wasn't allowed to invite black kids over to her house. Her father said they would steal their TV and their laptop. When he was dying he told her to find an older white guy with money and marry him. In a few years, Sierra thought she might take that advice, but in the meantime, she was going to have Joe.

The hours wore on, and then finally it was time to go home. Taking the stolen chips and dip, Sierra left the pharmacy and drove home. She realized she was humming "Maneater" by Hall & Oates and laughed at how excited she was. She headed straight to the shower and shaved every inch of her body. Then she went to study the bottles of top-tier booze in her bar. Aviation Gin. Aperol. Stoli. Myers's Rum. Now mixers: Coke, seltzer, orange juice, limes, lemons. Beer in the fridge: Fat Tire, Blue Moon, Corona. She really didn't know what Joe drank. He had been drinking Corona the other night at the Dragger Inn. Was that his go-to? She preferred he drink something stronger than beer, so she took the Corona out of the fridge and hid it under the sink.

She set out a bowl for the chips and one for the dip. Right before eight o'clock she would pour out the chips. Not much of a spread. Oh well, she hadn't invited him here to eat. Although men were always hungry. Should she order pizza? Maybe after the seduction.

She went into her bedroom, into her enormous closet, and ran her finger across the silk shirts hanging in one section. What color would Joe like? Cassie had that crazy multi-colored hair. Maybe he liked lots of color. Black was always seductive. White set off her black hair. She had bought a sparkly silver shirt just because she liked the way the light danced on it. That was a definite possibility. It was also low-cut. Joe must be starved for boob after dating Cassie with her little-boy body. She decided on the silver shirt, tight black jeans, and bare feet. Sparkly earrings and a toe ring completed her outfit.

She spent a lot of time blow-drying her long hair and putting on gobs of black mascara. Red lip gloss, and voila! No man could resist her. It was almost time. She went into the living room, poured the chips into the bowl, and spooned the dip out of the can into a smaller bowl.

She felt really nervous. *Get a grip, girl. What's the worst that can happen?* He could storm out. Yell at her. Laugh at her.

The doorbell rang at 8:05. Inhaling deeply, Sierra went to the door.

Joe stood outside looking a little embarrassed. Bashful and adorable. "Hi," he said.

"Hi, c'mon in," said Sierra, holding the door open for him. She seemed to shimmer with her silver shirt, sparkly earrings, and shiny black hair.

"Wow! Nice place," said Joe. "Here, I brought wine," he said, handing her a brown paper bag. Joe was wearing a forest-green shirt that brought out the color in his eyes.

"Thanks."

Joe looked around at the pristine apartment. Sierra had lit a number of votive candles around the living room.

"Looks like a showroom," said Joe, smiling. "Am I early?"

"No, just the first to arrive. What can I get you to drink?" asked Sierra, heading over to the bar. "I probably have anything you can think of."

Joe sat down on one of the stools at the kitchen island. "How about a screwdriver? I used to drink that once in a while. Before I started saving all my money for school."

"Where's Cassie? I thought you might bring her," said Sierra, getting two glasses, the vodka, and the orange juice from the fridge.

"I thought you knew. Isn't that why you invited me?" Joe chuckled.

"Knew what?"

"That we broke up."

Sierra suppressed a small smile. "I'm so sorry," she said.

Joe laughed. "Liar."

Sierra joined him. "You're right. I don't give a shit. Just means you might be available." She gave him a look from under her thick lashes.

Joe laughed again. "So, who else is coming?" He took the drink that she handed him.

"Let's sit on the couch," she said, crossing the room to the leather couch. Her silver shirt shimmering in the light from the candles. She sat down and curled her legs under her. "C'mon. I won't bite you. Not yet, anyway."

Joe reluctantly went to sit on the couch. "What's going on here?"

Sierra held up her glass. "Cheers."

Joe clinked her glass with his. "Cheers."

"Can I ask you something?" Joe asked.

"Sure."

"How do you afford this place working at the pharmacy?"

"My dad left me a lot of money," she said hesitantly.

"Oh, sorry. When did he die?"

"When I was nineteen. No need to be sorry," said Sierra, taking a sip of her drink. She noticed that Joe had nearly finished his.

"Didn't get along with your dad?"

Sierra tried to decide how much to share. Joe was such a sweet guy, she decided the truth might help her seduction. "My mom died when I was four. A plane crash. And my father started sleeping in my bed when I was twelve."

Joe's face registered a swirl of emotion from revulsion to pain to anger. "Shit. That's horrible. I'm sorry."

Sierra took Joe's empty glass and her own over to the island for a refill. "So, enough about me. What happened with you and Cassie? You two were like the couple of the year."

Joe paused. "Sally. Sally happened to us. Cassie finally admitted that she would never leave her, and, frankly, I'm tired of the constant bullshit. It all came to a head the other night."

Sierra went back to the couch with their drinks. Bending over more than necessary to hand Joe his drink and give him a peek at her cleavage.

"Isn't there a home she can put that old woman in?" said Sierra with a disgusted tone.

"No money," said Joe. "I admire Cassie, I really do, but I can't take it anymore. I just can't. Sierra…"

Sierra had curled up closer to Joe, and she reached out and touched one of his curls. "So soft," she whispered.

"Sierra, did you set me up? Is anyone else coming to this so-called party?"

"Would it be so terrible if it was a party for two?"

Joe bit his bottom lip and then downed half of his drink. "I don't think I'm ready. We just broke up."

Sierra put her glass down on the coffee table and touched Joe's lips with her forefinger. She moved her hand to the back of his head and gently nudged his face toward hers, moving in to kiss him. He pulled away and stood up.

"You know, you were the final straw."

"Me?" Sierra said, surprised. She chuckled. "Why?"

Joe ran his hand through his curls, pushing them away from his forehead. "Because we had drinks at the Dragger Inn. And you told her. You made sure she knew." Joe suddenly sounded angry.

"Joe, baby, if your relationship can't survive a few drinks, well…I don't know what to tell you." Sierra stood up and looked up at Joe with wide, innocent eyes. "Joe…"

Joe grabbed his coat. "I don't know why I came here. I have to go."

"Joe, that's crazy. You didn't break up because of me. Grandma was always going to be between you two. That has nothing to do with me," said Sierra, feeling her cheeks grow hot.

"And now, you've basically laid a trap to get me here alone." Joe shook his head, and his curls went flying.

"But you broke up! And not because of me. You said yourself it was because of Sally. You can be here with me. It's okay. Baby, it's okay." Sierra walked toward Joe and put her arms around his neck. "It's okay. Whether you stay here or not, it's over between you and Cassie." She reached up, standing on tiptoes, and kissed him softly on the lips. He didn't resist. She put her hands in his hair and pulled his mouth down to hers and kissed him deeply, making him drop his coat.

"Cassie just makes me feel bad," Joe said. "No one can be as good as she is."

"Let's have another drink, Joe." Sierra took Joe's hand and pulled him toward the couch.

"Yeah, why not?" asked Joe, allowing himself to be brought back to the couch.

Sierra made Joe comfy on the couch and went to make two more drinks. When she came back she gave Joe his drink and he downed it in two gulps. He looked over at Sierra, and when their eyes met, she climbed into his lap. At some point later, they made their way into the bedroom.

In the morning Joe had to be at Home Depot early. He quickly found his clothes, got dressed, and left the apartment without waking her.

Ten minutes later, Sierra was awakened by a loud banging on the door. *Joe must have forgotten something or he misses me already!* Smiling with anticipation, she threw on her robe and padded to the front door.

"Miss me already, baby?" she asked, swinging the door open.

Rick burst into the apartment, pushing Sierra back, away from the door.

"R-Rick..." she stammered in shock before he shoved her down onto the floor. He slammed the door, the windows shook. He locked it and turned back to Sierra.

You're a Natural

On Wednesday Cassie said goodbye to the Ladinskys and left the pharmacy. On Thursday she went to the *Tinden Record* at nine o'clock sharp for her first day as a reporter. Sally was still in the hospital for another week, and then she would go to a short-term rehabilitation center for a week or two. This gave Cassie some time to get used to the demands of her new job. She was so busy that she was mostly able to bury the pain of her broken heart. Thoughts of Joe would surface unexpectedly— mostly images of him wrapping his long, strong arms around her and pulling her into his chest for a hug—and Cassie had to force herself to think about her new life as a reporter to take her mind off him.

Cassie parked her little green Honda in the parking lot beside the *Record*. She still couldn't believe that she had her own car. *Exciting!* Taking a moment, she ran her hand over its shiny hood and allowed herself a little smile. She also took a minute to savor walking into the *Record* as an employee and climbing the creaking staircase to the paper's offices. She hoped that Luke Miller remembered that he had hired her. He hadn't sent her a formal letter or even answered her thank you email.

Cassie entered the reception area and approached the woman sitting at the desk, who was drinking her morning coffee and reading the paper. A quick glimpse around the newsroom showed Cassie that she was the only one there.

"Good morning. I'm Cassie, the new reporter," she said.

"Oh, hi! Luke said you were coming one day this week, but he couldn't remember which day! I'm Sadie, the receptionist. How are you?" Sadie spoke in a rapid-fire way, smiling constantly.

"It's great to meet you, Sadie! Am I early? Where is everybody?"

"Yes, the reporting staff officially starts at ten with the editorial meeting every morning, but it's good you're here because you have forms to fill out." With this, Sadie produced a manila folder with Cassie's name on it and handed it to her. "I'll show you to your desk."

Cassie followed Sadie to the last desk in the last row of desks. It looked like it hadn't been dusted since the paper opened in 1921.

Sadie looked disapprovingly at the desk, running her finger through the soft gray dust. "Tsk, tsk, and we do pay a service to dust every week. Well, I'll get you some paper towels to wipe it down. Fill out all the forms before the meeting if you can." She walked away.

Cassie spent the better part of the hour filling out the various forms. She had to think long and hard about who her emergency contact would be. She finally settled on Sally with Frank Jaworski as a backup. *Last week I would have put down Joe,* she thought, and then quickly turned her attention back to the forms. She finished with fifteen minutes left until the editorial meeting to try to clean up her desk. Sadie had brought her paper towels and Windex.

When she stood up to clean her desk, she noticed that the newsroom was starting to fill up. Reporters were wandering in, getting coffee, and reading the paper. Many of them were middle-aged men, but there were also a few young women and a few young men. Cassie noticed that everyone was dressed very casually and that one young woman had a ring in her nose. She started to relax a little.

At 9:55, one by one, they all started to walk to the conference room. Cassie followed along and took a seat next to the girl with the nose ring. As she was just about to introduce herself, Luke came into the room and took the seat at the head of the table.

"Good morning, everybody! How's it going?" he asked the group, smiling as his eyes met Cassie's. "I want everyone to say hello to Cassie

Pennebaker, our new reporter. She's taking Claudia's position on local news. Welcome, Cassie!" he said, flashing her his dimples.

"Hi! Hey!" She looked around the table at the smiling faces of her new colleagues greeting her, smiling shyly as she did.

"Okay. Down to business. Cassie, we meet at ten every morning to give updates on our stories and get assignments. Everybody introduce yourself to Cassie as we go around." Luke's bright white teeth flashed as he spoke.

Cassie listened as each reporter gave their update. Each started by giving her their name and beat. Many were working on long-term projects, but most of the young reporters were waiting for assignments. When everyone had given their updates and Luke had laid out his thoughts for the front page, he started to give out story assignments.

Hanging on every word that was spoken, Cassie waited eagerly for her first assignment. A store opening went to Rob, a twenty-something with a goatee; an animal adoption fair went to Cyndi, an early thirty-something with acne; and the planning meeting of the College Women's Club for their upcoming annual fundraiser was tossed to Alyssa.

"Sam," said Luke, pointing to the girl with the nose ring, "I want you and Cassie to cover the accident out on Route 1 this morning. A pedestrian was hit by a car. Interview the police, the hospital, family. Get a photo of the scene. You know the drill. Stay together. Don't divide it up today. Sam, show Cassie how it's done. Okay?" Luke paused to look around the table. "Anything for the good of the cause? No? Okay. Go get 'em!"

Cassie waited for Sam when everyone piled out of the conference room. "Hi," she said tentatively as Sam came out.

"Hi. Do you have a car?" asked Sam, looking tired.

"Yeah, I can drive," volunteered Cassie.

"Good. I need to take a little nap on the way. My baby was up all night."

"How old's your baby?" Cassie asked as she followed Sam down the hall.

"Six months. I just came back to work last week. Go grab your coat and get a reporter's notebook from Sadie."

As Cassie drove out to Route 1, Sam closed her eyes and was instantly asleep. Luke had texted them the exact location of the accident, and as Cassie approached the spot she saw police cars, yellow tape, and orange cones blocking off the area. She pulled into a Target parking lot next to the accident and looked over at Sam, who was snoring slightly. *Nothing like sleeping on the job.* Touching her lightly on the arm she said, "Sam, we're here."

Sam winced and opened her eyes. "Okay, go over there to the scene, tell the police you're from the *Record*, and find out as much as you can. You know, who, what, where, when, why. Find out if it was a hit and run. What hospital did they take the victim to? You got it?" Sam's bloodshot eyes had already started to close. "I'll be here if you need me." Sam lowered the back of the car seat and was asleep again in an instant.

Cassie shrugged, grabbed her reporter's notebook, which was slim enough to easily fit in her hand, and a pen from her backpack, and went over to the scene. She looked around at the police milling about, trying to decide who was in charge. Finally, a burly officer approached her. "Can I help you?" he asked.

"Good morning. My name is Cassie Pennebaker and I'm with the *Record*," Cassie said, trying to sound as official as possible.

"New at the *Record*?"

"Yes, first day, actually," Cassie said with a smile. "Can I ask you a few questions?"

"Anything for the *Record*," he said, smiling back.

After getting all the facts from Sergeant Jackson, Cassie felt very proud of herself. As she left she took a photo of the skid marks on the road with the yellow police tape to one side.

When she got in the car, Sam opened her eyes. She looked a little better from her half-hour nap. "How'd it go? Read me your notes," she ordered.

Cassie gave her a rundown of the accident and read her a quote from the sergeant.

"You're a natural," Sam said without enthusiasm. "Now I need coffee, and then we'll go to the hospital."

For the rest of the morning and into the afternoon—with a pit stop at Taco Bell for lunch—Sam told Cassie what questions to ask whom, where to go, and gave her photo suggestions. Cassie drove where Sam told her to go and interviewed the people Sam told her to. Sam slept, looking a little better after each short nap.

On their way back to the *Record*, Sam sat up, stretched, and yawned. "Oh my God. Now I feel almost human. I'm telling you, having a baby and working is hard. You work all day and then you're up all night with the baby. No time to actually sleep. Cassie, thanks. I know I wasn't the best mentor today," said Sam.

"No worries. I think I got what we need," said Cassie with a smile.

Back in the newsroom, Cassie wrote a first draft of the story. As she waited for Sam to mark it up before they submitted it, there was some commotion in the newsroom. Cassie overheard Luke telling one of the reporters to give him three hundred words on the robbery.

When Cassie left the *Record* at six thirty that night she was bursting with excitement. She danced to her car and sang with the radio at the top of her lungs all the way to the hospital. It wasn't until she was walking into the hospital that she remembered it was her twenty-first birthday.

Unannounced

"**W**hat's the matter? Only you can show up unannounced?" Rick growled as Sierra tried to get back on her feet. "And look at this place. Swanky. You're a rich bitch, slumming it when you visit me."

"Rick, what do you want? How did you get my address? Get out!" screamed Sierra.

Rick slapped her hard across the face. "Shut up, bitch! I followed you after our little hookup at the Dragger Inn. When I pulled up I saw Joe leaving. What, are you shacking up with Cassie's boyfriend now? I mean, I know you're a slut…"

Sierra leaped up at Rick and scratched his face with her nails, drawing blood. He grabbed her arm and twisted it behind her back. "Where's the bedroom? This way?" Rick pushed Sierra in front of him toward the hallway. She tried to fight him, but he was much stronger. He pushed her into the bedroom and down on the bed. She was only wearing a T-shirt under her thin satin robe. Holding her down he unzipped his pants and took her from behind. Barely breathing, her face buried in the pillow. Sierra tried to resist.

"What's the matter? You like it like this," he hissed into her ear.

When he finished he held her down under his weight and whispered in her ear, "Here's how this is gonna go. I want that ruby ring you've been flashing around, and any others you have and all your cash." He picked up his head and looked around the room. A large jewelry box sat on the top of the dresser. "Is it in there? Is it in the box?" When she didn't answer he grabbed a handful of her hair and pulled her head up, rough. "We can do this the easy way or the hard way. Which is it?" He yanked again on her hair.

"Take it. Take the whole box. Just get the fuck out of here," screamed Sierra.

"Where's the cash?"

"I don't carry any cash."

Rick got up and went over to the jewelry box. When he opened it he saw treasure—rubies, sapphires, an emerald, gold. He closed the box and tucked it under his arm. As he turned around, Sierra swung a baseball bat hard at his head. He held up one hand, caught the bat, and pulled it out of her grip. Keeping his eyes glued on Sierra, he squatted down and put the jewelry box on the floor. Without missing a beat, he sprang up and punched her in the face.

"You fucking bitch! You want a fight? We can fight. It'll be my pleasure." Fire in his eyes, a wicked sneer on his face, he beat Sierra with the bat until she lay lifeless beside the bed. Even then it was hard to stop, but he forced himself. He grabbed the box, saw a dark brown leather tote on a chair beside the dresser, threw the box in it, and went to look for Sierra's purse. *She must have a few bucks.* He looked around the living room, did not see her purse, and decided it was better to just get out with the jewelry. He looked at Sierra lying in a broken heap and gave her one last kick in the ribs. *Fuckin' bitch!* He left the apartment, closing the door tight behind him.

❖ ❖ ❖

Sierra opened her eyes as best she could, searing pain tearing through her skull. When she lifted her hand up to her face, every muscle in her body ached. Her hair was matted with blood, and it took her a moment to remember that Rick had done this to her. She listened intently to see if he was still there. After a few minutes of hearing nothing, she tried to get up. She pulled herself up to a kneeling position with the help of the bed, then dragged herself onto the bed. When she moved her right arm she saw stars. Her eyes were swollen from the beating and her lip was split. Like a drunk, she bobbed and weaved into the kitchen to find her phone and called 911.

I Thought It Was You

Joe drifted through the day at Home Depot in a fog. Sleeping with Sierra, as sexy as she was and as single as he was, was a bad move. He hadn't had time to shower before work, and every time he moved he smelled Sierra. It made him feel dirty, utterly alone, and empty as he helped customers find the right light bulb and answered questions about screwdrivers. He just wanted to get away from Tinden. He just wanted to go to Boston and focus on school and his career. Focus on himself. No mentally deficient grandmas, no hitmen living next door, no girlfriends with too much responsibility.

It was also Cassie's birthday. Was he supposed to send her a text? *Hi, happy birthday! Slept with Sierra to celebrate.* They had talked about celebrating her big day before they broke up. Maybe going out to dinner. He had saved enough money to buy her a necklace that she had admired one day in the jewelry store downtown. She never wanted Joe to spend money on her, so he had remembered when she had pointed it out in the window.

Doesn't matter now. Joe tallied up the months until he could pack up his car and drive to Boston. Maybe he could move up early. Or maybe he should knock on Rick's door and take him up on his offer to get rid of Sally. He felt like he was coming unglued, jittery, couldn't concentrate. He went to the staff restroom and washed his face and hands.

When he thought about Cassie's situation from her point of view, he couldn't fault her. As she said, she couldn't just leave Sally alone in the apartment; she would definitely die. There was no one else to ease Cassie's burden, but one day, Sally would die. Joe looked at himself in the mirror, thinking of his deep love for Cassie and how that couldn't just disappear overnight. *Are you willing to wait until Sally dies?* She could live another ten years or more. No, he wasn't willing to wait. It was just an impossible situation. And now that he had slept with Sierra, would Cassie ever take him back? He wouldn't blame her if she never spoke to him again.

He went back out on the floor and started to restock light bulbs, putting them in straight rows. The section was in the back of the store, and Joe could pass time without being bothered. But thoughts of last night, images of Sierra, kept creeping into his brain. What had he done? He was supposed to sort the bulbs by wattage, but now he didn't care. He just crammed them onto the shelf willy-nilly.

The long afternoon wore on. Close to quitting time, Joe's phone started to vibrate in his pocket. It was Sierra. Joe frowned but picked up the call.

"Sierra, I'm at work. Can't really talk," he started.

Sierra half-whispered, "Joe, he raped me and beat me with a baseball bat."

"What? Who?"

"Rick. I'm in the emergency room at Sullivan. Can you pick me up, Joe?"

"When did it happen? How did—"

He could hear Sierra weeping pitiful sobs. "He banged on the door right after you left and I thought it was you. I opened the door. He forced...hit me with the bat...forty-five stitches...broke my arm and three ribs..."

"Okay, Sierra, I'm coming. I'll be there as soon as I can."

After they hung up, Joe stood staring at his phone. Holy shit. He had always been so worried that Rick would do something like this to Cassie. But going to the hospital only added another layer to his pseudo-relationship with Sierra. He didn't want a relationship with Sierra, but how could he just leave her at the hospital? Somehow, he felt a certain sense of responsibility.

He told his supervisor that he had a family emergency and he had to leave a little early. It was almost six o'clock. Joe jogged out to his car. He thought about stopping at his apartment for a shower but decided to go straight to the hospital. He hoped that Sierra had called the cops and that Rick had been arrested. He tried to remember if he had seen anything suspicious when he left Sierra's this morning, but his mind had been so absorbed with thoughts of Cassie and Sierra that he couldn't even remember the walk to the car.

He parked his car in the hospital parking lot and went into the hospital. He was always struck by how deserted the place was and wondered how they kept it going. Following the signs to the emergency room, he walked down the empty corridors until he came to a locked door. Finally, a nurse let him through on her way out, and he went to the nurse's station to ask where she was. The nurse pointed to a closed curtain.

He was not ready for what he saw when he pulled back the curtain. Last night he had made love to a beautiful woman, and now he stood before a mangled face that he didn't recognize. Two black and swollen eyes, a split lip, a shattered nose. A large patch on the side of her head had been shaved to stitch up a gash. One arm was in a sling. Two fingers on the other hand wore silver splints.

"Oh my God, Sierra!" Joe uttered.

She tried to open her eyes. "Joe." She reached out to him with her unbroken arm.

"I can't believe this." Joe's face was pinched with pain. "Tell me you had him arrested."

"They're looking for him." Her words were broken. "Joe, I can't go to my apartment. I can't be alone. Can I go home with you?"

"Of course," Joe said. "But are they keeping you tonight? For observation or anything?"

"No, I can go and I want to get out of here," Sierra insisted.

Joe watched tears fall down her bruised cheeks. "I hope they're giving you something for the pain."

The nurse came in and gave Joe a number of prescriptions and a discharge packet. "Are you her boyfriend?" she asked.

"No, just a friend," said Joe.

The nurse looked displeased with this piece of information and turned to Sierra. "Do you feel comfortable going home with this man?"

"Yes," said Sierra.

"Do you have a mother or a sister we can call?"

"No, Joe will help me. I just want to go," said Sierra, putting her legs over the side of the bed and sitting up. "Oh, dizzy." Sierra's head wobbled on her neck.

"I'll get a wheelchair," said the nurse, turning around quickly, sneakers squeaking. She came back in two minutes with the wheelchair.

"Take it easy," said Joe, helping Sierra into the chair. "Lean on me." He put his arm around her and helped her up. She pointed to her black watch wrap on the back of the visitor's chair, and he wrapped it around her shoulders. They headed slowly out into the hallway. Joe wheeled her carefully down the hall, and when he looked up, he saw Cassie coming toward them. He felt his cheeks grow hot. *What a nightmare!* He wanted to be anywhere except where he was.

Cassie glared at Joe with a look on her face that he had never seen before. Her nostrils flared, her cheeks were flushed, and her tiny hands were clenched into fists. But when she shifted her gaze to look at Sierra in the wheelchair, a look of horror and disbelief replaced the anger.

"Sierra! What happened to you?" Cassie asked, raising one hand up to her mouth.

"Rick. Rick did this to me," said Sierra, her words slurring from her swollen lips.

Joe felt like a traitor. His heart cried out for Cassie even though he was there for Sierra. How had his world turned upside down? The walls started to close in and he had to get out of there. "We have to go, Cass," said Joe and moved the wheelchair down the hallway.

When he opened the outside door and pushed Sierra into the night wind, he looked back and caught a glimpse of Cassie still standing in the hallway looking devastated. Like a truck had run her over. As he helped Sierra into his car he realized he hadn't even said happy birthday.

Earl's Pawnshop

While the police were ransacking Rick's apartment, Detective Herman Deegan sat in his car and smoked his cigar. He thought about Rick Smollett. Ex-Marine. Master marksman. Rapist. Thief. General lowlife. Unemployed. Desperate. Violent. He thought about Sierra Kole. Shit, Rick could have killed that girl. Beating her with a baseball bat. Add psychopath to the list. Deegan had seen a lot of assault cases, and the way this girl looked was one of the worst. She told him she knew Rick from the pharmacy and the Dragger Inn. But she also knew his home address and what kind of car he drove. Was there more to their relationship than she was saying? She had said that he had shown her his guns one day. A rifle and a Beretta. Where were they when he had shown them to her? Was this a romance gone bad? She said no.

Deegan started his car and, on a hunch, drove over to the pawnshop on the outskirts of town. The real seedy one run by Earl, a liar and a cheat. If Rick wanted to pawn the jewelry, he would probably go to Earl's Pawnshop. Earl wouldn't ask any questions. Deegan pulled into the parking lot, cigar in one hand, trying to avoid the beer cans, trash, and potholes. He pulled into a parking spot and tamped out his cigar in an ashtray he kept on the passenger seat for this purpose, and put the rest of the cigar in his coat pocket.

Earl's Pawnshop was a single-story, free-standing building badly in need of a paint job. In the window the sign said, "We'll help you stay afloat. Cash for gold and diamonds." Earl advertised that he would hold customers' possessions for three months, but since most of his clients never came back for their things he usually tried to move the merchandise after a few weeks.

A bell jingled over his head as Deegan walked into the dark shop. Earl was sitting behind the counter, and a man fitting Sierra's description of Rick was nervously shifting his weight from one foot to the other while Earl looked at a piece of jewelry through his jeweler's loupe.

"Morning, Earl," said Deegan slowly, placing himself squarely in the middle of the doorway so that no one could get in or out of the shop.

Earl's back straightened when he saw Detective Deegan. "Morning, Detective," he said, looking up at Rick. Earl had lost his two front teeth in a brawl a few years back and had them replaced with gold ones. When he smiled they shone in the dim light. "What brings you out here?"

"Just checkin' in," said Deegan, keeping his position in front of the door. "We're lookin' for a guy. A guy who stole some jewelry this morning from a young woman. Beat her up real bad." Deegan moved his jacket back for easy access to the gun at his hip.

Earl put the piece of jewelry on the counter, and Deegan saw it was a ruby ring surrounded by a halo of diamonds. The ring fit the description Sierra had given him earlier of one of the pieces in her jewelry box. Deegan slowly moved his hand onto his gun.

"Hey, buddy," he said to Rick. "Do you mind turnin' around?"

Earl pushed back in his seat. Rick didn't turn around. The air was electric with tension.

"Hey, you in the Army jacket. You Rick Smollett?" Deegan took a step forward, adrenaline pumping through his veins. "I asked you to turn around, and now I'm telling you to turn around and make it slow." Deegan took his revolver out of the holster.

Rick put his right hand into his jacket and when he pulled it out, Deegan saw a glint of metal. The butt of a pistol. Deegan fired one shot through the back of Rick's head.

Earl screamed and fell off his chair. "What the fuck? Deegan, man, what the fuck?"

Rick fell over the counter, blood running out of his head, down the back of the counter onto Earl's boots and the floor. A sickening sweet smell of blood was added to the booze and sweat that emanated from his pores. Deegan quickly approached the body and checked the neck for a pulse. When he was confident that Rick was dead, he turned and picked up the Beretta that had slipped out of Rick's hand. He checked the chamber. It was loaded. He closed his eyes and sighed in relief, quickly saying two Hail Marys.

"I had no idea. No idea. He said it was his mom's jewelry," stammered Earl, who had gotten up from the floor, eyes bulging out of his head, holding his hands up for Deegan to see.

"Shut up," commanded Deegan. He pulled out his phone and called it in. Within minutes they heard police sirens.

The squad cars arrived, and Earl's became a crime scene. Detective Deegan, pale but still swaggering, heart thumping, made his way to the parking lot, where he took his cigar out of his pocket, licked the tip, and lit up.

Sacrifice

Seeing Joe with Sierra left Cassie speechless, breathless, numb. It was like Sierra had stolen a part of Cassie's being. The part that made her whole. She kept hearing his words over and over in her mind, "We have to go, Cass." *We.* As in Joe and Sierra. Last week he would have said *we,* as in he and Cassie. Were they together now? Sure, she and Joe had had a fight, but was that it? He had replaced her with Sierra in a day? She navigated the halls of the hospital in a trance, finding her way to Sally's room.

Sally was asleep. Cassie pulled the chair in the corner of the room close to the bed and sat looking at Sally. She had given up Joe for this. To sit here with this woman who brought her tremendous pain. Who caused her constant worry. Who stole her time and her dreams. Her dream to be a foreign correspondent. That was all it would ever be, a dream. How could it ever be a reality with Sally? Resentment fought with unbreakable love in her heart.

Cassie took Sally's hand in hers. Worn, with chipped nails, Sally's hand was so familiar to Cassie that it made her cry. Some of her earliest memories were of Sally braiding her pigtails with these hands. Making her mac and cheese. Tying her sneakers. Were these memories why she couldn't leave Sally? Cassie stared at Sally's pain-ravaged face and let the tears come. Was her love for Sally so strong that she would sacrifice Joe and their future together, a degree from a top school, and an exciting career to stay in Tinden and take care of Sally?

When Jillian had left Cassie and Sally to fend for themselves, a bond had been forged between grandmother and granddaughter that was so strong, Cassie couldn't break it for Joe or even for herself. They became central to each other's lives. It was as though her sacrifice was not a choice, it was her fate. It didn't mean that she didn't love Joe. She did. But not to the exclusion of Sally.

Sally wasn't just family. Being tied to someone by blood did not necessarily mean that she would sacrifice herself for them. No, family alone was not enough. It was because Sally was always there for her. Cassie never thought for a minute that Sally would leave her or kick her out of the apartment. She and Sally were each other's constants. Everything was shared between them. Love, unconditional and unwavering.

Joe was the one with the dream of going to BU, and Cassie was beginning to see that Joe wanted to move to Boston to put distance between Cassie and Sally so that Joe didn't have to put up with their relationship. Joe could learn to be a reporter right here in Tinden if he wanted to. But moving hundreds of miles away? She had seen that before, when Jillian and Jake had moved to Australia. Jake had moved Jillian away from her daughter and mother, and now Joe was making a similar move. If Joe truly loved her, they could work it out. Go to school closer so that Cassie could also be there for Sally. If Cassie was really a priority to him, then Sally would have to be part of that. But Joe didn't want Sally in his life. He didn't understand her and didn't want to understand. There was no hope for Cassie and Joe's relationship. She could see that clearly now.

How quickly he had turned to Sierra for comfort. *To Sierra!* That empty shell of a person who only dated people she couldn't have. But now she had Joe.

And I have you. Cassie leaned down and kissed Sally on the cheek. *And you have me.*

Get Some Blood

C ops were swarming all around the apartments when Cassie got home from the hospital. She had to show them her ID to get past them and into her apartment, but when she left in the morning, just one squad car was posted outside. She wondered if Rick had been caught.

When she got to the *Record* on her second day, the sleepy atmosphere that had greeted her the day before was now charged with the excitement of a real story. Rick Smollett had been shot and killed by a detective in a rundown pawnshop on the outskirts of town.

As the reporters filed into the conference room for the ten o'clock meeting, Cassie was feeling a wide range of emotions. She couldn't believe that Rick was dead. Even though she should have felt only relief, somehow news of his being killed by the detective also scared her. She was torn between divulging all she knew about Rick and Sierra to the reporters or keeping it to herself. Someone at the paper would soon realize that Rick was her neighbor.

Luke was already in the conference room monitoring his phone. Before the last of the reporters took their seats, he was eager to give an update and get his staff out in the field. "Good morning, everybody! Glad to see we're all here. I'm sure you've all heard that a woman was raped and beaten with a baseball bat yesterday and that the intruder stole her jewelry box. The suspect, Rick Smollett, was then shot and killed by Detective Herman Deegan at Earl's Pawnshop. Smollett made a move and Deegan took him out with one shot to the head. Turned out Smollett had a loaded Beretta in his hand." Luke paused here and looked around the table at his team. His eyes sparkled and Cassie could tell that he was excited by the story.

"Tom," Luke said to one of the older reporters, "give me six hundred to eight hundred words on the overall story for the front page. Colin, let's do a profile of this Detective Deegan. You know him?"

"Oh yeah, he's a tough old-timer. Been around as long as me," said Colin, who was one of the older reporters.

"Cyndi, go over to Kensington Apartments and interview folks about Rick Smollett," Luke continued. "Talk to the groundskeeper, Frank Jaworski, he knows everybody."

Cyndi nodded and nervously touched an angry-looking pimple on her cheek.

"Sam and Cassie, go out to Earl's and see what's going on. See if you can find Earl and get a firsthand account of what happened," said Luke. "Okay. Anything else for the good of the cause?" Luke looked around the table. "All right, go get the story. And get good art. Get a photo of our hero, Detective Deegan. See if they'll let you take a photo at the pawnshop. Get some blood if you can." Luke raised his eyebrows.

Sam winced. "Really?"

"Yeah, hopefully they haven't cleaned it up yet. You get it, Cassie, if Sam's too squeamish." Luke smiled at Cassie.

As the reporters filed out of the conference room, Cassie hung back, telling Sam she'd catch up with her in a minute.

Luke looked up from his phone. "What's up? Great story for a newbie." Luke's ridiculously attractive dimples were on full display.

Suddenly Cassie felt tongue-tied. "So, I kind of know Rick and the woman he beat up."

Luke took a second to consider what she was saying. "How do you know them?"

"Uh, Rick is—was—my neighbor. A real asshole. Scary asshole. And Sierra—that's the woman he beat up—used to work with me at the pharmacy. Well, she still works there. I think. They were..." Cassie stopped.

"They were..."

"They used to hook up. She would go to his apartment in the middle of the night. I never really understood why she was with him, because he was disgusting. Anyway, I just needed to tell you since I'll be covering part of the story."

"Interesting," said Luke. "What do you know about Smollett?"

"He used to work construction, but I think he got fired recently. He was a veteran. A Marine. Had a couple of guns. Divorced. He killed my cats."

"He killed your cats?" asked Luke.

"It's a long story."

"Maybe we should interview you, but I don't think I want to do that when you've only been here two days. We'll check out his discharge status and try to track down the wife. It doesn't surprise me that the victim knew this guy. Most victims know their attackers," said Luke. "Do you think the woman would want to talk? Would she give you an interview?"

Cassie laughed harshly. "No, I don't think Sierra will be talking to me. I saw her leaving the hospital last night when I was going in to visit my grandmother, and her whole face was black and blue and swollen, and her arm was in a sling. She was a mess and she was with…" Cassie's voice trailed off.

"Who was she with?" asked Luke, looking intrigued.

"Well, she was with my ex," said Cassie, cheeks blushing.

"Well, it sounds like there is a lot of history between all of you. None that we want to get into for our story. By the way, the *Record* doesn't name victims or possible victims because that can discourage survivors from coming forward. We usually only name a victim if they want us to, like if they want to tell their story." Luke gathered his papers, and as he stood up Cassie realized how tall he was.

She smiled up at him and wanted to bite her nails.

"Nice job on the hit-and-run story yesterday," Luke said as they walked out of the conference room together.

Cassie could smell the musky soap he used. "Thanks." She smiled at the compliment. "Hey, Luke…"

"Yeah?"

"Maybe we could do a story on services for victims," said Cassie.

Luke smiled. "Cover Earl's today and let's see what tomorrow brings. If the story has no legs, we'll see if we can squeeze something in."

Cassie nodded and started back to her desk, where Sam was sitting with her coat on.

"Sorry, I had to talk to Luke for a minute," said Cassie.

Sam looked at her with bleary eyes. "And I need to get in your car and take a nap. I looked up the address for Earl's," she said as she got up and started to walk out. "You're welcome!"

Cassie followed Sam out of the newsroom. It was kind of nice to have Sam with her, even though Cassie knew she would make Cassie do all the work. She decided to think of Sam as a sleep-deprived fairy godmother who showed her where to go and told her what to ask, and then slept until she did it. As they drove out to Earl's, the storefronts got more dilapidated. She was happy she didn't have to go to the pawnshop alone, even though when Cassie looked over, Sam was snoring soundly.

As Cassie pulled into the pawnshop parking lot, she saw that the front door of the shop was cordoned off with yellow police tape and that two police officers were huddled by the door comparing notes. The door behind the tape was open, and Cassie thought she might have a chance of getting a photo if she could get the permission of the officers.

She parked and nudged Sam's shoulder. "Wake up, Sleeping Beauty. Although you snore more like the Beast."

"You're mixing your Disney movies," said a sleepy Sam, surveying the scene out of her window.

"So, the one on the right is Officer Bell. He's great. Start with him," said Sam, yawning and snuggling into the seat.

"Okay, but don't drool on my new car."

Sam opened one bloodshot eye. "I'll try not to."

Cassie shook her head and wondered if all new parents were this tired as she grabbed her notepad and headed over to the officers. "Good morning!" she said brightly, giving the officers a big smile. "How's it going? Pennebaker, from the *Record*." She flashed her press credentials, savoring the act. Her press badge had become her most cherished possession.

"Officer Bell, and this is Officer Kimble. What can we do for you?"

"We're writing a story on Rick Smollett and what happened here. I wanted to know if I could speak with Earl. Get a firsthand account of what transpired between Smollett and Detective Deegan. Is he around?"

"No, the shop's closed until further notice," said Officer Bell.

"Can I look inside? Maybe take a photo?"

Officer Bell looked at Officer Kimble, who shook his head slightly. "I'm sorry, Miss Pennebaker, but we can't let you in. Forensics is expected any minute. You can take a picture of the front of the shop if you want," he offered.

"Okay, can you confirm that Detective Deegan shot and killed Rick Smollett?" asked Cassie.

"Yes, I can confirm that the suspect, Rick Smollett, reached for his firearm when he was told to turn around, and that Detective Deegan fired one shot, thus subduing the perpetrator," said Officer Bell.

Cassie furiously wrote down this quote in her reporter's notebook. "And he died instantly?"

"Yes, he died instantly with his hand still on the firearm."

"And Earl was there?"

"Yes, Earl was looking at the stolen jewelry that Smollett was trying to pawn."

"And Rick...I mean Smollett, was taken to the ME?" She had heard that question on *Law and Order*.

"Yes, that's correct."

Cassie wished that Sam would wake up and help her out here. "Okay, thanks. I'll take a few photos of the front door."

"Sure, I was just leaving anyway," said Officer Kimble, who took his leave, got in the squad car, and drove slowly out of the parking lot.

While Cassie was taking the photos of the outside of the shop, getting as close to the door as she could, she saw Sam walking toward them, looking like she had just combed her hair and applied new lip gloss.

"Officer Bell, my favorite!" she sang when she was about six feet away. "How have you been? I haven't seen you since, what? The Bayona robbery?"

Officer Bell's face lit up, eyes sparkling when he saw Sam. "Sammy! How you been?" he chuckled.

"Well, the baby's trying to kill me. Never sleeps. I'm sure he's sleeping now, but he never sleeps at night. How's the old ball and chain?"

Officer Bell smiled. "She's great!"

Sam turned to Cassie. "Jakey here, I mean, Officer Bell, is a newlywed. Wed to my best friend, Sara."

"Congratulations!" Cassie offered.

"So Jakey, listen, it's Cassie's first week on the job, and it would really be big for her if she got a shot inside. Did you guys clean it up yet?"

Cassie could see Officer Bell tense up. "No, we haven't. The investigation is ongoing."

"So what if we just snuck in the back, didn't touch a thing, and took a quick shot? Huh? Whaddaya say?" Sam gave Officer Bell a wide smile.

"Sammy, I don't know. I don't want to get in trouble."

"No one else is here…"

"Okay, but go quick. My replacement will be here in five—"

Both Cassie and Sam exclaimed in unison, "Thank you!" They started to move around the back.

"Don't touch anything!" yelled Officer Bell after them.

The young women entered through the back door. It was dark, dusty, and gray. They walked through the back stockroom that was full of old paintings in gilt frames, tarnished silver candlesticks, and brass bed frames, and into the main shop, which was marked up with yellow tape and police markers. Cassie saw the dark stain of blood that started on the counter and dripped down the back onto the floor. She quickly took a lot of different photos.

"I got it," she told Sam.

Cassie came out of the pawnshop experiencing a swirl of emotions—satisfaction that Rick was gone and wouldn't be able to intimidate her anymore, but also sadness that he had been shot in this brutal fashion. The whole affair was a tragedy borne of his pain and Sierra's pain. She left the shop feeling like she had been at the frontlines of a conflict. Did she and Joe really have to go to Africa or the Middle East to find compelling stories? Was being a foreign correspondent her dream? Or *Joe's* dream? For her, the stories of Tinden were enough. She didn't have to go any farther to cover the human experience.

Possibilities

Cassie had never seen an ambulance gurney like the one wheeled into Sally's room to move her from the hospital to the rehab center. Bright yellow legs with a thick black leather mattress and enough restraints to keep Sally strapped on even if it accidently turned over. She could tell that the two paramedics, Chester and Marshall, were pleased with their shiny state-of-the-art equipment. Marshall had proudly told Cassie that he and Chester were the only two on their squad who were experts in how to use the equipment.

"Your chariot awaits," said Chester to Sally as she pulled the blankets up to her neck and burrowed down in her hospital bed. If looks could kill, Chester would be six feet under.

"Cassie, we don't need that thing to get me home. You take me. You take me, Cassie," Sally ordered. "We don't need that thing. Take it away."

Cassie smiled at Chester and Marshall, who seemed unsurprised that Sally didn't want to go on the gurney. "Gram, you can't walk yet. I can't take you by myself. These guys are going to help me. Okay, Gram?"

"No, it is not okay," Sally said emphatically. Cassie could see that Sally was working herself into a rage. She knew that Sally's anger was always about control. It was about every time in her life when she'd had no control over what happened to her. Chester and Marshall moving her today was just another log on the fire that continually burned in Sally's brain.

Cassie gave a nod to Chester to do his job. No amount of talking to Sally would calm her down. The men started to wrap Sally's blanket under her on all sides, swaddling her arms into the blanket so she would be restrained when they moved her onto the gurney.

"Stop! Don't touch me!" screamed Sally.

"Gram, it's okay," comforted Cassie.

When she was all tucked in, Chester and Marshall moved into position, one on each side. Sally glowered at one, then the other. They lowered the protective sides of the hospital bed and grabbed the bottom sheet.

"On my count," said Marshall.

"No, I'm not going with you!" screamed Sally.

"Gram, please," said Cassie.

"One, two, three," said Marshall.

They moved Sally in one swift motion onto the gurney. Working quickly, they locked her into the restraints that formed the spokes of a wheel across her chest. It all happened so fast that Sally had momentarily been silenced, but once she realized she couldn't move she started to protest.

"Cassie, are we going outside? Is it raining? Have you checked?" Sally started to sound panicked.

"The sun is shining, Gram. Don't worry. I'll be with you," Cassie said, glancing at her phone. Today was Saturday and she wanted to get her chores done. She also wanted a cigarette.

"How much longer do you think this will take?" she asked Marshall.

"It's a quick ride. Maybe an hour to get her upstairs to her bed," he replied.

"We don't live upstairs Cassie. What's he talking about?" asked Sally.

"You have to go to rehab before you can go home, Gram," said Cassie in the calmest tone she could muster. "You can't go home until you can walk."

"I can walk!"

"Okay, Gram," said Cassie, biting the nail on her pinky.

"Let's go," said Chester. They took Sally out of the hospital room, down the hall to the elevator, and out to the ambulance. Cassie watched as the gurney was loaded into the truck.

"Hop in," said Chester, holding out his hand to help Cassie into the back of the ambulance. "It's a big step," he said with a grin. She looked up at him and he winked at her.

Cassie smiled. She had been with Joe for such a long time that she had forgotten how to act when cute guys were nice to her. She thought she might be blushing.

"You work around here?" Chester asked as they rode to the rehab center.

"Yeah. At the *Record*. I'm a reporter," said Cassie, sitting up a little straighter.

"Is that right? Cool," said Chester, giving her a big grin.

"Cassie, where are we going?" wailed Sally.

"To the rehab center," said Cassie. Turning back to Chester, she said, "I know she's a handful. Thanks for being so patient with her." She smiled at Chester and he smiled back. As they drove through the quiet town, she realized that the world was full of possibilities.

Ground Rules

It had started to rain as Cassie came out of the rehab center, big sloppy drops rolling out of the sky, and by the time the Uber picked her up to take her back to the hospital where she had left her car, it was pouring. As she watched the wind make the weeping willows dance on the hospital grounds, her problems flickered in and out of her mind.

Her cuticles stung from constantly chewing on them. She looked down at her swollen and bleeding fingers as she pressed the button to start the ignition. Her index finger on her left hand was bleeding the worst so she stuck it in her mouth and sucked on it as she slowly made her way out of the parking lot. Glancing at the digital clock on the dashboard she realized she had an entire day to fill. Yes, she still had all her chores to do, but no one was putting any pressure on her to be anywhere or do anything for them. No Joe, no Gram, not even the cats to feed. This was a new feeling for her. Exciting, but scary at the same time. She could decide for herself—and only herself—what she wanted to do.

As she slowed down to turn into her street and begin the endless chores she always had to do on her day off, she couldn't make the turn. Her arms simply wouldn't move the steering wheel in the direction of the street. She flicked the blinker off and drove right past Kensington Terrace. She had no idea where she was going, but she wasn't going to the apartment to clean the bathroom and do the laundry. For once in her life she was not going to do what she was supposed to do. She would play hooky. She was going to play hooky from her life. She felt an adrenaline rush burst inside her chest at the idea of doing something, anything for herself.

A tremendous weight lifted from her shoulders. She pulled over, turned her phone off, and threw it in the back seat of the car. With a smile, she put the radio on and turned up the volume. "Blurred Lines" was blaring, and Cassie sang along with Robin Thicke and Pharrell. She and Joe had loved this music video, and she knew every word of the song. A visual of Joe dancing to the song with an ice cream cone ran through her mind, but she stopped herself. There would be ground rules. No thoughts of Joe. No guilt about taking the day for herself. No thoughts of Gram. No lists of things she should be doing. Cassie was the only person she would care about for the rest of the day.

Where would she go? The only place she had ever gone for pleasure was Joe's apartment. To see him. To be with him. But there had to be a place she could go that would make her happy. Shopping. Other girls liked to shop. Cassie thought about going to the mall. She could walk through the stores, try on clothes, she could even buy something. She had money saved. Fifty dollars spent on a shirt or a new pair of jeans wouldn't break her. So the mall was an option. Where else did she like to go? The library or Barnes & Noble. She loved Barnes & Noble. She could walk through the shelves, sit on the floor, and read the first chapter of different books until she found one she wanted. She could buy it no matter what it cost.

Stopped at the traffic light, she looked out the window and saw a Starbucks. She had never had a Starbucks coffee. Joe always said that people who spent five dollars on a cup of coffee were stupid. Well, today she would be stupid. She pulled into the lot. The rain had stopped as she parked the car. She studied the mermaid on the sign. Why a mermaid? What did mermaids have to do with coffee? Feeling intimidated, she got out of the car, crossed the parking lot, and pulled open the door. The smell of burned coffee and hazelnuts hit her in the face. There were five or six people standing in line studying their phones. She entered the coffee shop and looked around. Bags of branded coffee were stacked impressively on shelves to left. The line formed in front of a refrigerated counter on her right.

"I'll have a tall Spiced Pumpkin Caramel Macchiato," said the young man who was next in line.

"Five seventeen," said the girl behind the counter, her voice monotone. "What's your name?"

"Sam," said the young man, giving the girl a ten-dollar bill.

Cassie listened to the people place their orders. She had no idea what to get. They all seemed so confident. It was like a cult. A cult she did not belong to. Each person before her knew how to order from the menu overhead. She stepped out of the line to study her options, telling the girl in back of her to go before her. She went to stand by the shelves of Starbucks-branded mugs and thermoses and scanned the overhead board for a small coffee. Seeing no "small" option she realized that "tall" must be "small." So millennial. Everyone was special, no one was small. She got back on the line.

When it was her turn, she said, "I'll have a tall mocha coffee." She said it with disdain. It seemed the right attitude to have.

"Four ninety-seven," said the girl.

Cassie handed her a five and pushed Joe's comment out of her mind. Everyone was allowed to be stupid once in a while.

"Name?" said the girl.

"What?" asked Cassie.

The girl was holding a cup and a pen. She looked at Cassie through her thick bangs. "What's your name?" she asked with an exasperated tone. "For the cup?"

"Cassie," she said, reaching out for the cup.

The girl pulled the cup back. "You pick up your coffee down there. After they brew it." The girl rolled her eyes.

"Oh." Cassie looked over and saw that all the people who had been ahead of her in line now formed a disorganized semi-circle around the far end of the counter. "Thanks."

"Next," said the girl.

Cassie joined the people who had ordered and were now studying their phones again, standing in the loose semi-circle. As their names were called they silently went up and got their order. Since Cassie had purposely left her phone in the car, she now felt awkward standing and waiting without it. She glanced around at the people standing with her. A young man in khakis and a polo shirt. A young woman wearing a mustard-colored coat and tortoiseshell glasses. A mom with two silent little boys, both playing games on their phones. And a woman in her mid-thirties, who had a brisk haircut, a strand of pearls, and a suit.

Cassie watched the crew make the coffees. They had many different pitchers, shakers, whipped cream makers. There were three of them. All with slightly different jobs at different stations. One of the girls had a bright magenta streak on one side of her hair. Cassie had noticed a small smile on the girl's face when she looked at Cassie's rainbow-colored hair.

"Cassie!" called the girl with the magenta streak, not waiting for Cassie to come for the coffee, but placing the cup on the counter and moving on to the next order.

Cassie went over and picked up the cup. "Thanks," she said in the general direction of the girl and went to find a table in the small seating area. There was one small table for two in the back corner, and Cassie took the seat by the wall so that she could watch the crowd. She took the lid off the coffee cup, and the steam from the hot liquid rose up. It smelled like a mixture of chocolate and coffee, and Cassie eagerly tried to take a sip, but it was too hot. She warmed her hands on the cup and tried to be comfortable. Tried to fit in. Here she was, sitting in Starbucks. Kind of like sitting at the cool kids' table at school. Only she had never been invited to sit with the cool kids and didn't know how to act.

The woman with the pearls was now looking for a seat. Cassie saw her narrow down her options. There was a seat at the table for four with the mom and two kids, but Cassie could tell the woman rejected this option. Cassie watched as the woman approached her table.

"Do you mind?" asked the woman, pointing to the empty chair with her coffee.

Cassie, assuming this was normal in the culture of Starbucks, nodded that it was fine, even though she preferred that the woman sit elsewhere.

The woman's perfume filled the air around their table. Mixing with the smell of the coffee and the mocha. Cassie noticed that the woman wore a large diamond ring and a diamond-studded wedding band. Her suit was tailored, a gray-and-black plaid, and the silk shirt she wore matched the gray in the suit perfectly. Cassie wondered what she did for a living. She looked out the window and tried to figure out which building she worked in.

"I like your hair," said the woman, barely looking away from her phone.

"I like your haircut," Cassie responded, venturing a sip of her coffee. She wrinkled her nose at the bitter taste.

"Two sugars and some cream will help it," said the woman.

"I'll get used to it," Cassie said. "You work around here?"

The woman looked away from her phone and focused on Cassie. "Yes, my office is across the street. I'm a lawyer."

"What kind of law?"

"Do you want to be a lawyer?"

"No. I'm a reporter."

The woman smiled, and Cassie noticed how white and straight her teeth were. "That would explain the questions."

Cassie smiled.

"I'm a criminal lawyer. Mostly white-collar, but I get my share of low-level drug dealers, thieves, and other lowlifes. Everyone deserves fair representation."

"What kind of a case are you working on today?"

"Assault. It's a 'he said, he said.' My client says the other guy started it, but he's bigger and stronger, so the other guy looks worse than my guy. It's his first arrest, so I'm hoping the judge will give him a slap on the wrist. Maybe some community service. What about you? Are you in school?"

"Yes. Community college right now," said Cassie. "But I'm also a reporter for the *Record*. Where'd you go to school?"

The woman hesitated a beat. "Harvard." Cassie thought she detected a bit of embarrassment.

"And law school?"

"Harvard."

Cassie had never spoken to anyone who went to an Ivy League school before. She studied the woman's eyes for some sign of what it meant to have gone to Harvard. The woman was obviously smart, tough, confident. But Cassie felt she could hold up her side of the conversation.

"So, is that your dream? To be a reporter?"

Ground rules, Cassie. No talk of Sally. "For a long time, I wanted to be a foreign correspondent, but now I think I want to stay here and cover social services."

The woman smiled. "Ahh...to be so young and just starting out. So many possibilities. I'm jealous. You get locked in quick. My husband owns his own law firm, so we're not going anywhere. Our life will play out in New Jersey. Now I have a daughter, who's two, and Dan, my husband, wants another one soon."

Cassie felt giddy. Did this woman just say she was jealous of her? No one had ever said they were jealous of her. She felt...what was it? Yes, she felt like a normal person. A person whom other people did not feel sorry for. She felt tingly, safe, protected, like her future was bright. That pain might not be around every corner.

"What's your name?"

"What?" Cassie had been so deep in her own world that she had temporarily blanked out the conversation.

"Your name..."

Cassie smiled. "Cassie."

"Well, Cassie, I'm Gwen and I have to go now and meet my client. It was great meeting you and I'll look for your byline."

"Yes, Cassie Pennebaker."

"Okay, Cassie Pennebaker. Nice to meet you."

"Yes, thanks. You too."

Cassie sat at the table in the back of Starbucks bursting with happy feelings. She looked at the clock on the wall and noted that she had hours to do whatever she wanted to do. Closing her eyes, she decided she wanted to continue to not live her actual life but this invented life. She decided to head to the mall.

The Right Thing

"Front page byline again," Joe muttered to himself as he sat waiting for class to start. He couldn't believe that he was actually jealous of Cassie's success at the *Record*. For the last month she had a front-page story at least two times a week, and he had to admit, they were good. She always went the extra mile, got the extra quote, gave salient details.

He always knew she was good. And he missed her. He missed her opinionated remarks. He missed her planning and her sense of mission for the day. He had to admit he even missed the drama and the constant crises. He would not go as far as to say that he missed Sally, but he did wonder how she was.

He had only seen Cassie once after he saw her in the hospital when he was leaving with Sierra—a memory that still made him squirm—and that was on the day she came to get her stuff at his apartment, and Sierra had been lying on his couch in a black teddy. Awkward couldn't begin to describe how they had all felt. Even Sierra had reached for his afghan to cover herself. As Joe watched Cassie go around picking up her things and throwing them in a box, he couldn't believe this turn of events. What was he doing with Sierra? How had that even happened? He had finally gone in the kitchen to do the dishes and wait until Cassie left.

After he heard the door close, he had gone into the living room and sat in the chair across from Sierra. He still felt guilty when he looked at her swollen eyes and broken nose. Guilty that she had let Rick into her apartment thinking it was him.

"Well, that was weird," said Sierra. "She really should have called before she came. Don't you think?"

Joe gave her a hurt, bewildered look.

"What? You think it's okay that she just barged in here and started taking things?" asked Sierra, trying to lift herself up on her good arm to look at Joe.

"I don't want to talk about it. I have to go to work," Joe had said, grabbing his jacket and heading out.

That was the only time he and Sierra had mentioned Cassie. After a week at Joe's they had moved to Sierra's apartment. Sierra had said that she really needed to get back to civilization, and Joe woke up each morning saying that this would be the day that he would tell her he was leaving and going back to his apartment. But each day she would need him to bring her a prescription or take her to a doctor's appointment or go to the grocery store, and then he would cook dinner, and then it was time to go to bed, and he hadn't left.

Even when he was at work, Sierra was constantly texting and calling Joe, asking him to buy her ice cream on the way home or pick up her pain medication. He had slipped very easily into being at her beck and call. *Joe, sweetheart, get me a glass of water with ice. Joe, honey, can you run me a bath? And make the water a little less soapy than you did last time. Lover, pick me up at 1:15 to take me to the doctor and please don't be late.* Joe realized his situation, although short-term, was not unlike Sally's constant demands on Cassie. It was easy to feel that he needed to do anything Sierra asked. It was hard to say no.

He never had any time for himself. The day before he had been planning on going to the library at lunchtime to pick up a book he needed, but instead, Sierra had called and asked him to go and get her a special sandwich that she liked, and the next thing he knew he was in line at Feast ordering a smoked turkey, Jarlsburg, pickle, and avocado on wheat. He was going a little crazy. He hardly had time to do his homework or work on articles for the *Record*. He turned down a number of assignments from Luke so that he could dote on Sierra. However, Sierra was not Joe's girlfriend or a relative. She was just a girl who he had slept with once before the attack and then had asked for his help.

But now a month had gone by, and Joe was determined to end this thing with Sierra. He thought of it as a "thing" because he couldn't say that they had a real relationship. Staying with her was just the right thing to do until she was better. Her face was still a little lopsided, but better every day. The cast was coming off her arm next week, and she had cut her hair into a layered bob to hide the bald spot where the stitches were, so Joe felt the time had come to gently disengage.

After class tonight he would just say that it was time for him to go back to his own life. They could still be friends, but he had to focus on his move to Boston and getting ready for college. He stopped at the liquor store on his way to her apartment and bought a bottle of Cabernet, then headed to Sierra's with determination.

He let himself in with the key she had given him and heard laughter as he opened the door. The foyer led into the living room, where Sierra was sitting on the couch with a man in his early forties and laughing at some story he was telling her.

Joe stood in the foyer holding the bag with the bottle of wine and stared at them.

Sierra turned to Joe with her most dashing smile and said, "Joe, come and meet Thurston."

Joe hesitated, this was his opportunity. "Hello, Thurston," he said. "How are you?" Joe looked from Sierra to Thurston and noticed that they both had bare feet. "I can't stay. I just dropped by to pick up a few things," he said and headed into the bedroom, where he found the bed unmade. He grabbed his duffel bag from the closet and threw his clothes in. By the time he went back into the living room, his anger had solidified.

On his way out he dropped Sierra's keys on the small table by the front door and turned to face her.

"Joe, what is wrong with you? Come and have a glass of wine," she said with a flip of her hair. Thurston yawned.

Joe looked at her and felt like a fool. "I hope Thurston can take you to the doctor tomorrow," he said as he let himself out.

Invitation

C assie and Sally sat at the table in their apartment eating Cheerios and bananas before Cassie had to go to work. Sally had spent a few weeks in rehab, and now that she was home she could get herself around the apartment with her walker, and Cassie could see that she was getting stronger every day. Spending her nights in her own apartment made her mornings much easier. Sally seemed more relaxed than she had been when Cassie ran in for a half hour here and there.

Cassie had worked a deal with a woman in the apartments named Judith, who spent four hours with Sally each day making her lunch and doing light housework. Cassie was surprised that Sally let her into the apartment and accepted her help.

"Judith is coming this morning. You guys can watch MTV together," said Cassie.

Sally stopped chewing her banana. "What's she making for lunch?"

"Whatever you want. We have the usual." Cassie got up to bring her bowl and coffee mug into the kitchen.

"I don't need her to be here, you know," said Sally defiantly to Cassie's back.

"I know. After she leaves just take a nap until I get home. Okay?"

"I'll have to get through five hours," said Sally, staring at the television.

"Have to get ready for work, Gram." Cassie went into the bedroom to find some clean clothes and brush her hair. When she went into the bathroom to brush her teeth, she studied her multi-colored hair and wondered why she had ever decided to dye it that way. She had noticed Luke looking at it the other day, but she couldn't read his expression. Was he thinking, "Cool" or "Jeez, why does she do that to her hair?"

"Okay, Gram. Gotta go." Cassie bent down to give Sally a kiss on the cheek.

"Let's check and see if it's raining. Cassie, look out the window."

"Bright and sunny," said Cassie.

"I asked God to keep you safe while you're driving and while you're at work," said Sally.

"Okay, thanks, Gram. Bye." Cassie smiled at Sally.

"I'll ask him again and count my buttons. Cassie, wait, take these dishes away," said Sally.

Cassie quickly went over to Sally, got the dishes, and brought them to the kitchen. "Okay, now I'm late. Gotta go," she said with an annoyed tone. "Bye."

Once in the car she drove to the *Record* and got into the conference room just in time for the editorial meeting. It was a slow day, and she could tell that Luke was having trouble finding enough good stories to hand out to the reporters. After the meeting, Luke approached her.

"Hey, Cassie, do you have a few minutes?" he asked.

"Sure," said Cassie with a smile.

"In my office." Luke led the way down the hall.

"Was I bad?" Cassie giggled.

"Not that I know of. Have a seat," Luke said, pointing to the chair in front of his desk. When they were both seated, he looked at Cassie.

Cassie raised her eyebrows as if to say, "Okay, go ahead."

"So, Sam is leaving. Her husband got a new job that pays a lot more money, so instead of sleeping in your car…" Luke stopped there and gave her an accusatory look.

"I…she didn't always sleep in my car…"

"She's going to stay home with her baby, and that leaves me free to hire another general assignment reporter. You've said on a number of occasions that you want to do more reporting about services that are offered in the community, and I think that's a great idea. I'm thinking that you can train the new person, and then start writing some of the stories you want to write. What do you think?"

Cassie found herself speechless.

"Hello? Did you hear me?" asked Luke.

"Oh my God! Are you serious? That would be amazing," said Cassie, leaning into the desk and smiling ear to ear. "Thank you. Thank you, Luke. I don't know what to say."

"You're welcome! We'll start looking for a new reporter right away. Why don't you come up with a list of possible articles and we'll talk it through?" Luke smiled with his deep dimples.

Cassie tried not to swoon. "Yes! I have so many ideas. I'll write them up. This is so great. Thanks again!" Cassie got up to leave.

Luke suddenly looked less confident than he usually did when he said, "Hey, a bunch of us are going across the street to get a drink after work. Do you want to come?"

Cassie looked into his bright blue eyes. "Sure. I'd like that."

On her way back to the bullpen, Cassie's skin was tingling. It felt so great to actually get something that she wanted. It felt like winning the lottery. She couldn't believe that she had an opportunity to write the stories she wanted to write and an invitation from Luke.

Goodbye

I t was Luke who told Cassie that Joe was leaving. "I'm losing my best stringer," he had said with a frown as they sat in his office before the editorial meeting one morning. She had taken to arriving early and having a cup of coffee with Luke before the others arrived. Cassie looked up from her paper. "Joe Darby," he said.

When Cassie heard Luke say Joe's full name, she felt a little stab in her heart. Of course she had known this day would come, but she liked to think of Joe at Home Depot or in his apartment so that she could, if she wanted to, go see him.

For the rest of the week she wondered when he was leaving. She thought about going to his apartment to say goodbye. Her stomach ached when she thought about him driving up to Boston without her, discovering the city without her. She had known for months that he would be leaving at some point, but now that it was a reality she felt panicky. What had she given up?

On Saturday morning, she was sitting with Sally watching MTV and writing out her to-do list when there was a knock on the door.

"Who's that?" asked Sally, always suspicious of visitors.

"I don't know," said Cassie, going to the door. The first thing she saw when she opened it was Joe's curls, then his beautiful smile as he stood on her porch. He was wearing her favorite Nirvana T-shirt and cargo shorts.

"Hi," he said.

"Who is it, Cassie?" asked Sally impatiently.

"I'll be right back, Gram," Cassie said, slipping out the door. The sun was bright; Cassie put her hand up to shield her eyes. "Let's go sit on the back porch," she said. They walked around the apartments to the back and sat down on Cassie's back steps.

Once they were settled Joe asked, "How've you been?"

"Good. Working a lot. Taking care of Gram. You know the drill. I hear you're leaving," said Cassie.

Joe laughed. "Wow! Word travels fast. Yeah. Leaving tomorrow…but wanted to say goodbye." They both stared straight ahead for a few minutes. Finally, he said, "I like your hair, but I kind of miss the streaks."

Cassie smiled and ran her hand over her light brown hair. "Decided to go natural. Takes less time and people take me more seriously. At work, I mean."

"I've been reading all your stories. You've been on the front page an impressive number of times." Joe smiled.

"You've been keeping track?"

"Sort of," said Joe with an awkward grin. "I like to keep my eye on the competition."

"Luke told me you were his best stringer."

"Stringer, not reporter."

Sitting with Joe, Cassie wished that the moment would never end, but there were so many unanswered questions. After a while she asked the question that had plagued her for months. "So, Joe…why were you with Sierra at the hospital after Rick beat her up? I mean, I guess I have no right to ask, but—"

"She called me. Said she'd been beaten up. I felt like I had to go."

"How is she?"

"She's seeing a therapist. She has lots of things to work out. She told me that her father used to rape her after her mother died."

Cassie stared down at her hands. "That is so horrible," she said, shifting on the stair so that she could see Joe's face. The face she loved and missed kissing. "I've been doing a lot of research on PTSD and I think that Sally, Sierra, and even Rick, all suffer, or suffered in Rick's case, from the same thing. Trauma. I've learned a lot about Sally's childhood and the abuse she suffered, and Sierra obviously suffered from her father's abuse, and Rick had trauma from his tours in Afghanistan. People always say that children are resilient, but the truth is they're not. Neither are adults. We're all fragile."

"Well, at least in Sally's case, she's lucky because she has you to take care of her," said Joe, putting his arm around Cassie's shoulders and pulling her to him. Cassie folded herself into Joe's embrace and smelled his familiar scent, closing her eyes to drink it in.

Finally, she asked, "When are you leaving again?"

"Tomorrow. Tomorrow morning. I have an appointment to look at an apartment tomorrow night. Then I'll spend the next few weeks looking for a job before school starts."

Cassie smiled and tears sprang to her eyes. Sitting up, she reached out and squeezed Joe's hand.

"You could still change your mind and come with me…" Joe's voice was uncertain.

"I made the choice I had to make. She was always there for me. Now I need to be here for her."

"I know, but Cassie…I do love you," whispered Joe.

Cassie stood up and ran her hands through his hair. "I know," she said. "I have to go back in…"

Joe got up and took Cassie in his arms and they hugged, holding each other tightly. When Cassie felt that she couldn't take it anymore she pulled away and walked back up the stairs to go in the back door. "Goodbye, Joe. Send me a text and let me know how you're doing."

Joe looked up at her, his eyes filled with tears. "Yeah, I will." He turned and started walking around the apartments and back to his car. Cassie went back inside, shut the door, and leaned against it to steady herself, crying silently. Tears washing her cheeks. Her chest ached for what couldn't be. Joe had been her first serious relationship and it wasn't ending due to lack of love. It was ending because neither of them was willing to give up something that was important to them. They both had commitments to something or someone else. They both had to be true to themselves first.

When she finally felt numb to the hurt she'd known had been coming for a while now, she focused on gathering her strength. For Sally. For herself. She dried her face with a paper towel, went back into the living room, and sat down next to Sally, finding comfort with the one person who had never left. Time would heal her broken heart.

❀❀❀

Walking around the apartments, Joe couldn't breathe—why was he leaving her? Why was he leaving the woman he loved? He made up his mind to go back to the front door and beg Cassie to come with him. But as he got to the front of Cassie's apartment and looked in the window, he saw Cassie and Sally sitting together, laughing over something on the TV, and he understood in a way he hadn't before that Cassie was where she was meant to be.

The End

Who should make a woman's most private decision?

The Recovery Room

By Ann Ormsby

One

The recovery room at the clinic out on Route 54 had eight small stalls, each just big enough for a bed and the nurse to stand beside it. The room was kept very cold, so the women were all swaddled in cotton, waffle-weave blankets that were heated in a large warming cabinet at the back of the room. The nurses had a special way of replacing the used, cool blankets with new, hot ones without ever exposing the women to the cold air. Yellow curtains with white and blue flowers surrounded each bed for privacy. Patty, the head nurse, had chosen yellow because it was hopeful. She had said it made her think of the sunrise.

On this particular morning, two women were already in recovery. Now, just being wheeled out of the procedure room and down the hall to the recovery room, was a young girl, Clara Mahoney. She was only 16 years old, and the man who had come with her was in the waiting room pestering the receptionist.

"How is she? Is it over yet?" he had started asking, about ten minutes after Clara had been called in by the nurse.

"No, not yet. Sit down. Relax. She'll be fine," said Kathleen, the receptionist, hunching over her paperwork.

Michael Russo could not sit down. He stood in front of the nurse's window, craning his neck to see into the inner depths of the clinic. Frustrated by the floor-to-ceiling file cabinets blocking his view, he turned on the heel of his army boot and started to pace in front of the first row of chairs lined up auditorium-style in the large room. His black hair, slick with gel, glistened under the harsh fluorescent lights and the smell of disinfectant filled his nostrils. He was oblivious to the stares of the other patients, who worried that he would stomp on their feet as he assaulted the gray, industrial-grade carpet. A young man with crossed legs and a book in his lap cleared his throat as Michael marched by. Their eyes locked for a moment and Michael sat down, pulling on his mustache. Feeling as if the situation were out of his control, he rested his head on the back of the chair and forced himself to silently count, visualizing each number behind his closed eyelids.

Michael had met Clara two months earlier. It had been a warm spring night, one of the first of the season when the air smells sweet. After work he had headed to The Sportsman, the one working-class bar in town. When he walked in, he saw his buddies playing pool in the back but decided to have a quiet beer first. Jay, the bartender, flashed his crooked smile and gave him a draft Budweiser. Michael usually knew everyone who hung out at the bar, but there were some new faces there that night. Young faces. A whole pack of little girls. He saw them, five or six of them stuffed into one of the wooden booths by the jukebox. He scanned the table of silky hair and spaghetti straps. The girls' slim, tanned arms glowing from the light of the candles. Their silver jewelry shimmering. He chuckled at his interest in these girls and looked away. He took a long pull on his beer. Okay. Who was that at the pinball machine? Long legs. Tight blue jeans and a soft, loose blouse. Curly dark hair fell almost to her waist. He couldn't see her face. He grabbed his Bud and walked over to the pinball machine. As he did, she lost her ball.

"Damn!" she swore, banging the top of the game with her fist. "I didn't get the highest score," she said to no one in particular.

He leaned on the Ms. Pac-Man game next to the pinball machine she was playing and watched her with amusement. "I'll play you. I have the second highest score on that machine," he bragged.

She turned to look at him. She was still pouting over her lost ball. His heart skipped a beat. She was almost ripe, still a girl, just moments away from being a woman. Minus the eye makeup she would be fabulous, he thought. Her lips were so pink and so full, he stared at them and his mouth ran dry.

"Okay, but I warn you. I'm good," she said slightly slurring her words and holding out her hand for him to give her coins for a new game. He laughed at her presumption, but reached into his pocket and pulled out a handful of change. She picked out two quarters and put them in the machine. His palm tingled when her soft fingers touched it. She had made no attempt to introduce herself, being more interested in playing pinball than in meeting him.

"Ladies first," he said, but she was already pulling the lever to play the first ball.

Michael was fascinated. Of course, he was 23 and this girl was way too young for him, but it was only a game of pinball. He watched her manipulate the flippers. She was pretty good. He hoped he could beat her. After three humiliating games for Michael, he wanted to stop playing. "Let's get a drink," he suggested.

"Can't stand to lose again?" she taunted. She smiled at him in a slightly condescending way, her eyes twinkling. He noticed that she had two deep dimples.

"I'm letting you win," he lied, and laughed at himself. He took her arm and guided her to where he was sitting at the end of the bar.

"Really?" she laughed at him, but allowed herself to be escorted to a bar stool with a dirty, red leather seat. Clara, never having been in a bar before, was amazed at all the tools the bartenders used to make drinks. She watched Jay, the bartender, pour liquor from exotic-looking bottles into shot glasses and stole a cherry from the plastic box containing sticky fruit and sour lemons. At the center of the bar was a row of beer taps. Michael was amused by her interest in these common things.

"Don't get out much?" he asked. Immediately, Clara's face changed. She frowned slightly. "It's okay," he said, smiling. He ordered another beer for himself and a Tequila Sunrise for her. She already felt more than a little giddy from the first one. She took a sip from the tiny cocktail straw and looked up at him as she did. She had just begun to realize her effect on men and, like a child with a new toy, she played him. He was amused but excited by her at the same time.

"What's your name?" he asked.

"Clara."

"I'm Michael."

"You really suck at pinball," she said with a smile, fixing her eyes on him. He looked over at Jay, who tipped his chin toward Clara and smiled. Michael tipped his chin back.

She finished her drink. "I need'a go see my friends." She pointed to the table of girls that now had a ring of young men standing around it. "Thanks for the drink, Michael." She touched his shoulder and he flinched. She laughed. He watched her walk over to the table and join the other girls, noting that she was greeted by warm hellos from the men.

"Jailbait, that one," said Jay.

"All of them," said Michael. "Don't you proof these girls? How are respectable men supposed to relax and just have a drink?" Michael laughed. "I should call the police."

"Ha, ha," said Jay.

At that point Michael's friends had finished playing pool and came over to chat with him. As the night wore on, he couldn't stop himself from looking over at Clara. He was never able to catch her eye. He wished she would play pinball again. While his friends talked of their day, he could hear her laughing in the background. Not being able to help himself, he glanced in her direction and saw her look up at one of the guys with the same alluring look she had given him earlier. Michael felt his cheeks grow hot.

Meanwhile, Clara was enjoying herself, flirting with the young men at the table, but for some reason she peeked over at Michael to see if he was still there. She knew that if she went over to play pinball, he would come to her. She thought he'd drive her home if she asked him. A rugged young man bought her another drink. Very drunk at this point, she suddenly felt as if she had had enough and tried to look at her watch, but the room was too dark.

"I'm gonna go home, Lin-na," she said abruptly to her friend, her words slurring into one big sound. Linda, equally as drunk, ignored Clara and laughed as one of the young men kissed her ear. Clara rose unsteadily and walked over to Michael. "Take me home," she demanded. Michael's friends howled with laughter as Michael quickly stood up. They slapped him on the back and hooted. "They're just jealous," she said. It came out "ja-wus." He laughed and put his arm around her to hold her up.

They walked outside into the parking lot to his red Mustang, and he helped her into the passenger seat. He ran around to the other side of the car and jumped in. After he put the key in the ignition, he looked over at her and saw that she was leaning back against the black leather seat with her eyes closed. Her lips were slightly parted, and he realized that she had passed out. He didn't know where she lived, and he didn't want to deliver her in this condition to her parents. With his luck, her father was a cop.

It was 11 p.m. according to the dashboard clock. Did she have to be home at midnight? He vaguely remembered midnight being the magic curfew hour. He decided to take her to his apartment and let her sleep for an hour. Driving through the quiet streets of Litchfield, she never moved. He parked his car in the lot in front of his apartment building and carried her up the stairs to the second floor. She was light, but her long legs kept hitting the wall and he hoped that snoopy Mrs. Stockwell, his neighbor, didn't see him carrying a drunken teenage girl into his apartment.

When he reached his door, he put her down, and then swung her over his shoulder so he could find his keys. Once inside, he put her on the couch and rolled up an old sweatshirt to put under her head as a pillow. She was totally unconscious. He felt kind of nervous, as if he were kidnapping her. If she had been five years older, it would have been different. He went into the kitchen to grab a beer. When he came back to the living room, he decided to watch television and wake her up in an hour to take her home. She was taking up the whole couch, so he lay down on the floor in front of her and turned on a rerun of *Seinfeld*.

Bored and stuck in his apartment, he turned around to look at the sleeping girl. He ran his finger down her cheek, noticing how rough his own skin looked next to hers. He wanted to wake her up. Without thinking, he leaned over and kissed her on the lips. She turned her head a little and a silky strand of hair fell across his hand. Rising up on his knees, he leaned down, breathing in her apple-scented shampoo. He kissed her again, this time with more force.

He felt himself stirring, but since she did not respond, he turned abruptly, sat back down, and looked at the television.

Seinfeld segued into *Friends*. He watched the show as long as he could and then turned back to the girl. She opened her eyes and he rose up on his knees to look down at her. She stared up at him, her gaze looked unfocused. Bending down, he kissed her, forcing his tongue in her mouth, and his hands reached under her shirt before he could stop himself. She didn't scream or struggle, but lay lifeless, as he climbed on top of her. He took her silence as submission. When he rolled over on his side to unzip his jeans, and then hers, she kept her eyes closed, arms stiff at her sides. She didn't stop him, but she did nothing to help him, as he struggled to pull her tight pants off. The skin on her thighs was so soft, and the smell of her hair was so overpowering, that rational thought left him.

Clara didn't know what to do. Panic bubbled in her chest, draining her of the ability to move. At first, her Tequila-soaked brain tried to comprehend the dim light, the laugh track from the television, the unfamiliar smell of masculine sweat mixed with beer, and the freckles on the shoulder above her, gyrating. Gradually, she became alert, her survival instinct kicking in, and she knew she needed to pull herself together, to get out of the apartment. She didn't know this man. What else would he do to her? He didn't seem hostile or angry, but he was very strong and heavy. She could feel the hard muscles in his arms, chest, and thighs crushing her. His body shuddered, and he moaned, his face buried in her neck. She suddenly felt like she couldn't breathe. Tears started to stream down her cheeks.

He picked up his head when he heard her sniffle. "It's okay, Clara," he said softly. "Did I hurt you?" She winced when he said her name, and looked at him with frightened eyes. Michael's gut twisted. "I'm sorry," he whispered, putting his fingertips on her cheek to hold her face where he could see it. When she didn't answer, he asked more urgently, "Are you okay?"

"My parents…are waiting for me." She choked on her words, and then, afraid he might take this as a threat, she added, "I won't tell them."

Thinking fast, he said, "No, they would be angry at you for getting so drunk. You shouldn't tell them."

She finally steadied her voice and said, "I want to get up." Michael rolled off her toward the inside of the old gray velour couch, pulling his jeans up to cover himself.

She sat up quickly. "Yes. Can I use the bathroom?" she asked, grabbing her pants and underwear, which had fallen on the floor. He pointed to the door across the room. She got up, naked from the waist down, and walked to the bathroom.

Michael put his head down on the old sweatshirt he had made into a pillow for Clara and closed his eyes. *Shit. This could mean all kinds of trouble.*

In the small, dark bathroom that smelled like sour towels, Clara collapsed onto the toilet. She urinated and tried to wipe away the mess between her legs. Then, she hurriedly pulled on her underwear and her jeans. As she did, her cell phone fell out of the pocket, and she saw that it had run out of power. Taking some toilet paper and wetting it, she tried to fix her smudged eye makeup. As she ran her fingers through her hair to smooth it, she thought of her mother, who would be waiting up for her. She wanted to seek comfort in her mother's arms, but quickly realized she could never tell her mother the truth. It would be the crushing blow. Her mother wouldn't be able to endure it. Both of her children ruined. No, Clara had always been invisible, and what had happened here tonight would not change that.

When she was done, she came hesitantly out of the bathroom. "Can we go now?" she asked awkwardly, standing in front of the man. Gone was the bravado and confident attitude he had seen in the bar. She looked vulnerable and frail.

"Sure. Let's go," he said, using the remote to turn off the television and getting up from the couch. He took a step toward her to comfort her, but a flicker of fear crossed her face and he thought it was better to just get going. They left the apartment and got into his car. Once they were out of the parking lot, he asked tentatively, "Are you okay?"

She sensed he needed reassurance of some kind, so she said, "Yes. I'm okay," and gave him directions to her house in Sunken Meadow, an exclusive area of town. Ten minutes later, they pulled up in front of a white six-bedroom house with a three-car garage. Lights were on at the front door and glowed through the large front windows. Fancy landscaping ran across the front of the house and down the side yard to a high wrought-iron fence. Michael heard himself swallow hard. He was a carpenter who lived in a tiny apartment.

"Listen, you had birth control, right?" he asked.

"No," she said.

Buy *The Recovery Room* on Amazon.com.

Acknowledgments and Author's Note

This is the end of a long journey. It took me six years, and two efforts, to write this book having lost half of the original manuscript when my computer crashed in 2018 during a trip to Spain. But, with a little bit of perseverance, and a lot of help from the folks below, I finally finished it. At its core, this book is about family and my belief that family comes first. You don't get to choose the family you are born into or the problems that family members face, but you do get to choose how you respond to those problems.

My sister Mary struggled with PTSD her whole life and I did the best I could to support her. Mary's life-long mental illness and everything she went through taught me to be humble. I know that those who are different, who are less fortunate, who are suffering, should not be shunned, but helped. A kind word or gesture goes a long way. She reminded me every day that the world is a hard place, an unforgiving place, but her capacity to love and to enjoy my children and music also taught me that whatever life has done to a person we each have the ability to find joy.

I want to thank so many people who supported me in writing this novel. My first reader is always Lois Elson, my best friend since second grade, her enthusiasm for my writing always spurs me on. Thanks, Lo! Years ago, I met fellow writers, Rosanne Kurdstedt and Cheryl Sacra Paden and I want to thank them for taking the time to provide invaluable feedback. Early chapters were also workshopped with Richard Merli and the wonderful writers at Literary Lights. Thank you all for your insight and feedback.

The book would not be the same without the editing of Christie Stratos who pushed me to dig deep and show the emotions my characters were feeling and the credit for comma placement and proofreading goes to Anita Stratos. Thank you both for polishing the book with me.

Please check out my new website at annormsby.com that was beautifully designed by Chris Cadalzo with photography by Susan Cook. Both of these ladies are so easy to work with and deliver such great results. Of course, no one would be reading this book without Lois Hoffman who helped me with the publishing process and Robert Dweck who designed the beautiful cover and brought Cassie to life. Thanks to all of you. I appreciate everyone's work on my behalf.

And finally, a special thank you to my family: to my son William, my sounding board, to my son Charles, my technical consultant, and to my husband Larry, who didn't ask me to choose between him and Mary.

About Ann

Ann Ormsby is the author of two novels and many short stories that dig deep into family relationships. She has also written a number of opinion pieces about public policy issues. Her op-eds have run in the *New York Daily News*, *The Newark Star-Ledger, The Huffington Post, njspotlight.com, The Westfield Leader* and *The Alternative Press*. Her short stories have appeared in the *Greenwich Village Literary Review, Every Day Fiction, Pentimento Magazine, and October Hill Magazine*.

"I thoroughly believe that the family you are born into and how the people in that family treat you determine who you will become. Family members can either be our biggest supporters or the most savage and damaging critics, but I have found that most people can be saved by one strong, loving, positive relationship early in life," said Ann.

The Recovery Room, her debut novel, raised the question of who should make a woman's most private decision and tells the stories of three very different women struggling with an unintended pregnancy. The book is a must-read for anyone pondering the question of reproductive rights. The first chapter is included in this book.

Ann lives in the tri-state area with her husband and is the proud mother of two grown sons and one interesting cat who likes to take her on walks around their cul-de-sac.

Visit Ann's website at annormsby.com and follow her on Facebook, Instagram, and Twitter.

CPSIA information can be obtained
at www.ICGtesting.com
Printed in the USA
LVHW111410270521
688578LV00004BA/797